The New German Jewish Literature

Dialogue and Disjunction:
Studies in Jewish German Literature, Culture, and Thought

Series Editors:

Erin McGlothlin (Washington University in St. Louis)
Brad Prager (University of Missouri)

The New German Jewish Literature

Holocaust Memory, Solidarity, and Worldliness

Stuart Taberner

Rochester, New York

Copyright © 2025 Stuart Taberner

Some rights reserved. Without limiting the rights under copyright reserved above, any part of this book may be reproduced, stored in or introduced into a retrieval system, or transmitted, in any form or by any means (electronic, mechanical, photocopying, recording or otherwise)

This title is available under the Creative Commons license
CC-BY-NC-ND

This work was supported by the Arts and Humanities Research Council [grant number AH/V008536/1].

ISBN-13: 978-1-64014-179-7 (hardcover)
ISBN-13: 978-1-64014-215-2 (paperback)

Library of Congress Cataloging-in-Publication Data

CIP data is available from the Library of Congress.

The publisher has no responsibility for the continued existence or accuracy of URLs for external or third-party internet websites referred to in this book and does not guarantee that any content on such websites is, or will remain, accurate or appropriate.

For Ivor and Pip

Contents

Acknowledgments ix

A Note on Translation and on Terminology x

Introduction: German Jewish Identities in the Plural 1

1: Holocaust Memory: Adriana Altaras, Jan Himmelfarb, and Benjamin Stein 31

2: Solidarity: Mirna Funk, Kat Kaufmann, and Katja Petrowskaja 78

3: Worldliness: Channah Trzebiner, Sasha Marianna Salzmann, and Olga Grjasnowa 118

Conclusion: The Postmigrant Society and the Limits of Solidarity—After October 7, 2023 161

Bibliography 183

Index 211

Acknowledgments

This work was supported by the UK Arts and Humanities Research Council [grant number AH/V008536/1].

I am grateful to the Arts and Humanities Research Council for the award of a fellowship to allow me to work on this book. Without this support, progress would have been much slower and I would not have been able to receive generous feedback from colleagues at conferences in the United States and UK, especially Katja Garloff, Agnes Mueller, and Helen Finch.

I am also grateful to the University of the Free State in South Africa, where I am a Research Fellow. Its support has also been vital in allowing me to travel to archives in Germany. I am delighted to have this association with South Africa, where I have been involved in public engagement and Holocaust education activities for many years, especially with the Johannesburg Holocaust and Genocide Foundation. The JHGF does important work with all communities in South Africa, and indeed across the continent, on human rights and building resilience for democratic transformation.

The research presented here was completed in early 2024, following the vicious attack by Hamas on Israel of October 7, 2023, which killed more than 1,200 people, overwhelmingly Jews but also Arab citizens and migrant workers from around the world. Israel's response was ferocious and, by mid-2024, had killed more than 40,000 Palestinian residents of Gaza. Around the world, understandable outrage and legitimate criticism have often been drowned out by antisemitic provocations, on the one hand, and anti-Muslim prejudice, on the other.

A Note on Translation and on Terminology

Quotations from German-language scholarship are directly translated into English, without the German original. Quotations from literary texts and authors' essays and interviews are given in the original German, with the English translation in parentheses. The titles of literary texts are rendered in a plain translation, even where there is a published English version. All translations are my own.

In the groundbreaking collection of essays from 2002 that he edited with Sander Gilman, Hartmut Steinecke notes that the hyphenated adjective "German-Jewish" is "to a large degree ideologically and politically laden."[1] This book employs the term German Jewish—without the hyphen—not only to emphasize that in many of the texts examined there remains a tension, and a distance, between German and Jewish but also to signal that for at least some authors a primary concern is to explore Jewish identity both in its own terms and in its engagement with the world beyond Germany. For the same reasons, circumlocutions such as Jews in Germany are for the most part used in place of German Jews.

---

1   Steinecke, "'Deutsch-jüdische' Literatur heute," 10. See also Brenner and Frei, "German Jews or Jews in Germany?"

Introduction: German Jewish Identities in the Plural

This book argues for a new approach to the significant corpus of German-language fiction by self-identified Jewish authors that has appeared since around the early 2000s and which researchers now generally refer to as the New German Jewish Literature.[1] This approach draws heavily on recent sociological and ethnographic scholarship on the dramatic transformation of the Jewish presence in Germany, in order to interrogate key literary texts as dynamic interventions in the debates and controversies that are reshaping Jewish life in that country and across the global diaspora. In today's German Jewish novels, the book suggests, authors elaborate competing versions of what it means to live as a Jew in Germany and often reimagine what it means to be a Jew more generally. These rearticulations of Jewish identity typically involve a reframing of family history and traumatic memory, especially the Holocaust.

Reading recent German Jewish literary texts in the context of sociological and ethnographic insights into the transformation of the Jewish community in Germany and of debates about Jewish identity both there and globally reveals important shifts. Firstly, in the New German Jewish Literature, Jewish identity is now articulated not only—or even primarily—in relation to the country that was responsible for the Holocaust and to which Jews returned only with feelings of great ambivalence following the genocide. Jewish protagonists thus position themselves vis-à-vis other Jews, whether immigrants from the former Soviet Union, Orthodox, or liberal Jews, or they bypass faith altogether for a secular understanding of Jewish solidarity with other minorities. Secondly, transcending the understandable fixation on the uncanniness of Jewish life in the land of the perpetrators that previously characterized German Jewish fiction, many authors now articulate Jewish identity "beyond the nation." Jewishness need no longer be domesticated or integrated, therefore, but can (perhaps once again) become truly *worldly*. Thirdly, while contemporary German Jewish writing continues the post-Holocaust convention of working through traumatic family memory—whether direct experience of flight, ghettos, and camps, or the suffering of parents and grandparents—it now presents and represents the legacy of the genocide in a multitude of ways,

1 See, for example, Garloff, *Making German Jewish Literature Anew.*

with different implications for the framing of a Jewish identity. As will be discussed in subsequent chapters, how Holocaust memory is expanded, inflected, centered, or not centered within the literary text reflects but also evolves a variety of modes of Jewish engagement with others, including demarcation, retrenchment or alliance-building, and worldliness.

Reframing Current Scholarship

With its sociologically and ethnographically informed approach this book aims to build on, extend, but also reorient existing scholarship on the New German Jewish Literature. In essence, its ambition is to situate literary texts in relation to the diverse reality of Jewish life in modern Germany, more explicitly than hitherto and paying greater attention to the variety and nuance of their interventions in a Jewish conversation, taking place across the diaspora, about what it means to be a Jew today. Even as German Jewish writing presents—and perhaps even performs—Jewishness for an overwhelmingly non-Jewish readership, parts of it now also aspire to deploy an (assigned or chosen) "minoritarian identification" (Bhabha) more productively, to assert a Jewish identity and even a Jewish intervention in the world.[2] In 1995, author Maxim Biller declared that Germany was the only country in which an original, autonomous Jewish literature was possible, excepting Israel.[3] Thirty years later, the New German Jewish Literature has now fully emerged, and the mark of its originality and autonomy may be its gradual transcendence of its historically fraught German context and—as a tendency, at least—its *worldliness*.

In a field-defining intervention from 1995, Thomas Nolden identified the emergence of a Young Jewish Literature,[4] drawing a distinction between writers active in the postwar decades—mostly exiles from National Socialism or survivors of the ghettos and camps—and a new generation of self-identified Jewish authors, notably Maxim Biller, Ruth Beckermann, Barbara Honigmann, Rafael Seligmann, Esther Dischereit, Katja Behrens, Lea Fleischmann, Robert Menasse, Doron Rabinovici, and Robert Schindel. The work of this second generation after Auschwitz, Nolden argued, was marked by its "konzentrisches Schreiben" (concentric writing), as the children and grandchildren obsessively circled around the horrors endured by their parents and grandparents, and by how the traumatic legacy passed down by Holocaust victims continued to impact on those who came after. Commenting on the same group of writers a decade or so later, Stephan Braese suggested that they remained fixated on the incongruity of their presence as Jews in the country responsible

---

2   See Bhabha, "Speaking of Postcoloniality."
3   Biller, "Goodbye, Columbus," 93.
4   Nolden, *Junge jüdische Literatur.*

for the genocide. Writers of the second generation, consequently, "insistently speak about themselves as Jews, however incomplete this identity might be perceived. More specifically, they write about themselves as Jews in the concrete German present."[5] Finally, and emphasizing the apartness of second-generation authors from the country they grew up in, literary scholar Andreas Kilcher in 2002 described their physical or psychological "Exterritorialität" (exterritoriality), even as they wrote in German and cited German culture.[6] For some, like Biller, "exterritoriality" meant a form of (self-)estrangement in Germany (or Austria) while relentlessly confronting it with its Nazi past and exposing its hypocrisy in the present day. For others, it meant quitting the country—Honigmann moved to France; Fleischmann went to Israel—in order to continue the German and German Jewish literary tradition from outside the land of the perpetrators.

Certainly, many examples can be cited.[7] Biller's columns "100 Zeilen Hass" (100 lines of hate) in the monthly magazine *Tempo*, published between 1986 and 1997 (and collated in a book of the same name in 2017), assail not only German hypocrisy but also what the author sees as the passive acquiescence of the Jewish community, often Holocaust survivors. The same is true of his collections of essays, stories, and short novels throughout the 1990s, including, most notorious of all, *Harlem Holocaust* (1998), in which the American Jewish writer Warszawski exploits his German audience's insincere obsession with Jewish victimhood to satisfy his sexual perversions.[8] In Dischereit's *Joëmis Tisch: Eine jüdische Geschichte* (Joëmi's table; 1988), the protagonist reclaims her Jewish identity by interweaving stories of her mother's persecution with conversations with the non-Jewish Germans around her, while the autobiographically informed *Merryn* (1992) features a sixteen-year-old runaway who seeks out the site of her grandparents' deportation from Berlin.[9] Schindel's *Gebürtig* (native; 1992), Rabinovici's *Suche nach M: Roman* (Search for M: A novel; 1997), and Menasse's *Die Vertreibung aus der Hölle* (The expulsion from hell; 2001) exemplify these Austrian authors' focus on excavating traces of the Nazi past and the persistence of fascist mentalities in the present day. Honigmann's "trilogy of Diaspora," *Roman von einem Kinde* (Novel about a child; 1988), *Eine Liebe aus nichts* (a love from nothing; 1991), and *Damals, dann und danach* (Back then, next, and after; 1999), alternatively, constructs a German Jewish

---

5   Braese, "Writing against Reconciliation," 28.
6   See Kilcher, "Exterritorialitäten." See also Kilcher, "Was ist 'deutschjüdische Literatur'?"
7   See Morris and Remmler, eds., "Introduction."
8   See Chase, "Shoah Business."
9   See Nolden, "Contemporary German Jewish Literature."

identity outside of Germany but still immersed in the German language and in German culture.[10] (Honigmann left East Germany for France in 1984—after the war, her parents had preferred communism to Judaism). In these and other novels such as *Soharas Reise* (Sohara's journey; 1996), Orthodox as well as Sephardic and Ashkenazi traditions are explored.[11] Finally, Fleischmann marked her departure with *Dies ist nicht mein Land: Eine Jüdin verlässt die Bundesrepublik* (This is not my country: A Jew quits Germany; 1980) and today writes for German readers to "explain" Israel and Jewish customs. In 2006 Fleischmann published *Meine Sprache wohnt woanders: Gedanken zu Deutschland und Israel* (My language lives elsewhere: thoughts on Germany and Israel; 2006) with Chaim Noll, who quit East Germany for West Germany and then Israel after he detected anti-Jewish tones on the German Left.

Taken together, these authors demonstrate what ethnographer Dani Kranz characterizes as the second generation's "non-rootedness, or out-of-placeness, a non-identification with Germany."[12] At the same time, their self-understanding as German Jews, or even as Jews, can seem insecure. They are called upon—by non-Jewish compatriots, publishers, the media, and scholars—to speak for Jews in Germany even as their connection to, and even knowledge of, Judaism and Jewish culture is by definition interrupted.[13]

Katja Garloff's *Making German Jewish Literature Anew* (2022) is the most substantial study to appear to date on the subsequent development of German Jewish literary fiction from the early 2000s, as the authors discussed above evolved and were joined by new names, mostly younger immigrants from the former Soviet Union. Garloff identifies a caesura around the turn of the millennium after which second-generation writers—she discusses Biller, Dischereit, and Honigmann, along with the recently emerged Benjamin Stein—began more consciously and decisively to fashion a Jewish authorial identity through their literary work, public performances, and, most often, essays. This more assertive self-presentation, *Making German Jewish Literature Anew* implies, initiates, or at least anticipates, dynamic processes of "remaking memory" and "claiming places" more generally, perhaps because Jewish writers now feel less constrained to only ever write against—against German (and Austrian) repression of the Nazi past, against their parents' and grandparents' overwhelming trauma, and even against their own uncanny presence in the land of the perpetrators. Recent novels by Doron Rabinovici and Katja Petrowskaja, Garloff suggests, thus enact a "metamemorial

---

10 See Guenther, "Exile."
11 See Fiero, *Zwischen Enthüllen und Verstecken*, especially 91–100.
12 Kranz, "Where to Stay and Where to Go?," 188.
13 Nolden, *Junge jüdische Literatur*, 67.

shift in Holocaust remembrance," pointing toward the potential for more dynamic understandings of the genocide that, for example, might enable parallels between the Holocaust and other historical traumas.[14] (Rabinovici was born in Israel in 1961 and moved to Austria with his family in 1964. Petrowskaja was born in Ukraine in 1977 and settled in Germany in 1999). With regards to "claiming places," Garloff examines literary texts by Honigmann, Vladimir Vertlib, and Julya Rabinowich—Vertlib's family moved from Russia to Austria in 1981, via America and Israel, and Rabinowich arrived from Russia in 1977—and Lena Gorelik, Dmitrij Kapitelman, and Jan Himmelfarb, who came as children from the former Soviet Union in the early 1990s. The argument is that through their work these Jewish migrants lay a claim to belong in Germany (and Austria), and in German literature, often by reanimating historically Jewish spaces in German cityscapes and Jewish resonances in German culture.

In general terms, Garloff's *Making German Jewish Literature Anew* identifies a change in tenor in the evolution of German Jewish writing from the Young Jewish Literature of the 1980s and 1990s to the New German Jewish Literature that began to emerge from the mid-2000s. The more or less reactive stance that typified the early work of second-generation authors—writing against—has given way to greater assertiveness. Jewish writers no longer feel the need to justify their presence in Germany and German culture, neither to themselves nor to their non-Jewish compatriots, and they are reshaping memory and place in ways that point beyond the (natural) obsession with Jewish suffering and German perpetration.

Garloff sees "authorial self-staging and self-fashioning," then, as "a process of becoming: learning to speak German, practicing to be Jewish, moving from the past to the present."[15] This insightful summary of the gradual transformation of German Jewish writing since the early 2000s needs to be nuanced, however, both to account for the full diversity of authors who are now active—her study includes no German-born, third-generation authors, for example—and to properly appreciate how far German Jewish authors may have moved beyond the categories that scholarship has typically used to apprehend their work. For one, while it is self-evident that authorial self-fashioning establishes a stake in an overwhelmingly non-Jewish literary culture, careful attention to how protagonists position themselves within texts suggests two important correctives to the conventional approach of reading German Jewish literature primarily in relation to the majority—for all that nearly every reader will be a non-Jewish German, of course. First, there is no single, homogenous

14 Garloff, *Making German Jewish Literature Anew*, 10.
15 Garloff, *Making German Jewish Literature Anew*, 27–28.

Jewish identity being staged. Second, the plurality of Jewish perspectives across recent texts references debates in the Jewish world as much as the need to define either apartness from, or integration into, wider German society. The same can be said with regard to "claiming places." In her close readings of Vertlib, Rabinowich, Gorelik, Kapitelman, and Himmelfarb—all originally from the former Soviet Union—Garloff speaks of "migration narratives" and "arrival narratives," which again suggests that protagonists are primarily focused on Germany as their ultimate destination, even as they now more confidently assert a Jewish presence. What is perhaps under-appreciated, however, is the degree to which some recent novels also articulate Jewish identity beyond Germany. A close reading of a broader selection of texts can engender a new perspective on German Jewish writing, and specifically its striving to be worldly.

This worldliness is at least implied in Garloff's discussion of key works by Rabinovici and Petrowskaja, and specifically how they tentatively propose comparisons between the Holocaust and other atrocities. Here, Garloff invokes Daniel Levy and Natan Sznaider's thinking on "cosmopolitan memory"[16] and Michael Rothberg's notion of "multidirectional memory."[17] These are not the same, of course. The concept of cosmopolitan memory, developed during the benign geopolitical context of the immediate post-Cold War period, refers to a commitment to universal human rights underpinned by the globalization of Holocaust memory, whereas multidirectional memory references how the Holocaust is invoked, in a noncompetitive way, to draw attention to other historical traumas. Both, however, suggest an opening-out of Holocaust memory to the global and the potential for solidarity with other minorities. Yet in limiting her analysis to Rabinovici and Petrowskaja, Garloff may not be able to show just how prevalent this rethinking of the Holocaust as cosmopolitan/multidirectional memory has become, or its far-reaching implications for the rearticulation of Jewish identity.

The close readings presented in later chapters of recent novels by Sasha Marianna Salzmann and Olga Grjasnowa—in addition to Petrowskaja—thus present a corrective to Garloff, who most likely underestimates the worldly orientation of German Jewish writing, but also to other scholars who may *over*estimate its instinctive solidarity with other minorities. Reading recent texts as emerging out of and engaging with real-life debates in the German Jewish and global Jewish communities moderates the tendency in articles by Bühler-Dietrich, Maria Roca Lizarazu, J. Rafael Balling, Francesco Albé, and others to remove Jewish protagonists from their concrete social and political contexts—in their communities, and in Germany—and to idealize them as "nomadic subjects" (Rosi

---

16 Levy and Sznaider, *The Holocaust*.
17 See Rothberg, *Multidirectional Memory*.

Braidotti's term)[18] and thus as somehow "naturally cosmopolitan."[19] Contemporary German Jewish writing, this book argues therefore, is increasingly characterized by its exploration of the tension between insisting on the Jewishness of the Holocaust and emphasizing its universalistic implications, and more generally between Jewish self-sufficiency and cosmopolitan engagement on behalf of others.

Jewish particularism versus Jewish universalism, in fact, both invokes an age-old thematic in Jewish culture and thought and goes to the heart of the modern-day debate about what it means to be a Jew that is occurring in Germany and across the diaspora more broadly. In a final reconceptualization of existing scholarship, then, the present book explores how elements of the New German Jewish Literature pose even bigger questions about Jewish identity after Holocaust memory. If Holocaust memory increasingly functions simply as a reference point for solidarity with others—and faith and religious ritual are largely absent for the secular majority—what is left of Jewishness other than a vaguely defined sense of a Jewish ethical commitment to "repairing the world," typically summarized in the expression *tikkun olam*? This question is addressed in chapter 3.

The Paradoxical Normality of Jewish Life in Germany

As described above, this book aims to contextualize the New German Jewish Literature in relation to the debates on Jewish identity that are animating Jews in Germany and, in several aspects at least, also globally. These debates can be summarized under three headings: the paradoxical normality of Jewish life in Germany today; the demographic transformation of the Jewish community; the diaspora as the repository of "authentic Jewish values." This and the following sections address each in turn.

Jewish life in Germany eighty years after the Holocaust is vibrant, self-confident, and diverse. An existing community of only 30,000 in the late 1980s was swollen following the arrival of 220,000 immigrants from the former Soviet Union at the end of the Cold War, taking advantage of Germany's commitment to accept Jews, and their non-Jewish family members, as automatically qualifying for asylum. These are the "Jewish quota refugees"—*jüdische Kontingentflüchtlinge*—admitted under the same legal provision that had allowed entry for Vietnamese boat people

---

18 See Braidotti, *Nomadic Subjects.*
19 See Buehler-Dietrich, "Relational Subjectivity." See Roca Lizarazu, "'Integration'." See also Roca Lizarazu, "Ec-static Existences." See Balling, "Intimate Associations." Albé, "Becoming Queer."

in the mid-1980s.[20] Now, 120,000 people—the eighth largest Jewish presence anywhere in the world—belong to Orthodox, Conservative, and Reform congregations,[21] and tens of thousands more can claim a Jewish heritage.[22] Indeed, Orthodox Judaism is undergoing a revival in Germany[23] even as the Liberal/Reform movement has become reestablished in the country where it originated, and lesbian Jews, secular Jews, interfaith couples, and converts are also catered for, for example in the Ohel Hachidusch in Berlin.[24] As Melanie Eulitz puts it, "there are different ways to live Judaism in Germany today."[25] Whatever congregation they belong to (or none), Jews are visible in politics and the media and are not afraid to challenge the majority on the Nazi past, antisemitism, and racism more generally. Jews in Germany are writers, filmmakers, and playwrights.

In the postwar decades, the Eastern European survivors who had ended up as displaced persons in the American, British, and French occupation zones (West Germany from 1949) mostly hoped simply to rebuild their lives and not draw attention to themselves.[26] The same was true of those German Jews who had fled the Nazis or survived in hiding and who, after 1945, chose to live in the country that had killed their families.[27] In the Soviet zone, later East Germany, emigrés returned to help build socialism and saw their Jewishness as secondary to their ideological convictions. Over time, the Jewish communities in the two Germanys aligned themselves with their respective states while also remaining somewhat apart.[28] Today, the majority of Jews are committed to participating in German society as Jews, and as German Jews. The protagonist of Rafael Seligmann's 1989 novel *Rubinsteins Versteigerung* (Rubinstein's auction)

---

20 See Belkin, "Jüdische Kontingentflüchtlinge und Russlanddeutsche."

21 The relationship between these different strands is not always harmonious. The *Union progressiver Juden in Deutschland* (UPJ), for example, has often been in conflict with the more observant umbrella body *Zentralrat der Juden in Deutschland* and, in April 2023, the *Jüdischer Liberal-egalitärer Verband* broke away from the UPJ following allegations of misconduct on the part of a prominent rabbi.

22 This is according to the World Jewish Congress in 2023. See https://www.worldjewishcongress.org/en/about/communities/de. Last accessed July 25, 2024.

23 See Arfa, "Modern Orthodox Jewish life."

24 See https://www.ohel-hachidusch.org/index.html. Last accessed July 25, 2024.

25 Eulitz, "Die jüdisch-liberale Bewegung."

26 Wolffsohn, "Jews in Divided Germany (1945–1990)." See also Brenner, "East European and German Jews."

27 See Kauders, *Unmögliche Heimat*.

28 Sinn, "Returning to Stay?"

declares "Ich bin ein deutscher Jude" (I am a German Jew),[29] having grown up in the country, and the writer Maxim Biller—a "Deutscher wider Willen" (a German against his will)—is no less German: "Ich habe in diesem Land Abitur gemacht, ich habe hier Hashisch geraucht und Sex gehabt [. . .] und manchmal [. . .] fällt mir ein, daß ich besser Deutsch spreche als die meisten Deutschen."[30] (I did my school leaving exams in this country, I have smoked hash here and had sex [. . .] and sometimes [. . .] I become aware that I speak German better than most Germans). As discussed below, identifying as a German Jew is by no means always comfortable—the self-description of the protagonist of Esther Dischereit's *Merryn* (1992) as an "integrierter Fremdkörper"[31] (integrated foreign body) resonates still—but it is a significant reorientation, nonetheless.

This "new positioning," as Y. Michal Bodemann describes it,[32] can be dated back to the time of reunification in 1990; however, it does not relate solely to that seismic political transformation but rather incorporates more gradual attitudinal shifts. For the last thirty years, the last Holocaust survivors have been fading away and their children and grandchildren are rethinking their relationship with the country that perpetrated the crime. Immigrants from the former Soviet Union, who were often greeted with suspicion by members of the established community, bring different historical experiences, including the Red Army's victory over Nazism and communist repression. (Throughout this book, the term "established community" is used to render the German *alteingesessene Juden* and to distinguish them from Soviet-born Jewish immigrants). In 2021, Rabbi Mordechai Balla was appointed as the first rabbi in the German armed forces since the First World War.[33] In 2019, the American philosopher Susan Neiman asserted in *Learning from the Germans* that there was much to absorb from Germany about confronting difficult pasts, including, for America, the legacy of slavery.[34]

The opening in June 2023 of the Pears Jewish Campus in Berlin was a bold affirmation of the Jewish presence in the land of the perpetrators almost eighty years after the World Jewish Congress had declared "the determination of the Jewish people never again to settle on the bloodstained soil of Germany."[35] Costing $44 million and equipped with a gym, baseball court, movie theater, music studio, and kosher deli, the center is run by the Chabad-Lubavitch, a Hasidic movement based in

---

29 Seligmann, *Rubensteins Versteigerung*, 189.
30 Biller, "Deutscher wider Willen," 121.
31 Dischereit, *Merryn*, 117.
32 Bodemann, "A Reemergence of Jewish Life?," 48.
33 Schwartz, "Germany's 1st post-WWII Military Rabbi."
34 Neiman, *Learning from the Germans*.
35 Cited in Brenner, *In the Shadow of the Holocaust*, 1.

the United States that engages in energetic outreach around the world, including twenty cities in German.[36] Likewise, young Israelis are moving "back" to the country that their grandparents fled, rejecting the militarization of Israeli society and its high cost of living, and, in some cases, on account of Berlin's lively gay and lesbian scene.[37] The extent of their identification with Germany is debatable,[38] and they may be more interested in their present-day roots in the Middle East and historical connections to Europe than in Germany today, as Hadas Cohen and Dani Kranz argue.[39] There are signs, though, that Israeli Jews, along with others, are beginning to reshape German Jewish identity. Julius Schoeps relates how "next to the Russian Jews, a large number of Israeli and American Jews have found their way to unified Germany, with most opting to live in metropolitan centres such as Berlin, Frankfurt, and Munich," continuing: "Some are descendants of the former *Yeckes*, and it will be very interesting to see how all these different groups of Jews will constitute a new German Jewry."[40] (Yeckes, also yekkes or jeckes, are Jews of German origin.) Y. Michal Bodemann suggests something similar when he notes how diversity in Jewish culture often develops "outside of the big established centres of Jewish life, first and foremost outside of Israel itself" and adds that Germany is one such "periphery [. . .] used by Israelis and North American Jewish artists, scholars, and writers as a laboratory to experiment within their respective fields."[41] Embodying this diversity in Germany are Tomer Gardi, the Israeli author of the novel *Broken German* (2016),[42] the Israeli playwright Yael Ronen, the Israeli comedian Shahak Shapira—who performs in English but tweets in German—and Deborah Feldman, the American author of the 2012 English-language bestseller *Unorthodox* who now publishes in a Yiddish-inflected German. As described below, the contribution of the much larger number of Russian-speaking Jews who arrived after 1990 is also vital.

The magazine *Jüdisches Berlin* (Jewish Berlin) publishes articles in German, Russian, and Hebrew and is one of a number of journals dedicated to Jewish news, politics, and culture, for example *Jalta: Positionen zur jüdischen Gegenwart* (Positions on the Jewish present), which appeared between 2017 and 2020 and now continues as a book series.[43]

36 Axelrod, "Chabad Opens Germany's Largest Jewish Center."
37 See Amit, *A Queer Way Out*.
38 See Hochman and Heilbrunn, "'I am not a German Jew'."
39 Cohen and Kranz, "Israeli Jews."
40 Schoeps, "Saving the German-Jewish Legacy," 55.
41 Bodemann, "Introduction," 2–3. See also Kranz, "Das Körnchen Wahrheit."
42 See Almog, "Politics and Literary Capital."
43 There has been a lively Jewish press in Germany since the 1980s. See Bodemann, "A Jewish Cultural Renascence in Germany?"

More generally, Jewish journalists, writers, and activists are present in the mainstream media, demanding a proper reckoning with the past and an end to antisemitism in the present. In 2020, Ronen Steinke, who writes for the *Süddeutsche Zeitung* on law, human rights abuses around the world, and right-wing extremism in Germany, published two books that sparked intense debate, *Terror gegen Juden: Wie antisemitische Gewalt erstarkt und der Staat versagt* (Terror against Jews: How antisemitic violence is growing stronger and the state is failing) and *Antisemitismus in der Sprache* (Antisemitism in language). Comedian Oliver Polak is even more outspoken in his stage shows and his books, *Ich darf das— ich bin Jude* (I'm allowed, I'm a Jew; 2008), *Der jüdische Patient* (The Jewish patient; 2014),[44] and *Gegen Judenhass* (Against hatred of Jews; 2018). Other Jewish voices speak out in solidarity with Muslims, including Palestinians,[45] for example Max Czollek, Sasha Marianna Salzmann, and Yael Ronen, whose play *Dritte Generation* (Third generation; 2008) stages the intersections between historical traumas and features German, Israeli, and Palestinian actors.[46] At the community level, Ármin Langer founded the Salaam-Schalom initiative in Berlin's Neukölln district in 2013 to counteract dominant narratives in the media—including from Jewish leaders—that Muslims were inveterately hostile toward Jews. (Langer's book *Ein Jude in Neukölln: Mein Weg zum Miteinander der Religionen* / A Jew in Neukölln: My path to a dialogue of religions, appeared in 2016.) In 2022, the writer, social scientist, and public figure Dmitrij Belkin helped to establish *Schalom Aleikum*—later adopted by the Central Council of Jews in Germany[47]—as an organization dedicated to Jewish-Muslim dialogue, mutual understanding and liberal values, but also to reinforcing contemporary political norms, including a clear disavowal of antisemitism and an unconditional acceptance of Israel's right to exist.[48]

The Austrian radio presenter Julia Stallinger explores Jewish identity and culture for a non-Jewish audience in a popular and accessible fashion,[49] as does Debora Antmann, who writes for the online magazine *Missy* about being Jewish, disabled, and a lesbian.[50] In fact, both the cultural and institutional structures of Jewish life in Germany are

---

44   See Battegay, "German Psycho."
45   See Atshan and Galor, *The Moral Triangle*.
46   See Popescu, "Performance, Memory and Identity."
47   See https://www.denkfabrik-schalom-aleikum.de. Last accessed July 25, 2024.
48   Belkin, "Der Dialog muss weitergehen."
49   See https://www.freie-radios.online/radiomacher_in/julia-stallinger. Last accessed July 25, 2024.
50   See https://missy-magazine.de/blog/category/kolumnen-und-kommentare/kolumnist_innen/debora-antmann/. Last accessed July 25, 2024.

increasingly accommodating of queerness. The *Keshet Deutschland* organization, for example, serves the "interests of lesbian, gay, bisexual, trans, inter, and other queer people inside and outside the Jewish community."[51] In 2022, Helene Shani Braun, a lesbian, was training to be Germany's youngest rabbi, evidencing the growing diversity of the Jewish presence in the country. As an example of this, Shneer cites the *Limmud Deutschland*, a three-day festival that has taken place annually since 2007: "there are no hierarchies, no titles, no membership dues, and no tests to determine Jewish observance [. . .] one of its most radical acts is its official tri-lingualism: German, Russian and English."[52] Shneer also notes tensions, of course. Orthodox Jews do not attend the *Limmud*, and Russian-speaking Jews, it is believed, may be less welcoming of gays and lesbians. Together, the presence of Orthodox, Conservative, and Reform branches, the contributions of Russian, American, and Israeli immigrants, and the visibility of queer Jews confirm the new diversity of Jewish life in Germany.[53] At the same time, as Körber notes, relations between the different branches, between the established community and Soviet-born Jews, and between more traditional congregations and gay, lesbian, secular, convert, and *non-halachic* Jews are often fraught: "In the conflicts and in and around Jewish communal life it becomes clear that the pluralization of the Jewish community has also made many things more difficult."[54] Jews in Germany, in sum, are not homogeneous.

Likewise, the fact that Jews are fully engaged in German politics, society, and culture does not mean that Jewish life in Germany is now entirely normal. (Jewish normality should not in any case be measured by the extent of Jews' participation in the non-Jewish German mainstream.) Recent controversies and conflicts point to the continuing salience of the Holocaust in German discourse, sensitivities on the subject of Israel, an intense focus on who is and isn't a Jew, and antisemitic tropes or even violence. Both online and on the street, right- and left-wing conspiracists compared COVID-19 restrictions in 2020 and 2021 with the persecution of Jews in the Nazi period.[55] In intellectual circles and the broadsheets, the withdrawal of an invitation to speak for the Cameroonian political theorist

---

51   See https://keshetdeutschland.de/de/unsere-vision. Last accessed July 25, 2024.

52   Shneer, "The Third Way," 115–16.

53   See Jungmann, *Jüdisches Leben in Berlin*; Katlewski, *Judentum im Aufbruch*; Rosenthal and Homolka, *Das Judentum hat viele Gesichter*; and Shneer, "Russischsprachige Immigranten."

54   See Körber, "Puschkin oder Thora?"

55   See "German call to ban 'Jewish Star' at Covid Demos," BBC, 07.05.21. Online at: https://www.bbc.co.uk/news/world-europe-57020697. Last accessed July 25, 2024.

Achille Mbembe in 2020[56] and the publication of the German translation of American literary scholar Michael Rothberg's *Multidirectional Memory* (2009; *Multidirektionale Erinnerung*, 2021) initiated controversies about solidarity with Palestinians; whether criticism of Israel is automatically anti-Jewish; the relationship between the Holocaust and colonial atrocities perpetrated by European powers (including the extermination of the Nama and Herero in German Southwest Africa); and whether the insistence on the uniqueness of the Nazi genocide is part of a self-congratulatory narrative of Germany's "successful confrontation" with the past.[57] In August 2023, Deputy Minister President of Bavaria Hubert Aiwanger was revealed to have written a pamphlet mocking the Holocaust as a schoolboy, provoking a crisis in the state's ruling coalition through the summer.[58] More generally, in Germany as elsewhere, the backlash that began in the early 2000s against globalization, open borders, and liberal politics frequently resorts to the negative trope of the "cosmopolitan Jew."[59]

On October 9, 2019, during the Yom Kippur holiday, twenty-seven-year-old Stephan Balliet attempted to break his way into the synagogue in the east German town of Halle. Frustrated in his efforts to gain access, Balliet shot dead two people nearby and then injured two others. Federal investigators identified an antisemitic motive, including a manifesto which named his ambition to kill as many non-whites as possible, preferably Jews. The attack took place against the backdrop of a steep increase in hate crimes against Jews in Germany (and across Europe) over recent years, and some commentators specifically blamed the far-right Alternative für Deutschland for inciting hostility toward people perceived as foreigners.[60]

This is the paradoxical normality of Jewish life in Germany. On the one hand, Jews are more assertive than they have ever been since the reestablishment of the community in the late 1940s and 1950s, and more present in German politics, media, and culture. On the other hand, anti-Jewish tropes—and anti-Jewish violence—are on the increase. In late 2023, following the ferocious Israeli military response to the murder of more than 1,200 Israelis by Hamas on October 7, a huge rise in anti-Jewish sentiment across German cities was reported, continuing and even escalating as the conflict intensified in early 2024. In Berlin, the Star of David was daubed on the doors of apartments with Jewish residents, pro-Palestinian activists handed out sweets, and antisemitic slogans were

---

56   See Sznaider, "The Summer of Discontent."
57   See Rothberg, "Lived Multidirectionality"; and Biess, "Holocaust Memory."
58   See Wilke, "Bavaria Premier Keeps Deputy Aiwanger in Office."
59   See Jacobs, "Globalisation, Anti-globalisation and The Jewish 'Question.'"
60   See Koehler, "The Halle, Germany, Synagogue Attack."

shouted at rallies.⁶¹ It remains to be seen, of course, how the most heinous mass killing of Jews since the Holocaust—and Israel's subsequent brutal assault on Gaza—impacts over the longer term on how Jews in Germany see themselves, their connection to the Jewish homeland, and their relations with other minorities (especially Muslims). The conclusion to this book assesses current responses and speculates on what October 7 might mean for the trend toward worldly engagement.

The Demographic Transformation of the Jewish Community

In his contribution to Hans Otto Horch's *Handbuch der deutschjüdischen Literatur* (Handbook of German-Jewish Literature; 2016), Jakob Hessing emphasizes the significance of the fall of the Berlin Wall in November 1989 and Unification a year later as a "historical and sociological paradigm shift" for Jews in Germany.⁶² Most immediately, the reemergence of a Germany as a fully sovereign nation provoked "skepticism, suspicion, fear,"⁶³ in Hartmut Steinecke's words, and fears of a reversion to extreme nationalism and rabid antisemitism⁶⁴ for Jews everywhere, but especially in the country responsible for the Holocaust. Over the longer term, however, the geopolitical convulsions of 1989–90 would prove to be less decisive than generational and demographic transformations. Certainly, as later chapters show, Unification hardly features in contemporary German Jewish literature, which is largely made up of family narratives. Similarly, the fall of the Wall appears as a parochial concern in novels by Soviet-born writers, who are generally more focused on repression in Stalinist and post-Stalinist Russia and, naturally, the mass immigration to Germany.

The generational shift that took place in the 1980s and 1990s was from a community dominated by survivors of the Holocaust to their children and then grandchildren, now reaching maturity and starting to rethink their relationship to Germany. Writing in 1998, Micha Brumlik went so far as to assert that the Holocaust had become less centrally defining for younger generations and that social, cultural, and economic integration was now paramount.⁶⁵ The close readings in this volume nuance this claim and suggest instead that the focus of second- and third-generation Jewish writers is now on balancing a fierce insistence on the right to remember, and to remind about, the past with a conditional

---

61 See Chazan, "Israel-Hamas War."
62 Hessing, "Aufbrüche," 244.
63 Steinecke, "Geht jetzt alles wieder von vorne los?" 163.
64 Gilman, "German Reunification and the Jews."
65 Brumlik, *Zuhause, keine Heimat*.

accommodation with Germany. Recent novels, then, evidence a more reflexive, more differentiated attitude than those of the 1980s, when the urgency to confront German (and Austrian) hypocrisy—e.g., as seen in the Bitburg controversy, the Waldheim scandal, and the *Historikerstreit* (historians' controversy)—provoked a combative response from emerging authors such as Maxim Biller, Henryk Broder, Rafael Seligmann, Robert Menasse, Doron Rabinovici, and Robert Schindel.

The fact that the last survivors of the Holocaust are now passing away also shapes how younger Jews grasp their familial connection to the genocide and how it is communicated in the present and then into the future, in Germany and across the world. At the same time, Germany itself is also changing. If Jews in postwar West Germany were expected to serve the "politically symbolical function" of proving the country's democratic rehabilitation, as Karen Körber describes it, then since Unification there has been a "gradual political and legal recognition that Germany could handle diversity and immigration as a modern pluralistic state."[66] Younger German Jews especially are reimagining their place in a society that, to use the term popularized by sociologist Erol Yıldız, is now postmigrant,[67] that is, self-consciously aware of the multiplicity of voices that constitute its public sphere and the need to navigate difference. This diversity includes ethnic minorities from around the world and, of course, several hundred thousand coreligionists from the former Soviet Union. (The situation of Jews in this postmigrant society is explored further in the conclusion.)

The arrival of Russian-speaking Jews after 1990 was not without precedent. A first wave had come to Germany after the Bolshevik revolution of 1917, a second wave in the immediate postwar period, and a third wave fled Soviet repression in the 1970s. (Biller's family was part of this third contingent.) What was different about the fourth wave, however, commencing in the late 1980s and accelerating following unified Germany's adoption of a policy of unrestricted Jewish immigration introduced by the German Democratic Republic in its dying days,[68] was the very large number of arrivals—dwarfing the existing community—and the motives for migration. Refugees after the war and in the 1970s had fled antisemitism, whether in the form of hostility and even violence when they tried to return to their homes across Eastern Europe or in the form of witch hunts, scapegoating, and persecution in the Soviet Union. After 1990, in contrast, *jüdische Kontingentflüchtlinge* were more likely to be driven by the hope of a better life in Germany, given the political and

---

66 Körber, "Conflicting Memories."
67 See Yıldız and Hill, eds., *Nach der Migration*.
68 See Tress, "Soviet Jews"; Dietz, "German and Jewish Migration"; Göttsche, Eberle, and Brückner, "Immigration into Germany."

economic insecurity in the Soviet successor states, and were less likely to feel a strong attachment to Judaism. Many Soviet-born Jews went instead to Israel or the United States, of course, and for the majority the motive was not religious but economic.[69] This distance from Judaism was in part a consequence of the Soviet policy of treating Jews as a national minority—with a marker in their passports—while repressing religious or ethnic identity.[70] And it was in part a function of what Benjamin Pinkus identifies as the negative nationalism of what remained of Soviet Jews' connection to their origins, that is, an association of Jewishness with the experience of marginalization and harassment rather than positive aspects of Jewish culture and practice.[71] In her account of her new life in Germany, *Ich bin es, jüdische Kontingentflüchtlingin* (I am a Jewish quota refugee; 2006), Alexandra Grushko describes this initial reluctance to embrace a Jewish identity—and the tensions that emerged with the established community.

Indeed, much of the existing scholarship, especially focusing on the first twenty or so years of post-Soviet Jewish settlement, highlights the gulf between the new arrivals from the former Soviet Union and the existing postwar community in Germany.[72] Weiss and Gorelik, for example, claim that "many of the refugees rejected parallels drawn between their own experiences and those of the Eastern European Jews who had arrived in Germany after the war."[73] Certainly, attitudinal surveys from the 1990s appeared to confirm a lack of interest in Judaism among the new arrivals,[74] a strong attachment to Russian language and heritage,[75] intense connections to the Russian diaspora around the world,[76] and a marked sense of social alienation, especially among older people, whose German was generally poor and who struggled to find work commensurate with their qualifications.[77] (It is worth noting here that *jüdische Kontingentflüchtlinge* were part of a much larger migration of Russian speakers to Germany after the collapse of the Soviet Union. From 1991, around 1.8 million *Russlanddeutsche*—ethnic Germans—were also welcomed.[78] In Kat Kaufmann's 2015 novel *Superposition*, the Russian Jewish protagonist feels most connected to a fellow migrant from the former Soviet Union—an ethnic German.) Early studies, therefore, reflected

---

69 See Cohen, Haberfeld, and Kogan, "Who Went Where?"
70 See Becker, "Migration," 20–23.
71 See Pinkus, *The Jews of the Soviet Union*.
72 See, for example, Schoeps, "Russian-Speaking Jews."
73 Weiss and Gorelik, "The Russian-Jewish Immigration," 402.
74 See Ben-Rafael, "Russian Jews in Germany," 93–108.
75 Judith Kessler, "Homo Sovieticus."
76 See Ben-Rafael, "Russian-speaking Jews."
77 See Remennick, "'Idealists.' See also Remennick, "The New Russian-Jewish Diaspora," and Tress, "Germany's New 'Jewish question.'"
78 See Panagiotidis, *Postsowjetische Migration*.

and even intensified widespread doubts about Soviet-born Jews' willingness to integrate as Jews.[79] Robin Ostow describes how the *Jüdische Allgemeine*, an important mouthpiece for the established community, lionized the newcomers as a potential renaissance of Jewish existence in Germany while also running stories suggesting that many of them were criminals.[80] And even if there were a welcome revival of Jewish life, it would be something different. The historian Dan Diner famously declared that the arrival of "the Russians" meant that the "history of Jews in the Federal Republic of Germany has come to an end."[81]

A specific complaint leveled by members of the established community against Soviet-born immigrants was their apparent lack of commitment to German Jewish memory culture.[82] As Oliver Lubrich frames the concern, recently arrived Soviet-born Jews seemed to display "indifference to German-Jewish traditions and [a] distanced attitude toward the Holocaust."[83] Indeed, members of the existing community noted that their coreligionists preferred to celebrate the Red Army's victory over Nazi Germany on May 8 each year rather than commemorate the genocide. This was one aspect of a larger disconnect between different historical experiences. "While other Jews in Germany experience the Second World War as the great trauma," Y. Michal Bodemann and Olena Bagno summarize, "this is not necessarily so for the Russian Jews; for them, present-day Russian anti-Semitism and earlier the Gulag, have often been the greater traumatic experience."[84] For many descendants of the victims, references to the Soviet experience implied a diminution of Holocaust memory.

In all these ways, Soviet-born Jews were a disappointment to the survivors who had rebuilt the community after 1945, but also to the non-Jewish population more broadly,[85] who, as Sveta Roberman puts it, made "no particular demands on the newcomers, with one exception: Germany expected them to be Jewish."[86] The newcomers were disappointed too, insofar as they rejected the expectation imposed on them to rebuild Jewish life in Germany.[87]

---

79 Becker, "Migration." See also Tress, "Foreigners or Jews?"
80 Ostow, "The Post-Soviet immigrants."
81 Dan Diner, "Deutsch-jüdisch-russische Paradoxien."
82 See Schoeps, Jasper, Vogt, eds., *Russische Juden in Deutschland*.
83 Oliver Lubrich, "Are Russian Jews Postcolonial?"
84 Bodemann and Bagno, "In the Ethnic Twilight," 163.
85 See Körber, "Zäsur." See also Körber and Gotzmann, eds., *Lebenswirklichkeiten*.
86 Roberman, "Performing Jewishness," 187.
87 See Roberman, "Haunting Images."

More recent ethnographic and sociological research, however, suggests that "homo Sovieticus" (Kessler)[88] is not as one-dimensional as early studies imply, and that dispositions are changing quite rapidly, particularly among the younger generation. In an article published in 2003, just a few years after government policy had become much more restrictive and immigration had largely ended, Barbara Kietz notes that the new arrivals had "introduced new social and political elements into Jewish communities," including a more secular outlook, Russian culture, and distance from the way Jews had previously interacted with Germany, and concludes that "all these elements reshape Jewish communities in Germany, also making them, in all probability, less traditional and more pluralistic in the long run."[89] In a retrospective from 2008, Julius Schoeps and Olaf Glöckner describe continuing tensions with the established community, the existence of "Russian colonies," ignorance of Jewish rituals, and high unemployment, but they also note key successes, including the stabilization of a population in decline and a cultural and religious revival.[90] Eliezer Ben-Rafael even suggests that for many Russian-speaking Jews, "Germany provides the conditions to re-attach themselves to Jewishness—and as a corollary to Israel as a focus of all-Jewish solidarity—even among the sons or daughters of mixed families and those who live with non-Jewish partners."[91] Judith Kessler argues that younger Soviet-born Jews have developed a more "dualistic orientation," acquiring "the competence and cultural savvy to be successful within the new environment" and being more likely than their parents to be interested in Judaism and Jewish politics.[92] And Dani Kranz focuses on how "Russian Jews" in their twenties and thirties—along with young Israelis—are shaping a dynamic, diverse, and hybrid Jewish culture. "Forget Israel," Kranz quips: "The Future is in Berlin!"[93]

Moreover, many Soviet-born Jews *do* have a family memory of the Holocaust, or at least of fighting the Nazis. "Most Soviet Jews of the older generation lost relatives in mass executions of Jews during the German occupation of the western parts of the USSR in 1941–43," Larissa Remennick notes: "Thousands of Jewish women and children survived the war as a result of the organized evacuation of citizens from Moscow and Leningrad [. . .] Tens of thousands of Jewish men were recruited to the Soviet Army."[94] Indeed, as literary scholar Harriet Murav argues,

---

88 Kessler, "Homo Sovieticus," 131–43.
89 Tress, "Jewish Immigrants," 7.
90 See Schoeps and Glöckner, "Fifteen Years of Russian-Jewish Immigration."
91 Ben-Rafael, "Germany's Russian-speaking Jews," 78–79.
92 Kessler, "Homo Sovieticus," 140.
93 Kranz, "Forget Israel."
94 Remennick, "Idealists," 32.

it is of course not the case that Soviet Jews were not impacted by the Nazis' program of attempted extermination. The Holocaust, Murav summarizes, followed a "different trajectory"[95] in those parts of the Soviet Union occupied by the Germans. Mass shootings by *Einsatzgruppen* (mobile killing units) and their local accomplices in forests and ravines were the primary mode of killing rather the death camps in Poland that feature more prominently in Holocaust memory in Western Europe and the United States. As we shall see in later chapters, contemporary writers with a Soviet background are concerned to counter this Western ignorance of the "Holocaust by bullets"[96] even as they are also focused on "recovering" the specificity of their Jewish identity, including the genocide, from its partial occlusion under the communist system. As many historians have pointed out, the ethnic specificity of the Holocaust was generally downplayed, at least until the 1980s, with the victims generally categorized as Soviet citizens rather than Jews. Equally, the Soviet Jewish experience *was* part of the broader Soviet experience of the war, including combat in the Red Army or as civilians suffering German air raids, encirclements, or forced displacement.

In any case, as Franziska Becker notes, migrants' biographies are not simply a piece of luggage, "in which finished life-stories are placed, which just need to be unpacked."[97] Rather, the stories they bring with them interact with, are impacted by, and subtly alter what they encounter in their new environment. Karen Körber suggests that an examination of the family narratives of Russian-speaking Jews reveals "a process of reevaluation, deferral or overlapping of different memories enabling both the war and the specific fate of Jews to become visible." Just as important, she continues, "the experience of the present includes the encounter with Germany's writing of history and the identity of the Jewish communities in which the Holocaust has become an elementary part of the collective memory."[98] To illustrate these points, Körber cites Lena Gorelik, a Soviet-born writer who came to Germany in 1992 (and who is cited above, as an academic), and specifically the preface she wrote for the diary of Lena Muchina, who survived the siege of Leningrad as a girl. (The diary was published in German in 2013). For Körber, this is evidence for how Russian-speaking Jewish immigrants have contributed to the "pluralization of the Jewish community's communicative memory with their own painful, different experiences that also demand a place

---

95 Murav, *Music*, 151.
96 See Desbois, *The Holocaust by Bullets*.
97 Becker, *Angekommen in Deutschland*, 9.
98 Körber, "Conflicting Memories," 286. See also Körber, "Widerstreitende Erinnerungen."

around the central narrative of the Holocaust."[99] In an interview with the *Süddeutsche Zeitung* from 2014, in fact, Gorelik revealed that her own family had been trapped in Leningrad and argued that this episode of Nazi terror should also be commemorated on Holocaust Memorial Day.[100] In 2022–23, Gorelik toured Germany with the publicist Carolin Emcke and the actress Maryam Zaree, staging readings of texts by Holocaust survivors in a variety of venues.

Joseph Cronin gives further concrete examples of what has changed as Soviet-born Jews have adapted to norms of remembrance but also inflected them. He cites Rabbi Levy Barsilay, from Hamburg, who suggested in 2005 that the presence of immigrants from the former Soviet Union could encourage the established community to celebrate May 8, in honor of Jews who had resisted the Nazis in the ghettos or who had fought against them as soldiers in the Red Army. From among the new arrivals, Cronin refers to Larisa Fukelman, a Russian Jewish journalist who, also in 2005, and on the same occasion, noted that the Red Army's defeat of Nazi Germany sixty years earlier was not only a Soviet victory but also the end of the genocide of European Jews. What is happening, Cronin infers, is the emergence of a new kind of Holocaust commemoration as a result of changing attitudes in both groups, with "more encompassing forms which made space for Jewish heroes alongside victims."[101]

The analyses of literary texts in subsequent chapters provide further indications that over the course of two to three decades since their arrival in Germany, Soviet-born immigrants have developed a stronger sense of Jewish identity and are now articulating new versions of a (Russian) German Jewish identity. The newcomers are not only absorbing but also reshaping Holocaust memory culture, both from within and in dialogue with national and global discourses on the meaning of the genocide for the present day. More generally, Soviet-born writers embody the innovation and creativity that younger Russian-speaking Jews have introduced—reimagining the community into which they migrated, forging new alliances with other minorities, and opening German Jewish identity up to the world.

The Global Context

Bodemann is clearly correct when he says that Jewish identity and Jewish institutions in Germany especially are unavoidably embedded in "specific national, political, and legal contexts," including dependence on the financial support of the state and on a memory culture that is highly

---

99 Körber, "Conflicting Memories," 285.
100 Gorelik, "Jüdisch sein."
101 Cronin, *Russian-speaking Jews*, 80–83.

normative and cannot be ignored.[102] At the same time, it is important to stress that contemporary rearticulations of German Jewish identity do not take place solely in relation to the German (or Austrian) context. On the one hand, this reflects the fact that it is now generally easier to communicate, travel, and live across multiple places than ever before. On the other hand, it has to do with the familial connections to other parts of the world that shape the lives, and attitudes, of many Jews in Germany today. Soviet-born Jews visit friends and relatives in Israel and the United States as well as return "home" to Russia, Ukraine, and Belarus.[103] As Eliezer Ben-Rafael puts it, these immigrants to Germany "participate in transnational-diaspora structures that bind them to their counterparts in Jerusalem, Moscow, and New York,"[104] including non-Jewish Russian networks. And Jews who grew up in Germany also have family ties in other countries, of course. A common trope in texts by both Soviet-born writers and authors from the established community is travel to visit relatives in New York and Tel Aviv. In Austrian writer Doron Rabinovici's *Andernorts* (Elsewhere; 2010), the sociologist Ethan Rosen—a specialist in "transculturalism"—commutes between Vienna and Tel Aviv, though he finds that he is split even against himself in each location.[105]

For these reasons, any if not all the issues that dominate the discussion in Germany can also be considered to be local inflections of global debates across the diaspora, between the diaspora and Israel, and between Jews and non-Jews. Three themes that recur throughout recent texts evidence these intersections: who counts as Jewish?; Israel and its treatment of Palestinians; and the relationship between Jewish particularism and Jewish universalism.

As described above, members of the established community often doubted whether "the Russians" had a genuine attachment to Judaism. This was based on the newcomers' seeming ignorance of Jewish practice but also on the fact that the evidence of Jewish ancestry that they were required to show by the German state in many cases did not conform to Jewish law.[106] In the Soviet Union, Jewish ethnicity could be transmitted through either the father or the mother,[107] and the German authorities were even more expansive, "including also half- and sometimes quarter-Jews," Remennick notes. "On the other hand," she continues, "the Central Jewish Council of Germany and the local communities adopted a

---

102 Bodemann, "Globale Diaspora? Europäisches Judentum?," 172.
103 See Ben-Rafael, "Germany's Russian-speaking Jews," 78–79. See also Gitelman, "Homelands," especially 6–7.
104 Ben-Rafael, "Russian-speaking Jews in Germany," 185.
105 See Banki and Battegay, "Sieben Thesen," especially 45.
106 The German state has often been instrumental in defining Jewish identity since 1945. See Bodemann, "The State."
107 Shneer, "The Third Way," 112.

much more stringent religious definition, accepting in its ranks only those born of a Jewish mother."[108] Kessler estimates that by this definition as many as half the new arrivals did not count.[109] Again, as Weiss and Gorelik write, this was a major source of "tension between the Soviet-Jewish immigrants and the established Jewish communities in Germany, whose self-definition and identity is based on religious values."[110] Gorelik's 2005 short story "'Herr Grinblum, Sie sind kein Jude!'" (Mr. Grinblum, you are not a Jew!) plays on the irony that in the Soviet Union a Jewish patronymic would often mean discrimination, while for the Jewish community in Germany, having only a Jewish father was not sufficient.

Yet there were plenty of Jews already in Germany whose Jewishness did not fulfill strict *halachic* criteria. In large part, this has to do with the way the Holocaust had disrupted Jewish genealogies across Europe. It also has to do, however, with the long history of marrying-out and conversion out of Judaism. Exogamy is viewed differently by the various branches of Judaism, with Orthodox communities generally excluding those who chose non-Jewish spouses, but even Reform and Liberal Jews sometimes worry that the practice will lead to the gradual disappearance of Judaism. In Germany specifically, where marrying-out had become common before the Holocaust,[111] the dominance of Orthodox Judaism following the reestablishment of the community and the sensitivities associated with the Jewish presence in the land of the perpetrators combine to make the topic even more controversial. In 2021, Maxim Biller attacked the poet, stage performer, curator, and activist Max Czollek for having "appropriated" a Jewish identity based "only" on having a single Jewish grandfather.[112] Biller even compared Czollek to Benjamin Wilkomirski, the Swiss writer who had faked Jewish origins and a Holocaust biography.[113] Indeed, it was more likely the appropriation of Jewish suffering, as he saw it, that actually concerned Biller than any strict *halachic* definition. Czollek has become known for his mobilization of a Jewish biography—his grandfather was in exile in Shanghai—to side with marginalized minorities today. In July 2023, the journalist Fabian Wolff, who had built a career on criticizing Israel, admitted that he was not in fact Jewish. This revelation caused anxious reflection on the "special status" accorded to Jews in public discourse, and on who may speak as a Jew, and for Jews.[114]

---

108 Remennick, "Idealists," 31.
109 Kessler, "Homo Sovieticus," 135.
110 Weiss and Gorelik, "The Russian-Jewish Immigration," 386.
111 See Lowenstein, "Jewish Intermarriage" and Voigtländer and Voth, "Married to Intolerance."
112 See Bodemann, "Die Causa Max Czollek."
113 See Eskin, *A Life in Pieces*.
114 See Nutt, "Der Identitätsschwindel des Fabian Wolff."

Protagonists who do not fulfill *halachic* criteria are common in contemporary novels, in fact, often evidently incorporating their authors' own ambivalent status. Eva Menasse's *Vienna* (2005), for example, tells the story of her Catholic and Jewish family,[115] and in Mirna Funk's *Winternähe* (Near winter; 2015) Lola expresses the same anxiety about her identity as a *Vaterjüdin* (Jew by patrilineal descent)—and about what it means to belong to both the victim and the perpetrator collective—as Funk does in newspaper articles.[116] Among Soviet-born writers, the protagonists of Kat Kaufmann's *Superposition* (2015) and Dmitrij Kapitelman's *Das Lächeln meines unsichtbaren Vaters* (The smile of my invisible father; 2016) both suffer from the knowledge that, as *Vaterjuden*, they don't quite count.

Funk's Lola and Kapitelman's Dmitrij travel to Israel to discover the Jewish identity that they feel they lack. Like Mascha in the Soviet-born writer Olga Grjasnowa's *Der Russe ist einer, der Birken liebt* (All Russians love birch trees; 2012), they soon become witnesses to Palestinian suffering inflicted by the Jewish state, however. In the face of a sustained campaign of rocket attacks by Hamas and rising antisemitism in Europe, Lola's sympathy is largely with Israel—though she later quits the country and travels to Thailand—whereas Dmitrij and Mascha find Israeli ethnic-nationalism difficult to reconcile with what they take to be the fundamental message of the Holocaust, that is, the requirement to express solidarity with all victims. For Lola, loyalty to Israel as the refuge for Jews everywhere is paramount, even if she is ultimately disillusioned. For Dmitrij and Mascha, in contrast, Israel's treatment of the Palestinians is a betrayal of universalistic Jewish values and indeed Holocaust memory.

In these and other recent novels, the global context is the discomfort that many Jews in the diaspora now experience in relation to Israel's political shift to the right, its harsh treatment of Palestinians in Gaza and the West Bank (and discrimination against Israeli Arabs), and its encouragement of Jewish settlement in areas designated for a future Palestinian state, including the displacement of Palestinian residents.[117] In the United States, what Steven Rosenthal calls "the waning of the American Jewish love affair with Israel" had already begun in late 1990s and early 2000s,[118] in large part because of the Palestinian issue,[119] whereas the different European context meant that most Jews there were still broadly pro-Israel, fearful for its security, unconvinced by their governments' support, and alive to any potential resurgence of antisemitism in countries

---

115 See Hamidouche, "The New Austrian Family Novel."
116 See for example, Funk, "Am Ende."
117 See Schoeps, "Contemporary Philosophical and Ethical Fights."
118 See Rosenthal, *Irreconcilable Differences.*
119 See Waxman, *Trouble in the Tribe.*

with long histories of persecution and, today, large Muslim populations.[120] More recently, however, sentiments have shifted in Europe too; not only on account of the treatment of Palestinians but also because of successive Israeli governments' perceived lack of engagement with issues that are vital to younger Jews in the diaspora especially. These include the different affiliations of Jewish belief and practice, conversion, and the broader issue of "who is a Jew?"[121] At the same time, across the diaspora, Jews are sensitive to criticism of Israel, fearing that it all too often betrays antisemitism.[122] In Germany specifically, Jewish anxieties have increased since the summer of 2015 following the arrival of refugees from predominantly Muslim countries across North Africa and the Middle East.[123] Similarly, the surge in anti-Jewish incidents in response to Israel's invasion of Gaza in October 2023—itself a response to the massacres of more than 1,200 Israelis by Hamas earlier that month—has also caused great trepidation.

More generally, many Jews in both Europe and the United States may now perceive a conflict between their understanding of Jewishness as a cosmopolitan identity and what they see as the Israeli state's ethno-nationalism. This is essentially an expression of the tension between Jewish universalism and Jewish particularism that has long shaped Jewish thought and culture.[124] On the one side, therefore, there is an idealistic, even idealized vision of diasporic existence as the source of Jewish values, including openness to the world, acting as a bridge between cultures, and the belief in equality for all. This position is espoused by prominent thinkers such as Alan Wolfe in the United States[125] and Micha Brumlik in Germany.[126] On the other side, there is a pragmatic determination to pursue Jewish interests, even if this means disregarding the rights of others.[127] The contrast between the two standpoints also relates to different interpretations of the Nazi genocide. For some, the Holocaust

---

120 See Shain and Brisman, "Diaspora."
121 See Eytan, "Complexity."
122 See Schoeps, "Anti-semitism."
123 See Brenner, "A New German Jewry," especially 426.
124 See Lundgren, *Particularism and Universalism* and Hughes, *Rethinking Jewish Philosophy*. Before the Holocaust, this discussion was especially energetic in the German-speaking countries, including Moses Mendelssohn and the Jewish Enlightenment; the emergence of Reform Judaism; the historicizing study of Jewish texts pioneered by the *Wissenschaft des Judentums* (science of Judaism); Herzl's Zionist 1896 tract *Der Judenstaat* (The Jewish state); and Franz Rosenzweig, Martin Buber, and Gerschom Scholem on Jewish history, theology, mysticism, and scripture.
125 See Wolfe, *At Home in Exile*.
126 See Brumlik, *Kritik des Zionismus*.
127 See, for example, Gordis, *We Stand Divided*.

is an injunction to defend the dignity, human rights, and lives of all.[128] (Reference is sometimes made to Hannah Arendt's dictum that the Holocaust was a "crime against Humanity, perpetrated upon the body of the Jewish people".)[129] For others, in contrast, the genocide imposes an unavoidable obligation to put the security of Jews above any other concerns.[130] Following the Hamas atrocities of October 7, 2023, and Israel's assault on Gaza, killing tens of thousands of Palestinians, Jews around the world are being forced to consider their Jewish identity and attachment to Israel even more intensively, of course.

For many Jews in North America and Europe today, expressing opposition to Israel's treatment of the Palestinians is not only a matter of asserting an authentic—cosmopolitan—Jewish identity, however. It also reflects a more profound belief that Jewishness should be good for something, that is, that Jews are imbued with a special obligation to make the world a better place. This is often expressed with reference to the concept of *tikkun olam*[131] ("to repair the world") that originated in classical rabbinical literature and which, especially since the Jewish Enlightenment (*haskalah*), has come to imply Jews' responsibility to seek to right injustice.[132] *Tikkun olam* is often cited as a reason for the disproportionate involvement of Jews in progressive causes, from the mass movements for economic and political equality of the nineteenth and twentieth centuries, to civil rights campaigns in the 1960s, to agitating on behalf of refugees today. As discussed in later chapters, *tikkun olam* is one dimension, or manifestation, of what British historian Adam Sutcliffe terms "Jewish purpose."[133]

Holocaust Memory, Solidarity, and Worldliness

The Jewish community that now exists is thus quite different from the community that reemerged after 1945, largely dominated by Eastern European survivors with an Orthodox heritage and their descendants in the second and third generations. It is strikingly diverse—mainly immigrants from the former Soviet Union but also Israeli and American Jews, and even some German converts[134]—heterogeneous in its confessional

---

128 See Sznaider, *Jewish Memory*.

129 Cited in Sznaider, *Jewish Memory*, 119. See Sznaider, "Hannah Arendt's Jewish Cosmopolitanism" and Michman, "Particularist and Universalist Interpretations."

130 See Patt, *Israel and the Holocaust*.

131 See Krasner, "The Place of Tikkun Olam."

132 See Birnbaum and Cohen, eds., *Tikkun Olam*.

133 Sutcliffe, *What Are Jews For?*

134 See Steiner, *Die Inszenierung*.

affiliations, and globally oriented, intensively engaging with the diaspora, with Israel, and with Russian speakers around the world and with countries of origin. In addition, many younger Jews especially are active in political causes relating to gender and sexuality, racism, and migrants and refugees.

Recent German Jewish writing incorporates this diversity and offers the likely non-Jewish German reader an insight into the history, religious practices, conventions, and sensitivities of the minority. Some novels are accompanied by glossaries of Yiddish terms or integrate explanations of culture and customs, for example, while others draw on historical works to situate life stories within the contexts of Nazi persecution, the Holocaust, or Soviet antisemitism. Likewise, there are obvious references to lived experiences of migration, antisemitic prejudice, or the suffering of parents and grandparents. Yet the corpus comprises far more than fictionalized auto-ethnography or lightly reworked biography. Echoing Nolden's comment on the Young Jewish Literature, therefore, today's German Jewish fiction is not simply "minority literature," with individual works to be read solely as "sociological phenomena (which they also—but not only—are)."[135] The chapters of close reading of literary texts that follow thus highlight formal strategies and stylistic innovations and how these not only respond to but also creatively refashion social reality. These aesthetic features most commonly include a propensity to merge author and narrator; multiple, speculative, or even fabulated reconstructions of the Jewish past, including the genocide; a flagrantly pop aesthetic that similarly appears to undermine the sanctity of Holocaust memory; an emphasis on gender and sexuality relating to narrative stance and "voice"; and, in many novels, frequent intertextual allusions to German, German Jewish, and Russian literature.

Chapter 1, "Self-positioning and Holocaust memory," examines three novels that enact different artistic approaches but are all fundamentally concerned with how their Jewish protagonists position themselves vis-à-vis the non-Jewish majority and other Jews, whether the "Russians," the "Germans," or the Orthodox and (increasingly) Reform congregations that largely determine who does—and doesn't—count as a Jew. Adriana Altaras's 2011 *titos brille* (tito's glasses) is conventionally autobiographical, then, presenting an account of her parents' wartime experiences and their role in the reestablishment of the Jewish community following their move from communist Yugoslavia to West Germany in the mid-1960s. The impetus for this chronicling of postwar history—including the fate of Sephardic Jews during the Holocaust—is the arrival of immigrants from the former Soviet Union in her area of Berlin, which also appears to prompt the daughter to align herself more closely with the

135 Nolden, *Junge jüdische Literatur.*

non-Jewish majority. Soviet-born Jan Himmelfarb's *Sterndeutung* (Star reading; 2015), in contrast, combines ethnographical description, historical facts, and pure fabulation. The novel depicts its middle-aged protagonist's struggles to integrate into the existing German Jewish memory culture while narrating his obviously implausible recollection of his birth in 1941 and summarizing what he has read in academic works about the deportations and mass killings taking place around the same time. Finally, Benjamin Stein's 2014 *Das Alphabet des Rabbi Löw* (The alphabet of Rabbi Löw), which had already appeared in 1995 as *Das Alphabet des Juda Liva*, is analyzed as an act of literary and religious nonconformity, in which Holocaust memory still reverberates but is far less defining of Jewish identity. This scandalously inventive novel combines elements of Kabbalah with allusions to the German Jewish literary tradition, to contrive an unorthodox Orthodox Judaism for modern Germany.

The close readings presented in chapter 1 reference the key insights that have emerged in the introduction, namely that the pluralization of the Jewish community has been accompanied by a gradual accommodation with Germany; a growing impetus to look beyond the land of the perpetrators; and an increasing tendency to ask what it means to be a Jew beyond the traumatic legacy of the Holocaust. Further to this, however, the chapter develops an argument that protagonists' self-positioning vis-à-vis the non-Jewish majority and other Jews contributes to a broader process of expansion and differentiation with regard to German (Jewish) memory culture—even when this process is provoked by a pragmatic or sometimes even parochial desire to signal standing within the community. This often involves an element of transgression, as aesthetic, memorial, and group norms are tested and reframed.

Chapter 2 focuses on Jewish solidarity with migrants and refugees (especially Muslims), victims of state persecution, and other marginalized groups. As German Jewish writing looks outwards to include Soviet and Soviet Jewish histories and parallels with other atrocities—even including, for example, the genocide in Rwanda or the civil war in Syria—the tension between Jewish particularism and Jewish universalism comes into sharper focus. In Funk's *Winternähe*, then, Lola travels to Israel to flee German antisemitism and to affirm her sense of Jewish identity—she is Jewish "only" on her father's side—but soon discovers that her desire to experience a sense of belonging in the Jewish state is in tension with her empathy with Palestinians. After a few months, she flees to Thailand before ultimately returning to Germany. In Kat Kaufmann's 2015 pop novel *Superposition*, the twenty-something jazz musician Izy Lewin is unable (or unwilling) to transcend the specificity of her Soviet Jewish past in order to imagine a cosmopolitan oneness with her German peers, never mind solidarity with the homeless people, migrants, and gypsies who inhabit the margins of the narrative. Finally, Petrowskaja's autobiographically inspired *Vielleicht Esther* (Maybe Esther; 2014) recounts its Soviet-born protagonist's travels to recover family history across eastern Europe and her efforts to think through the near-extermination of European Jews as simultaneously particular and universal. Here too, it seems that the attempt to imagine the "as if" of empathetic identification with others can only ever be partially successful.

In the Young Jewish Literature, the focus was on Jewish victims and German perpetrators. To reprise Braese, authors wrote "insistently [. . .] about themselves as Jews [. . .] about themselves as Jews in the concrete German present."[136] In the New German Jewish Literature, in contrast, a multidirectional, cosmopolitan, or universalizing Holocaust memory can underpin solidarity with others and a readiness to defend general principles of anti-racism and anti-fascism. At the same time, chapter 2 argues, even as this reframing of the genocide makes possible a more outward-looking German Jewish identity, it might also obscure the Jewishness of the Jewish past—which Soviet-born writers especially may only recently have recovered in their own family histories—or dissolve it into the abstraction of politico-philosophical discourses on historical justice and universal human rights. Relatedly, there is a difficulty in how to render this panoramic perspective on the Holocaust in compelling literary form, when German Jewish writing has conventionally focused on the intimacy of traumatic memory transmitted down through the generations in families turned in upon themselves. As the scale changes to encompass "the world," new narrative approaches must be found.

Chapter 3, "worldliness," examines three novels that articulate a worldly Jewish identity beyond the fixation on family trauma and indeed beyond Holocaust memory itself, and—in the first—without "burdening" Jewishness with a "special mission" to mobilize in solidarity with others. (Jewish identity can be rooted in faith, of course, which is what Stein attempts in *Rabbi Löw*, with his unorthodox Orthodox Judaism.) Channah Trzebiner's *Die Enkelin, oder Wie ich zu Pessach die vier Fragen nicht wusste* (The granddaughter, or how I didn't know the four questions at Passover; 2013)—like Funk's *Winternähe*—features a young female protagonist struggling to honor her grandparents' trauma and to define her own, authentic way of living as a Jew in modern-day Germany. Trzebiner's literary alter ego Channah leaves behind her family's strict, patriarchal Orthodox Judaism in order to throw herself into consumer culture. Again similar to *Winternähe,* the attempt to give meaning to Jewishness without continually invoking the Jewish exceptionalism of the Holocaust involves a triangulation of Germany, Israel, and "the world," also referencing current debates across the diaspora about support for Israel given its treatment of the Palestinians and about where

---

136 Braese, "Writing against Reconciliation," 28.

Jewish values now reside. A distinctly, even provocatively, "pop" aesthetic underscores the aspiration to integrate into the global—or rather Western—mainstream while also communicating the protagonists' apparent transgression of the sanctity of Jewish memory.

The second novel considered in chapter 3 is Sasha Marianna Salzmann's *Außer sich* (Beside oneself; 2017), arguably the most experimental German Jewish text to have appeared in recent decades. The analysis of this novel suggests that Jewish worldliness can be "written back into" Jewish family history, as it were, once received narratives of nation, gender, and the imperative to integrate and conform have been queered to recover moments of difference, self-transcendence and self-transformation, and solidarity. The argument, then, is that *Außer sich* revives a Jewish worldliness that—unlike the ultimately superficial imitation of global consumer culture depicted in Trzebiner and Funk—is deeply rooted in Jewish thinking on the meaning and purpose of diaspora, including to exemplify the ideal of cosmopolitanism. Here, Holocaust memory may be less central, and Jewishness itself might specify an attitude of social and ethical engagement rather than Jewish ritual and practice, or even belief.

Chapter 3 concludes with a discussion of Grjasnowa's *Der verlorene Sohn* (The lost son; 2020), in which discernibly Jewish characters play only a small role, and asks whether the trend toward worldliness in recent German Jewish writing necessarily implies *self-effacement*, that is, the setting aside of Jewish concerns in order to attend to global histories and to mobilize on behalf of others. If Jewish identity is focused on solidarity rather than on faith, tradition, and heritage, or even the genocide, might it eventually fade from view entirely? (*Der verlorene Sohn* focuses on the fate of a young Muslim prince abducted by the Tsar in nineteenth-century imperial Russia.) Or can a *Jewish sensibility* suffice to underwrite the Jewishness of a text—and the Jewishness of a humanistic and, above all, universalistic mode of engagement with the secular? These questions are thought through with reference to Polish Jewish philosopher Isaac Deutscher's self-characterization as a "non-Jewish Jew."[137]

Chapters 1 to 3 build on the ethnographic and sociological scholarship reviewed earlier in this introduction to argue that the protagonists of contemporary German Jewish novels position themselves in relation to other Jews as much as the German majority; debate whether Holocaust memory can be mobilized in solidarity with others; and sometimes even gesture beyond the traumatic legacy of the genocide in order to establish, or reestablish, a Jewish worldliness that can be less burdened by the past and even point the way toward a more just and harmonious future for all humankind. The trend in today's German Jewish writing is an evolution away from a fixation on German perpetrators and Jewish victims toward

---

137 See Deutscher, "The Non-Jewish Jew."

a framing of Jewish identity as fundamentally and productively diasporic. This literary development, it can be argued, reflects shifts in Jewish self-understanding across a newly diverse and self-assertive community, but it also contributes to the reimagining of this self-understanding.

The conclusion reiterates these findings while drawing out resonances across chapters and between texts, with particular attention to the thematization in many recent novels of the relative privilege Jewish protagonists enjoy vis-à-vis other minorities by virtue of being, as it were, "white." This leads into a discussion of what sociologists Naika Foroutan and Erol Yıldız term the "postmigrant society."[138] To the extent that Jews now position themselves in relation not (only) to the white majority but (also) to the other minorities, including many Muslims, who together constitute Germany's social reality as an ethnically diverse European nation, there is the potential for new alliances and new forms of Jewish self-articulation. At the same time, differences persist, cultures and values may clash, and the global context—including, of course, the ongoing conflict in the Middle East—cannot be wished away.

After the Atrocities of October 7, 2023, and Israel's Assault on Gaza

This book was completed between late 2023 and mid-2024, that is, just as Jews and non-Jews around the world were reacting to the indiscriminate massacre of around 1,200 Israelis by Hamas on October 7 and to Israel's subsequent invasion of Gaza and the killing of tens of thousands of Palestinians. The final section of the conclusion discusses how these shocking events might qualify—or amplify—some of the developments outlined in this book. How did German Jewish writers respond in the immediate aftermath of October 7, and what can we speculate about the future of German Jewish identity as a renewed embrace of—or retreat from—worldliness and solidarity with others?

---

138 See, for example, Foroutan, *Die postmigrantische Gesellschaft* and Yıldız and Hill, eds., *Postmigrantische Visionen*.

1: Holocaust Memory: Adriana Altaras, Jan Himmelfarb, and Benjamin Stein

Academic analysis of German Jewish writing since the 1980s has tended to highlight its exploration of the inevitably fraught relationship between Germans and Jews, and especially the incongruity of living as a Jew in the land of the perpetrators. Likewise, sociologists writing about the small and relatively homogeneous Jewish community before its demographic transformation from the early 1990s have typically emphasized its simultaneous ambivalence toward and dependence on the non-Jewish majority. In general terms, therefore, social science and literary scholarship has focused on the instrumentalization of Jews to bolster postwar Germany's self-image as (now) democratic and tolerant, and focused on the majority's exoticization of Jews to imagine—that is, invent—a sanitized German past or to at least indulge in nostalgia for a time before the country's responsibility for the Holocaust.

For example, in an influential book published in 1996, sociologist Y. Michal Bodemann coined the term "Gedächtnistheater" (memory theater)[1] to describe how Jews are required to perform the role of admiring and appreciative witnesses to German contrition, and thereby to confirm the nation's transformation not only into a place where Jews could feel safe but also—non-Jewish Germans liked to think—into an example to the world of a successful confrontation with a "difficult past." (In recent years, "Gedächtnistheater" has been recast as "Integrationstheater" by the polemicist Max Czollek, to describe how migrants are compelled to "perform" German values in order to secure their acceptance.)[2] Other scholars, especially from outside Germany, have focused on the *cultural* appropriation of Jewishness that emerged from the early 1990s in the wake of Unification, generational change, and the global interest in Jewish and Holocaust history. Jack Zipes, for example,[3] noted a "fascination for things Jewish," as Jewish food, theater, and klezmer music was suddenly everywhere, along with a proliferation of Holocaust memorials, for example in the once heavily Jewish *Scheunenviertel* in East Berlin.[4] As

---

1   See Bodemann, *Gedächtnistheater*.
2   See Roca Lizarazu, "'Integration.'"
3   See Jack Zipes, "The Contemporary German Fascination for Things Jewish."
4   See Alt, "Yiddish."

Constantin Goschler and Anthony Kauders put it, "the intensified interest in everything Jewish [is] directed less at the Jews who now actually lived in Germany than at an imagined Jewry. Jews became a preferred object of nostalgia—along with windmills and water towers."[5] Similarly, Karen Remmler speaks of an "imagined cosmopolitanism that would return Germany to a sense of 'normalcy.'"[6]

The "fascination with things Jewish" extends to Jewish authors too, needless to say. Typically, publishers draw attention to a Jewish biography in marketing materials, including on a book's back cover or on the inside of the dust jacket. In part, this is a reflection of what Sander Gilman calls the "market value of ethnic literature";[7] more specifically, it relates to the particularly—or peculiarly—representative function that is expected of Jews in public discourse. Jewish writers are called upon to "speak for" Jews on television programs, in newspaper articles, at cultural events, and on anniversaries of key dates relating to Nazism and the Holocaust. Vladimir Vertlib's *Letzter Wunsch* (Last wish; 2003) is one of many contemporary texts that thematize this pressure to speak for all Jews for a non-Jewish German audience. In this novel, Gabriel Salzinger joins a live radio show to discuss his deceased father, who cannot be buried in a local Jewish cemetery because he is not held to be *halachically* Jewish (his maternal grandmother had converted in a non-Orthodox ceremony). Rather than engaging with his personal distress, however, listeners inundate Gabriel with their ill-considered opinions about Israel, Jewish community leaders, and antisemitism.[8] Similarly, from the younger generation, Dana Vowinckel satirizes the inclination of non-Jewish Germans to read Jewishness into everything a Jewish writer does or says. In her short story "In my Jewish Bag" (2022), for example, the entire contents of her bag seem to relate to her Jewishness, notably a pen, sedatives, and the Kippah she carries with her to express her "Sympathie mit Philosemiten"[9] (sympathy with philosemites). Here, the joke is a reference to the stereotype of Jews as neurotic scribblers and to the perversity of Germans who expect to be congratulated for their embrace of the victims. Vowinckel's first novel, *Gewässer im Ziplock* (Still water in a ziplock; 2023), is a portrait of Jewish family life that is itself evidently addressed to a non-Jewish German reader, complete with a glossary.

Maxim Biller has long railed against the opprobrium heaped on Jews if they fail to meet German expectations. Frequently styled in the German

---

5   Goschler and Kauders, "The Jews in German Society," 362.
6   Remmler, "Encounters Across the Void," 21.
7   Gilman, "Introduction," 24.
8   See Guenther, "The Poetics of Ritual in Diaspora."
9   Vowinckel, "In my Jewish Bag."

media as a *Provokateur vom Dienst* (provocateur by profession),[10] the author's truculent public persona and taboo-breaking journalistic and literary work undermine the majority's preferred image of Jews as purely victims, worthy of pity on account of their suffering and grateful for the care now lavished on them by the descendants of the perpetrators.[11] Biller's newspaper articles, essays, and short stories thus relentlessly expose the rank hypocrisy of a country that has still not fully acknowledged its Nazi past and the cravenness of the older generation of German Jews that desired only to prosper and not draw attention to themselves,[12] whereas many of his novels more specifically push back against the stereotype of the virtuous Jewish victim by presenting protagonists who are self-regarding, sex-obsessed, and even deviant. In the opening pages of *Die Tochter* (The daughter; 2000), for example, Motto masturbates to a pornographic film featuring the daughter that he has not seen for ten years. Later, he exploits the sexual availability of German women wishing to learn Jewish customs. In *Biografie* (Biography; 2016), Soli Karubiner— who shares key biographical details with Biller—quits Germany after a younger author threatens to release a video of him pleasuring himself in a sauna, and flees to Prague and Tel Aviv, also to escape his neurotic Jewish family. (*Biografie* was poorly received by critics, whereupon Biller accused them of antisemitism.)[13] In these two novels, as throughout his oeuvre, Biller is self-admittedly influenced by the scurrilously priapic fiction of Philip Roth.[14] In his 2009 autobiographical account of his emergence as a writer, *Der gebrauchte Jude* (the used Jew), Biller describes the scandalous appeal of Roth and other American Jewish authors and his own struggle to develop an authentic voice in a literary culture where he is always immediately co-opted as a "representative Jew."[15]

Biller's self-staging as an uninhibited but also overly sensitive, and above all, *ungrateful* Jew, however, is also directed against what he sees as the conformist quietism of parents and grandparents. *Der gebrauchte Jude* thus relates how young Jews in the 1980s desired to demarcate themselves

---

10   For Biller's own commentary on how he is received, see his 2018 essay "Wer nichts glaubt, schreibt" (He who believes in nothing, writes). A thoughtful reflection on Biller's public persona can be found in Stefan Willeke's 2017 article in *Zeit-Magazin*, "Der Unzumutbare" (The unreasonable one).

11   See Remmler, "Maxim Biller."

12   Biller's journalistic pieces and short stories are collated in *Wenn ich einmal reich und tot bin* (Once I am rich and dead; 1990), *Die Tempojahre* (Tempo years; 1991), *Land der Väter und Verräter* (Country of fathers and traitors; 1994), *Deutschbuch* (German book; 2001), *Bernsteintage* (Amber days; 2004), *Moralische Geschichten* (Parables; 2005), and *Liebe heute* (Love today; 2007).

13   See Platthaus, "Brauchen Kritiker jetzt einen Ahnennachweis?"

14   See Rubin-Dorsky, "Philip Roth."

15   See Codrai, "Lost in Third Space?"

not only from the non-Jewish German majority but also from the older generation that had reestablished the Jewish community after 1945 and now wished only to "fit in." In fact, Biller's *transgression*—not only of the expectations of the majority but also of the norms of "living as a Jew in Germany" established by the survivors after 1945—is exemplary of the aesthetic and ideological program of second-generation writers. Biller's friend and oftentimes rival Henryk Broder is comparably outspoken in his journalistic attacks on German hypocrisy and Jewish acquiescence,[16] and Rafael Seligmann too undercuts the idealization of the innately virtuous Jewish victim by both non-Jews and Jews in novels such as *Der Milchmann* (The milkman; 1999), in which it is hinted that the elderly protagonist Weinberg may have falsely claimed credit for an act of altruism in a camp fifty years previously. (Broder quit Germany for Israel in 1981, assailing the antisemitism of the German Left in an article titled "Warum ich gehe" [Why I am going]. He returned in 1993.)[17] Biller, Broder, and Seligmann have routinely been decried as *Nestbeschmutzer* (foulers of their own nests).[18]

Speaking to the BBC in 2012, Seligmann declared: "People feel it's not enough to have a 'Holocaust identity.' We are trying to show that the Jewish identity is broader [. . .] It's about culture and history and politics."[19] Indeed, the urge to disrupt and even subvert that characterizes the work of Biller, Seligmann, and other second-generation writers is not just an attitude *against* something. By challenging the majority's exploitation and exoticization of Jews and the conformity of their parents and grandparents, authors such as Biller, Seligmann, Barbara Honigmann, Robert Schindel, Esther Dischereit, and Doron Rabinovici also at least suggest that a more expansive depiction of the Jewish experience might be possible, even desirable—even if their own work remains largely fixated on the incongruity of living as a Jew in Germany (or Austria) after the Holocaust. In recent novels, correspondingly, Seligmann presents a *twentieth-century* Jewish story rather than simply the Holocaust and its legacy and suggests the affection that Jews once felt for the German language, German culture, and even Germany itself—and now might be able to feel once again. The first two installments of a planned trilogy of autobiographical novels, *Lauf, Ludwig, lauf! Eine Jugend zwischen Synagoge und Fußball* (Run, Ludwig, run! A youth between Synagogue and football; 2019) and *Hannah und Ludwig—Heimatlos in Tel Aviv* (Hannah and Ludwig—uprooted in Tel Aviv; 2020) thus relate his father's

---

16 See Dollinger, "Anti-Semitism."
17 Broder, "Warum ich gehe."
18 See Bower, "Rafael Seligmann (1947–)."
19 Seligmann, quoted by Steven Evans, "Anti-semitism still Haunts Germany."

Bavarian childhood, flight to Palestine, service in the British Army's Jewish Brigade, Israel's War of Independence, and Ludwig's return in 1957 to Germany with his wife Hannah and the ten-year-old Rafael. Similarly, Biller's *Biografie, Sechs Koffer* (Six suitcases; 2018), and *Sieben Versuche zu lieben* (Seven attempts to love; 2020), excavate family history in the communist bloc (including a relative who may have denounced a grandfather to the KGB), Soviet antisemitism, and flight to the West. This focus on Soviet and Soviet Jewish history aligns Biller, perhaps unexpectedly, with the cohort of Russian-speaking younger writers who immigrated as children in the early 1990s.

Transgression enables an expansion of the scope of Jewish memory and a more differentiated articulation of Jewish stances on life in Germany, the "function" of Holocaust memory, and Jewishness itself. It is a gesture of *self-positioning*, therefore, that authors—and, of course, the protagonists of their novels—enact in order to "try out" the various and sometimes competing versions of German Jewish and Jewish identity that have emerged over recent decades in consequence of the greatly increased size and diversity of the community, or to imagine (or revive) other potentialities of Jewish self-understanding entirely. Here, the term self-positioning is drawn from social psychology, and especially the work of Rom Harré and Luk van Langenhove. Self-positioning, Harré and van Langenhove argue, constitutes "the discursive construction of personal stories that make a person's actions intelligible" in relation to the "moral order within which the discursive process takes place," including forms of speech and behavior that challenge this order and assert novel articulations of selfhood.[20]

In later chapters, other modes of self-positioning will be discussed, including the (re)fabulation of Jewish family history both before the Holocaust and beyond its geographical extent, an embrace of a distinctly unOrthodox pop aesthetic, and the queering of Jewishness itself. In each and every form it takes, however, self-positioning describes how Jewish protagonists *triangulate* their Jewishness in relation to non-Jewish Germans and to other Jews with different cultural, religious, and historical experiences. Members of the established community reconfigure previous norms of engagement with the majority in order to reassert their position vis-à-vis the "Russians." The immigrants from the former Soviet Union, in turn, must define a *Russian* German Jewish identity against both non-Jewish and Jewish Germans united by their skepticism of the newcomers. Otherwise, Jews debate with one another and with the overwhelmingly non-Jewish society in which they reside about secularism, religious faith, and what constitutes Jewish identity today above and beyond Holocaust memory.

20   Harré and van Langenhove, "Varieties," 355 and 399.

This chapter examines three contemporary novels in which German-born, Soviet-born, and religiously-oriented Jewish protagonists triangulate their identities in dialogue—and often disagreement—with each another and with the non-Jewish majority. In essence, it is argued that the self-positioning in response to the pluralization of Jewish life in Germany that takes place in Adriana Altaras's *titos brille* (tito's glasses; 2011), Jan Himmelfarb's *Sterndeutung* (Star reading; 2015), and Benjamin Stein's *Das Alphabet des Rabbi Löw* (The alphabet of Rabbi Löw; 2014)—depends on but also promotes an "opening-up" of Holocaust memory, and of Jewish memory more generally. Subsequent chapters will then explore the tensions that arise in other texts when the legacy of the genocide is further universalized and an even more radical reorientation of Jewish identity toward "worldliness" is insinuated.

Jews, Germans, and "The Russians": Adriana Altaras's *titos brille*

Adriana Altaras was born in 1960 in Zagreb. In 1964, her father Jakob—a leading figure in the ruling Communist Party who had fought with Tito's partisans—was forced to flee Yugoslavia on account of the state's campaign of anti-Jewish persecution. Adriana was smuggled to Italy, where she remained with her aunt and uncle until 1967 when she joined Jakob in West Germany, along with her mother Thea, a onetime inmate of the Rab concentration camp established by the Italians in (now) Croatia, and a passionate communist and architect who had been prevented from leaving at the same time as her husband. In West Germany, the family settled in the city of Gießen, in Hessen, where Jakob had become a senior physician and professor at the university hospital. Over the following decades, Jakob refounded the local Jewish community (but failed to be elected as Chair of the *Zentralrat der Juden in Deutschland*), Thea became known for her research on destroyed synagogues across the state of Hesse, and Adriana established herself as an actress and theater director. Adriana Altaras also began to write and stage her own dramatic works, focused on the banality of German memory culture and antisemitism, notably *Jud Sauer* in 2002 (Sour Jew, invoking the notorious motif of "Jud Süß," or Sweet Jew, including the 1940 Nazi film of that name)[21] and the provocatively named comedy *Trauer to go* (Mourning to go; 2004). Only in her early fifties did Altaras begin to publish autobiographically inspired fiction, including *titos brille* (2011), *Doitscha: Eine jüdische Mutter packt aus* (Germans [in mock Yiddish]: a Jewish mother tells all; 2014), *Das Meer*

---

21 See Sheffi, "Jud Süss." See also Niven, *Jud Süß*.

und ich waren im besten Alter (The sea and I were in our prime; 2017), and *Die jüdische Souffleuse* (The Jewish stage-prompter; 2018).

In *titos brille*, Altaras offers an account of her parents' persecution by the Nazis and their Croatian allies during the war years, their flight from communist rule in Yugoslavia, the consolidation of the Jewish community in West Germany beginning in the 1960s, and the author's own recent interest in Jewish ritual and practice. First and foremost, the novel is a memorial of sorts, for the author's recently deceased mother and father but also for the survivors from across central and eastern Europe who reestablished a Jewish presence as well as the multiethnic, multilingual "Old Europe" that they embodied: "so sterben sie langsam, die letzten Überlebenden, nehmen das alte Europa mit und fürs Erste gibt es keinen Ersatz." (Now they are slowly dying, the last survivors, they are taking the Old Europe with them, and for now there is nothing to replace it.)[22] The tone of this overtly autobiographical narrative is largely elegiac and even melancholic, then, as in the quotation above, but there are also moments of wry humor and occasional flashes of indignation, pettiness, and even prejudice that allow the reader to believe that he or she is being given privileged access to Adriana's inner world.

It is the sudden presence of Russian-speaking Jews in the narrator's Berlin neighborhood, coinciding with the deaths of her father in 2001 and then her mother in 2004, that is the impetus for Adriana's retelling of her parents' escape from Yugoslavia and their contribution to the rebuilding of the Jewish community in Gießen and indeed nationally. She reports, for example, how it was "Jüdische Russen, russische Juden" (Jewish Russians, Russian Jews; *tb*, 102) who arrived en masse to snap up bargains when she was selling off the contents of her parents' home for the benefit of a Jewish charity. Here, the imprecision of their Jewish identity is intimated, but just as important is the symbolism. The newcomers, Adriana implies, are appropriating the legacy of the survivors who built the postwar community at a hefty discount and with little appreciation for its significance. Even as she is flogging her parents' mass-produced furniture and inexpensive prints of clichéd Jewish scenes (*tb*, 97), therefore, she knows that the burden of preserving their memory falls to her. "Wirst du das Erbe annehmen?," she imagines her dead parents saying to her: "Aber das ist doch gar keine Frage, oder?" (Will you take on the legacy? But there's no question that I will, of course?; *tb*, 85). This will be the work of a lifetime, or at least of the next twenty years, she calculates, including lecture tours to inform non-Jewish audiences about "das Leben jüdischer Migranten der Nachkriegszeit" (the life of Jewish migrants in the postwar period; *tb*, 99–100). At the same time, the second-generation narrator is oppressed by how banal her life appears to be in comparison

---

22 Altaras, *titos brille*, 82. Hereafter *tb*.

with what her parents went through: "Was für ein Leben! Wie klein und eindimensional mir meines erscheint." (What a life! How small and one-dimensional mine appears to me; *tb*, 100). In essence, Adriana feels duty-bound to communicate the legacy of the generation of survivors who refounded the community in Germany but is simultaneously also compelled to assert—or to at least try and define—her own German Jewish identity against the monumentality of what they experienced *and* against the superior numbers and entrepreneurial esprit of recently arrived coreligionists from the former Soviet Union.

It is only when speaking of the "Russians," in fact, that Adriana betrays distrust, jaundice, and even anger, jarring with her narrative's otherwise predominantly even-tempered tone. The Russians are now everywhere, it seems, including as servers and doormen at the funeral reception that followed her mother Thea's death (*tb*, 81). Adriana believes that this ubiquitous presence at community occasions has less to do with religious conviction than with jobs and control of resources. Referring to a power struggle that had involved her mother, Adriana reports how Russian immigrants had attempted to seize the presidency of the community and describes their mafia-like methods: "Sie schienen von der russischen Mafia inspiriert zu sein: Um 4 Uhr morgens bekam meine Mutter Pizzalieferungen, die sie angeblich bestellt hatte, wurde nachts alle zwei Stunden angerufen, bedroht." (They seemed to be inspired by the Russian mafia: my mother received pizza deliveries at 4 a.m. that she had allegedly ordered, she got phone calls every two hours through the night, and was threatened; *tb*, 110–11). The association of Soviet-born Jews with the Russian mafia features again later in the text, when Adriana mentions the children "russischer Abstammung" (of Russian descent) at her son's (Jewish) school, suggests that half of them have non-Jewish parents, and relates how some of their families are connected to organized crime. Her comment that she found the remaining Russians to be "ausgesprochen herzlich und gebildet" (decidedly warmhearted and well-educated) once these dubious characters had moved on is patronizing, to say the least, as is her amplification that she soon learned to drink vodka out of a tumbler (*tb*, 211–12).

Most obviously, Adriana positions herself in *titos brille* as the guardian of the memory of the existing community against the Soviet-born Jews arriving en masse after the end of the Cold War. Styling herself as a voice for German Jews who grew up in the shadow of the Holocaust, she feels duty-bound to attest to the traumatic experiences and hard-won achievements of the survivors and (later) refugees from communist antisemitism who reestablished a Jewish presence in the land of the perpetrators. *Their* story, Adriana implies, is a properly Jewish story, in sharp contrast to the "Russians," with their (seemingly) tenuous relationship to Judaism and their banal opportunism. At the same time, this insistence on the prior claim of the established community is more than a simple reiteration of postwar settlement, watchfulness against resurgent antisemitism, and growing assertiveness while remaining somewhat apart. Notwithstanding its mostly understated, reflective style, in fact, Adriana's retelling is subtly transgressive, as she positions herself not only against the influx of immigrants from the former Soviet Union but also—precisely via her purposefully low-key narration—vis-à-vis her peers in the second generation, with their angry outbursts against a non-Jewish majority that still refuses to accept full responsibility for the past, *and* vis-à-vis the Eastern European survivors who dominated the community after 1945 until recently.

In all this, the likely non-Jewish German reader is implicated not only as a fellow citizen to be informed about the customs and culture of a minority—although the meaning of the different foods at Passover is explained, for example (*tb*, 222)—but as a confidant and perhaps even an arbiter. For the most part, this potential intimacy is expressed diffusely, through Adriana's unselfconscious and self-disclosing narration of her own and her parents' life stories. This is the autobiographical pact, of course, as famously defined by Philippe Lejeune.[23] Occasionally, however, contextualizing references within the narration of family history permit the non-Jewish German reader to grasp more directly the "reasonableness" of Adriana's self-understanding as a Jew who feels *at home* in Germany, now more than six decades after the Holocaust, in the late 2000s. Her account emphasizes, for example, that her mother descended from *yekkes*—middle-class Jews from central Europe who identified with German culture before the Holocaust—and that Thea spoke German at home and went with her father to Vienna to watch German theater (*tb*, 162–66). Elsewhere, Adriana's allusions to Hitler's Ustaše collaborators in wartime Yugoslavia, (*tb*, 115), communist show trials in the 1960s, and present-day antisemitism in Croatia (*tb*, 150) and in France (*tb*, 174) seem to situate fascism, totalitarianism, and anti-Jewish prejudice as European and not just German phenomena. Finally, Adriana is married to a non-Jewish German. In her description of Georg as an affable, intelligent, and "etwas autistischer Westfale" (somewhat autistic Westphalian; *tb*, 53)—whose appearance is as stereotypically German as that of all of her prior lovers (*tb*, 42)—the reader will register affection, love, and Adriana's evident willingness to engage.[24]

Perhaps counterintuitively, therefore, the Jewish narrator's restrained aesthetic and suggestion of reconciliation may be best understood as a transgression of a transgression. It is most likely a repudiation of the

---

23 See Lejeune, "The Autobiographical Pact."
24 There is a long tradition of interfaith love stories, alluding to the intimate but frequently fraught relationship between Jewish and non-Jewish Germans. See Garloff, *Mixed Feelings*.

acerbic satire, provocation, and often hostility that typifies the work of second-generation writers such as Biller, Broder, and Seligmann and more generally a postwar tradition of German Jewish writing of raw emotion, and especially resentment, initiated by survivors such as H. G. Adler and Jean Améry.[25] Biller, in fact, is mentioned in *titos brille*, with Broder, in the context of a Jewish friend Raffi who is invited to polemicize on German television (*tb*, 38). Biller's *Der gebrauchte Jude* and Seligmann's *Lauf, Ludwig, lauf! Eine Jugend zwischen Synagoge und Fußball* and *Hannah und Ludwig – Heimatlos in Tel Aviv* were discussed earlier in this chapter as examples of their authors' recent willingness to (re-)imagine a place for Jews in post-Holocaust Germany, yet a complete rapprochement is not possible. Biller reclaims a Jewish voice in German *culture* but remains bitterly estranged from the country itself, and Seligmann's narration of his parents' return to the land of their birth is simultaneously an acid indictment of the antisemitism they encountered.

Adriana's self-consciously modest narrative thus implies a radical rearticulation of the Jewish identity of the second generation—a self-distancing from Soviet-born newcomers that prompts an unprecedented embrace of Germany, and of non-Jewish Germans. She even praises her "unerotisches Deutschland" (unerotic Germany) for its dogged persistence in confronting its Nazi past: "Es hat—zunächst verordnet, dann nach 68 geradezu in einem Aufarbeitungswahn—verhältnismäßig viel seiner dreckigen Geschichte thematisiert" (at first as a result of eternal pressure and then, after 1968, in feverish self-analysis, Germany has thematized a relatively large portion of its dirty past; *tb*, 175). (Adriana's more conciliatory tone, however, does not mean that she won't defend Biller, Broder, and all the other "angry" Jews against an acquaintance who accuses them of "tyrannizing" Germans; *tb*, 156.) Yet this is not the novel's only quietly daring intervention. The history of the postwar resumption of the Jewish presence that Adriana presents for her likely non-Jewish German reader subtly but unmistakably challenges key norms long defended by the community itself. This includes the narrator's allusions to corruption by prominent individuals; her rebuttal of Orthodox values regarding women; and—the bulk of her account—her depiction of Sephardic Jews from the Balkans, which offers a corrective to the conventional emphasis in German Jewish memory culture on the experiences of survivors from Orthodox eastern European backgrounds.

Daughterly loyalty, then, might have led Adriana to include an account of how her late father had accused senior figures in the community of corruption relating to German reparations for Jewish victims (*tb*, 28). (This refers to Werner Nachmann, president of the Central Council of Jews in Germany from 1969 to 1988, who in 1987 was found to have

---

25 See Finch, "Ressentiment."

embezzled 30 million DM.)[26] However, a later allusion to how her own rabbi profiteered from the sale of licenses to certify kosher food (*tb*, 230) shows that she is also determined to expose malpractice in the present day—airing the community's dirty washing in public will seem unforgivably treacherous to her fellow Jews. Nor does she even spare her father, in fact. Jakob is famous as the hero who fought with Tito—leader of the partisans fighting against the Nazis and later president of Yugoslavia—and rescued twenty-four Jewish infants (*tb*, 12–14), and rebuilt the Gießen community. Yet, Adriana reveals, he was also a womanizer whose several mistresses Adriana discovers after his death (*tb*, 30), cruel to his first wife and Adriana's half-sister Rosa (*tb*, 19–20), the father of a half-brother she has never met (*tb*, 55), and unreliable in his retelling of his exploits, possibly including the saving of the children (*tb*, 24). In summary, Adriana signals that she is prepared to step outside of the community and critique its image of itself, placing principle and unflinching honesty over blind loyalty to the clan.

More generally, Altaras's determination to participate on equal terms in the non-Jewish mainstream is an innovation that is a continuity, or rather—noting the paradox—a resumption of a continuity. Implicitly but certainly not unwittingly, therefore, the author revives the Reform Judaism that, by end of the nineteenth century, had to a large extent come to define the community: modern, enlightened, and perceiving no contradiction between being a Jew and being integrated with the non-Jewish majority, and even being a German patriot.[27] This is clearly different from the way her parents understood their presence in Germany—as survivors, resistance fighters, and exiles from postwar Soviet persecution—and it is different from other members of her own generation, like Raffi, whose lives are still overdetermined by the Holocaust past and by the need to be always vigilant against resurgent antisemitism. Less obviously, however, her embrace of the secular culture of the majority also presents a challenge to the strict religious conformity of the eastern European survivors who reestablished the community after 1941—and to the Orthodox and ultra-Orthodox Jews whose numbers are also increasing in Berlin in consequence of immigration from the United States and the new-found fervor of some Soviet-born Jews (*tb*, 211).[28] Here too, Altaras's values are "German values." She can't bear the chauvinism of her strictly observant coreligionists and their *halakhic* literalism, as she makes abundantly clear: "Was ist schlecht an Reformen? An Veränderung? An Frauen? Wir leben schließlich nicht mehr im Mittelalter." (What is wrong with reform? With change? With women? After all, we no longer live in the Middle Ages;

---

26 See Goschler and Kauders, "1969–1989."
27 See Meyer, *Response to Modernity*, especially 140–44.
28 See Schrage, *Jüdische Religion in Deutschland*, especially 50–53.

tb, 245). Indeed, her own commitment to Jewish ritual is lax, to say the least, notably her son's Bar Mitzwah, which recalls family traditions but has little religious meaning (*tb*, 251; 255). Above all, she is married to a non-Jew. Her transgression is not just intimacy with a German, therefore, but her flaunting of the prohibition on exogamy.

Ultimately, Adriana is *at home* in Germany. America and Israel feature as alternative destinations for the second-generation German Jew seeking either a less encumbered existence in the diaspora or the identity-affirming experience of making aliyah. However, she is repulsed by her American relatives, "eine amerikanisch-jüdische Variante aus 'Baywatch' oder 'Dallas'" (an American-Jewish variant from 'Baywatch' or 'Dallas,' *tb*, 217), who are all grossly overweight and who seem to view her and her children "als seien wir geradewegs aus dem Stetl geflohen" (as if we had just fled the shtetl; *tb*, 218), and her relationship with Israel too has always been "gelinde gesagt—schwierig" (to put it mildly—difficult; *tb*, 201). A disappointing sabbatical year in a kibbutz and then, in more recent years, the constant requirement to justify her decision to live in Germany and her growing discomfort with the militarization of Israeli society mean that she is always pleased to return to Berlin (*tb*, 201–8). When violence breaks out in the West Bank, her instinct is to worry about the increased security around Berlin's Jewish institutions, including her sons' school, and not to ponder the potential rights and wrongs of the decades-old conflict in the Middle East (*tb*, 209).

As intimated above, however, it is through her narration of her parents' Sephardic legacy that Adriana makes her most decisive contribution to a reframing of Jewish identity in Germany. Certainly, her comment that it would take more than twenty years to work through her mother's papers and to tour Germany to inform her non-Jewish fellow citizens about "das Leben jüdischer Migranten der Nachkriegszeit" (the life of Jewish migrants in the postwar period; *tb*, 99–100) indicates both the *diversity* of the community and the *extent* of the history that is still to be disseminated about less familiar groups. ("Migranten" here most likely refers to Jews who arrived as refugees from communist persecution in the 1960s and 1970s rather than to survivors who came immediately after the war.) Through her rendering of family history, correspondingly, Adriana suggests that Jewish life in Germany is more varied, more complex, and more contested than is normally conceded by the community itself or by the majority, and that this reality needs to be acknowledged by Jews and non-Jews alike.

Adriana's father Jakob, the reader learns, was from a Sephardic background, the descendants of Jews expelled from Spain and Portugal in the late fifteenth century who migrated across France, Holland, England, Italy, and into the Ottoman Empire, including the Balkans (*tb*, 22). Adriana recalls visitors to her childhood home speaking their Spanish

Jewish language (Spaniolish) with her father (*tb*, 206); later in her narrative, she tells of a cantor she knows in Berlin, who escaped Thessaloníki just before the Nazis exterminated its community of "Spanish Jews" in 1942 (*tb*, 93). In this way, Adriana alludes, albeit parenthetically, to the long and illustrious Sephardic history in the Greek city, and across the Balkans more generally, and invokes the near total destruction of this form of Judaism across Greece, Serbia, Croatia, and Macedonia. (The Jews of Bulgaria—a German ally—were largely saved following protests by politicians, clerics, and intellectuals.)[29] In general terms, this counters the global ignorance—even occlusion—with regard to the fate of Sephardic Jews during the genocide.[30] More specifically, it addresses the lack of knowledge in Germany given the usual focus on the Jews of eastern rather than southeastern Europe.

The narrator's efforts to expand German and German Jewish Holocaust memory are supported by a wealth of detail from her parents' extraordinary and yet vividly representative life-stories. Adriana recounts, for example, how Thea, her mother, and her mother's sister Jelka were driven from their home by German soldiers (Thea's father died of a heart attack following the invasion), captured by Croatian fascists (the Ustaše), and then interned in the Rab concentration camp by the Italians—although, for a short time, this actually protected them from the Nazis (*tb*, 67–69). With regard to Adriana's father, the reader discovers that Jakob was one of six sons, one of whom became a rabbi, one an engineer, and two became doctors. "Wahrscheinlich ging es in vielen sephardischen Familien so oder ähnlich zu," she comments (It probably happened like this in many Sephardic families; *tb*, 22), referencing the work of the well-known Sephardic writer Elias Canetti. A prolific author raised in the German language—along with Ladino, or Judeo-Spanish—Canetti will be familiar to many readers as a documenter of the rise of fascism and the fanaticism of the masses.[31] Elsewhere, Adriana tells of how Jakob joined the resistance, repaired Tito's glasses—hence the title of the novel—and was persecuted by the postwar regime after he accused the communist partisans of having murdered his brother during the war (*tb*, 25). (The story about Tito is probably one of her father's self-aggrandizing fabrications.) For his daughter, absorbing these tales as a child, Jakob is a Dr. Zhivago figure (*tb*, 28), enigmatic and full of charm.

Adriana's account of Sephardic Jews in the Balkans, including allusions to their near-extermination in the Holocaust, does more than simply complement the customary emphasis on the fate of Ashkenazi Jews from eastern Europe, however. It also *integrates* their Jewish suffering

---

29 See Levy, *The Sephardim in The Holocaust.*
30 See Abramson, "A Double Occlusion."
31 See Lorenz, ed., *Elias Canetti.*

into the "canon" of German and German Jewish memory. Adriana thus describes how Thea was forced to leave school and to wear the Star of David, aged fifteen, following the introduction of race laws in Yugoslavia, how she was placed in the concentration camp at Rab when she was seventeen—though the occupying Italians were less antisemitic than the Germans—and how she was overwhelmed by disgust for the humiliations she endured, for other inmates, and for herself (*tb*, 61–62). The daughter's more or less factual description of the sequence of events, moreover, is then immediately followed by passages of direct speech interspersed over several pages that reproduce her mother's own words, spoken many years ago in conversation with her family. The content largely overlaps with what Adriana has just reported, although key details are added, for example that twenty-eight out of thirty-three of Thea's classmates were deported (*tb*, 68–69), that the Germans launched a killing spree after the Italian surrender, and that Thea worked as a translator for the Americans after her escape (*tb*, 75–76). These are important elaborations of Adriana's previous summary—they emphasize that Sephardic Jews were also caught up in the Nazi killing machine—but just as significant perhaps is Adriana's choice to have her mother substantiate her previous narrative as an *eyewitness*. Quite apart from the immediacy that this brings to Adriana's invocation of the Holocaust in the Balkans, it also aligns her Sephardic story with a German and German Jewish memory culture that, historically, has relied very heavily on first-hand accounts of the ghettos and camps.

In fact, it is clear that Adriana is already well-versed—and deeply involved—in contemporary practices of Holocaust commemoration in Germany. Woven through her retelling of her mother's persecution, deportation, and internment—and indeed through Thea's ostensibly original account—is Adriana's simultaneous narration of her absorption of debates about German guilt, self-recognition within current discourses on the transmission of Holocaust trauma to the second generation, and finally her active participation as an author of memory texts. Her reproduction of Thea's eyewitness report, accordingly, is prompted by a discussion with colleagues about the building of a Holocaust memorial in central Berlin. (The Memorial to the Murdered Jews of Europe was inaugurated in 2005.) She mentions how she began to read scholarly literature on the theme of memorials and German commemoration culture as well as the Mitscherlichs' 1967 work *Die Unfähigkeit zu trauern: Grundlagen kollektiven Verhaltens* (The inability to mourn: Principles of collective behavior; *tb*, 67). At the same time, she relates the staging of her play *Trauer to go* (Mourning to go; 2004), itself written in response to the public debate on the Berlin Holocaust memorial:

> Das war mein Outing als jüdische Schriftstellerin in der Berliner Szene. Bis dato war ich zuständig gewesen für südländischen

Charme, italienische Lebensfreude, Ausländerinnen aller Colours. Und fürs Putzen, versteht sich. Jetzt war ich plötzlich *the second generation in person.*

[That was when I was outed as a Jewish writer in the Berlin scene. Until that point I'd been the go-to for Mediterranean charm, Italian vivacity, foreigners of all colors. And for cleaning, of course. Now I was suddenly the *second generation in person*. (*tb*, 63)]

With this production, Adriana suddenly becomes legible as a "Jewish author." She has swapped walk-on parts as any kind of "foreigner," including the ubiquitous cleaning lady, for a central role in German and German Jewish memory culture. Specifically, she is no longer simply an actress with a vaguely exotic Mediterranean appearance—her Sephardic Balkan background was entirely ignored—but is now a *representative* of the second generation. (Her use of English—"*the second generation in person*"—no doubt ironically references the pervasiveness of Anglo-American scholarship on contemporary German Jewish writing.) Adriana, in sum, believes herself to be engaged at the very center of German and German Jewish memory discourse, and at the center of German Jewish literature, even as she is simultaneously intent on reorienting it away from resentment and toward reconciliation.

In *titos brille*, a second-generation narrator asserts the prior claim of the established community to define Jewish identity against Soviet-born newcomers while also hinting at the existing diversity among Jews long resident in Germany—enriched by waves of migrants before the "Russians," including her own Sephardic family. At the same time, she also subtly positions herself vis-à-vis the eastern European Jewish survivors and their descendants who dominated that community since its reemergence after the war. Adriana asserts a liberal Judaism in place of the generally Orthodox tradition from which the survivors came, insisting for example on equality for women, and stresses the transnational, multicultural, and even *worldly* orientation of her Sephardic heritage, with family dispersed across the Balkans and beyond, conversant in multiple languages, and trading and traveling across borders. The reader might think, then, of reconstructed synagogues such as the *Neue Synagoge* on Berlin's Orianienburgerstraße, built in the neo-Moorish style adopted by German Jews in the mid-nineteenth century to reference the cosmopolitan tradition of the Jews of Islamic Iberia, who famously lived in harmony with their Muslim neighbors and overlords before their expulsion in 1492 following the Christian reconquest.[32] The allusion to the

---

32 See Efron, *German Jewry*.

multilingual Sephardic writer and humanist Elias Canetti invokes the same cosmopolitan sensibility.[33]

In the end, the reconciliation with the non-Jewish German majority that Adriana seems to embrace, symbolically expressed through her marriage to Georg, might even style the liberal—Reform—Judaism she champions as the more authentically *German* Jewish tradition, in comparison to the apparent opportunism of Russian-speaking interlopers *and* the atavism of Eastern European survivors and their descendants. Adriana's German-speaking grandfather, a *yekke* originally from Budapest, could not imagine that the Nazis would target him and his family (*tb*, 68); her aunt Julia was the embodiment of the Austro-Hungarian empire (*tb*, 940); and her mother Thea—who visited the theater in Vienna as a child—battled with the West German authorities to be acknowledged as a "Volksdeutsche" (ethnic German; *tb*, 163), given that her family, generations ago, may have hailed from Frankfurt. Thea was even buried on the *Tag der deutschen Einheit* (the Day of German Unity, the anniversary of unification on October 3, 1990), with a special dispensation for the ceremony to take place on a public holiday (*tb*, 80). Perhaps the most scandalous aspect of Altaras's deceptively understated *titos brille*, in sum, may be its hint that reconciliation is simply a much longed-for and greatly delayed *return* to an intimacy—even a "German-Jewish symbiosis"[34]— that was in any case always meant to be, notwithstanding the unfathomable outrage of the Holocaust.

Becoming a (Russian) German Jew: Jan Himmelfarb's *Sterndeutung*

In Altaras's *titos brille*, the depiction of Soviet-born Jews can appear one-dimensional and even clichéd. The same is true in other contemporary texts by writers from the pre-1990s community, including German-born descendants of Holocaust survivors and even a previous wave of Russian-speaking immigrants whose families fled Soviet antisemitism in the 1970s and 1980s. In *Die Enkelin* (the granddaughter; 2013) by Channah Trzebiner, for example, the third-generation protagonist lampoons the broken German and grotesquely hackneyed Jewish performance of a Russian friend's mother.[35] In Vladimir Vertlib's *Viktor hilft* (Viktor helps; 2018) the stereotyping is gentler but no less pointed. In this novel, Viktor fails to connect with a young Russian woman working at a service station. As a recent migrant whose family was no doubt primarily motivated by

---

33   See Esformes, "The Sephardic Voice."
34   See Benz, "German-Jewish Symbiosis" and Traverso, *The Jews and Germany*.
35   Trzebiner, *Die Enkelin*, 173–75.

the desire for a better life in Germany, Viktor implies, she is unlikely to be able to truly understand what it means to be a Jew, while his own flight from Russia twenty years earlier was prompted by direct experience of antisemitism.[36]

Vertlib, of course, migrated from Russia in the late 1970s, via Israel, Austria (for the first time), Italy, Austria (again), the Netherlands, Israel (once more), Italy (again), Austria (again), the United States, and finally, Austria (for good, in 1981).[37] Biller arrived in Germany with his Russian-speaking parents from Prague in 1970, and the Austrian writer Julya Rabinowich migrated with her family to Vienna in 1977, to name two other authors with a background in the Communist bloc—as already mentioned, Biller both references and fictionalizes family history in *Sechs Koffer* (2018) and *Sieben Versuche zu lieben* (2020), and in *Spaltkopf* (Split-head; 2008) Rabinowich tells the story of a seven-year-old Russian Jewish child who experiences the difficulty of living between histories, cultures, and languages in Vienna.[38] Even as these established writers anticipate the focus on the Soviet and Soviet Jewish past in fiction by more recently emerged authors who came as children in the 1990s, however, this does *not* mean that there is a shared understanding of German Jewish or even Russian Jewish identity. In their essays, interviews, and fiction, the two groups barely mention one other.

Scholarship on the first post-Soviet writers to make a name for themselves in the early 2000s typically focuses on their "Russianness," arguably replicating the reductiveness just described in the work of authors from the established community, and indeed in much of the sociological and ethnographic research conducted on the *Kontingentflüchtlinge* in the decade after their arrival. (This was discussed in the Introduction.) Lena Gorelik's début novel *Meine weißen Nächte* (My white nights; 2004), for example, is identified by Anke Biendarra as a paradigmatic "arrival narrative," focused on its Russian protagonist's confrontation with a hostile German bureaucracy, life in an asylum-seekers' hostel, and melancholic flashbacks to a Soviet childhood.[39] Alina Bronsky's *Scherbenpark* (Broken glass park; 2008) is discussed in similar terms, with an emphasis on the sexual exploitation of the young Russian woman who is its main character,[40] and the author's darkly comic tale *Die schärfsten Gerichte der*

---

36 Vertlib, *Viktor hilft*, 283–55.
37 Vertlib, "Nichtvorbildliche Lieblingsautoren," 198. This migration story is told in Vertlib's autobiographical novels *Abschiebung* (Deportation; 1995) and *Zwischenstationen* (Intermediate stops; 1999). See Gilman, "Becoming a Jew," especially 28–32.
38 See Krenz-Dewe, "Zum wechselseitigen Verhältnis" and Guenther, "Julya Rabinowich's Transnational Poetics."
39 See Biendarra, "Cultural Dichotomies."
40 See Mennel, "Alina Bronsky, *Scherbenpark*."

tatarischen Küche (The spiciest dishes of the Tatarian cuisine), published two years later in 2010, is regularly cited for its reproduction of familiar tropes, including Soviet corruption, exotic dishes, and a tyrannical Russian grandmother maneuvering to marry her daughter into a better life in the West. Finally, commentators invariably reference Wladimir Kaminer, who arrived in Germany in 1990 and quickly established himself in Berlin's literary and music scenes, including DJ'ing at the regular "Russendisko" at the Kaffee Burger club on Torstraße.

Kaminer, it is usually claimed, identifies above all as Russian, with Jewish themes being seen as peripheral in his collections of satirical short stories *Russendisko* (Russian disco; 2000), *Mein deutsches Dschungelbuch* (My German jungle book; 2003), *Es gab keinen Sex im Sozialismus* (There was no sex in socialism; 2009), *Onkel Wanja kommt: Eine Reise durch die Nacht* (Uncle Venya is coming: A journey through the night; 2012)—invoking Chekhov—and *Goodbye, Moskau: Betrachtungen über Russland* (Goodbye Moscow: Observations on Russia; 2017), which is prefaced with a quotation by the nineteenth-century surrealist Nikolai Gogol: "Oh, Russland, wohin rast du?/ Gib mir eine Antwort!"[41] (Oh, Russia, where are you headed so fast/ Give me an answer). Kaminer, the American scholar Sander Gilman claims, is "the representative RUSSIAN."[42] Gorelik too appears to be focused on Russia and on Russians in her novels *Verliebt in Sankt Petersburg: Meine russische Reise* (In love in St. Petersburg: My Russian journey; 2008), *Die Listensammlerin* (The collector of lists; 2013), and, most recently, *Wer wir sind* (Who we are; 2021), in which the author processes her migration thirty years previously, including the parents' difficulties in relating to their daughter as she becomes fluent in German and starts her own family in the new country. In *Baba Dunjas letzte Liebe* (Dunja's last love; 2015), Bronsky narrates the aftermath of the Chernobyl disaster and, in *Der Zopf meiner Großmutter* (The braid of my grandmother; 2019), the author comes back to the familiar theme of a Russian family's arrival in Germany in the early 1990s. In addition, Bronsky has published several books for young adults that feature one or more characters with a conspicuously Russian background.

A related focus of current scholarship is on what Adrian Wanner calls the performance of "Russianness for German consumption."[43] This refers, on the one hand, to the brazen self-stylization that characterizes, say, Kaminer's literary production and public appearances, such as his amplification of his Russian accent on stage. On the other hand, it refers to publishers' marketing strategies. Nora Isterheld, accordingly, discusses

---

41 See Lubrich, "Are Russian Jews Post-colonial?" Lubrich, in fact, argues that Kaminer is neither "Russian nor Jewish" (36).
42 Gilman, *Multiculturalism*, 216–19. See also Gilman, "Becoming a Jew."
43 See Wanner, *Out of Russia*, 50–88.

book covers featuring onion domes, titles that play on Russian stereotypes, and images of the author, for example a photographic portrait of the Ukrainian (non-Jewish) novelist Marjana Gaponenko that recalls a Russian noblewoman striking majestic poses. Russian phrases, in Cyrillic, also feature frequently, emphasizing the provenance of the author and "otherness."[44] At the same time, the performance of a Russian identity can also suggest a more meaningful invocation of Russian culture within European and global traditions. As noted above, Kaminer alludes to Chekov and Gogol, the title of Gorelik's *Meine weißen Nächte* is a translation of the name of Dostoyevsky's short story of 1848,[45] and Bronsky too alludes to Dostoyevsky throughout her oeuvre, including a prolonged intertextual engagement in *Dunjas letzte Liebe*.[46]

It is in the work of Olga Martynova that the most sustained engagement with Russian literature as *world literature* is to be found. A poet and novelist with a Jewish background, Martynova was already well established in Russian literary circles when she moved to Germany in 1991 with her husband, the lyricist Oleg Jurjew, and even after her emigration she continued to write poetry in Russian and to enjoy success in her country of origin. As Miriam Finkelstein argues, Martynova's work exemplifies the recent (re-)emergence of a Russian-German translingual literature, incorporating elements of both traditions and often with Russian lexical items (often in Cyrillic) strategically deployed.[47] Her *Sogar Papageien überleben uns* (Even parrots outlive us; 2010) is a densely poetic tale of how a Russian literary scholar, Marina, reconnects with a former lover during a lecture tour to Germany—allusions to Russian, German, and more generally European classics abound. The same is true of Martynova's second novel, *Mörikes Schlüsselbein* (Mörike's collarbone; 2013), which also features a Russian-German couple as well as an invented Russian poet, Fjodor Stein, whose first name recalls Dostoyevsky and whose surname suggests Jewish roots.[48] The title, of course, invokes the nineteenth-century German Romantic poet and writer of novellas.

Yet for all that they clearly thematize Russia, Russian literature, and Russian history, Soviet-born authors *also* evidence a profound interest in their Jewish identity—although this may be more overt in texts written from the mid-2010s.[49] Joseph Cronin, then, has argued for a reevaluation

---

44   See Finkelstein, "From German into Russian."
45   See Isterheld, "*In der Zugluft Europas*," 158.
46   See Pailer, "Female Empowerment."
47   See Finkelstein, "From German into Russian."
48   See Isterheld, "*In der Zugluft Europas*," especially 316–33. See also Lehmann, *Russische Literatur in Deutschland*, especially 356.
49   It is worth noting that around 1.5 million *Russlanddeutsche*—ethnic Germans—also arrived from the former Soviet Union in the 1990s, with writers also emerging from this cohort. Many tend to focus on the history of their community

of Kaminer's oeuvre, to highlight the author's concern with antisemitism in the Soviet Union, accusations leveled against the newcomers that they had falsified Jewish genealogies, and assumptions about their commitment to Holocaust memory, even if these themes are expressed only indirectly.[50] In Bronsky's *Der Zopf meiner Großmutter* too, the author plays on widely held beliefs, including across the established Jewish community, that the Jewish identity of a good proportion of the new arrivals was fraudulent. The grandmother can claim only a distant relative as Jewish, but this is good enough for her, her husband, and grandson to gain entry to Germany. Once there, the Russian matriarch curses "the Jews" also living in her asylum-seekers' hostel. In Gorelik's *Meine weißen Nächte*, the protagonist's brother goes to Israel to learn Hebrew. His interest is short-lived—he also expresses an interest in Buddhism—but the point is precisely the haziness of Russian Jewish identity. In subsequent texts, Gorelik explores Jewish identity in a much more dedicated fashion. In *Hochzeit in Jerusalem* (2007), Anja travels to Israel to discover what it means to be a Jew, especially a non-believing Jew who lives in Germany. Eccentric relatives create opportunities for amusing interludes, a contemplation of the global Russian Jewish diaspora, and reflection on the element of chance that meant that her family ended up in the land of the perpetrators. Five years later, *Lieber Mischa . . . Du bist ein Jude* (Dear Mischa . . . You are a Jew, 2012) demonstrates the author's evolving engagement with Jewish traditions and rituals.[51] Lydia Heiss describes this book, addressed to the author's son, as a "guide to being Jewish in contemporary Germany."

Martynova too, whose work was earlier described as profoundly influenced by Russian and European classics, also emphasizes the significance of Jewish authors, and even a specifically Jewish aesthetic, within European literary traditions.[52] Isterheld notes the echoes of Joseph Roth's *Radetzkymarsch* (Radetzky March; 1932) in *Sogar Papageien überleben uns*. (The Jewish Catholic convert Roth describes the disintegration of the Austro-Hungarian monarchy—Martynova depicts the decline of the Soviet Union.) Specifically, the German critic notes that the quotation that provides the title of the novel is taken from Roth's 1927 essay "Juden auf Wanderschaft" (The wandering Jews) in which he discusses the arrogance of German Jews in the 1920s as they deluded themselves

---

during Soviet times, namely deportation under Stalin or conscription into Hitler's army. Eleanora Hummel is the best known. But others such as Mitja Vachedin, Wlada Kolosowa, Katerina Poladjan, Alina Galkina, Dmitrij Wall, and Nellja Veremej deal with the absurdities both of life in the Soviet Union and arrival in Germany, with its attendant bureaucracy and discrimination. See Isterheld, "*In der Zugluft Europas*," 146–62, esp. 157.

50 See Cronin, "Wladimir Kaminer."
51 See Heiss, "Lena Gorelik's Autofictional Letter *Lieber Mischa*."
52 See Martynova's interview with Jo Frank.

that they were culturally and morally superior to the eastern European Jews (*Ostjuden*) arriving after the First World War and that they were safe in their embrace of German patriotism.[53] The parallel with attitudes in the settled German Jewish community toward newly arrived Soviet Jews in the present day is, if not explicit, then at least likely. The Jewish writers Osip Mandelstam, Paul Celan, and Rose Ausländer are also invoked.[54] Elsewhere, in a special issue on "Jewish literatures of the present" in *Jalta*—a magazine dedicated to German Jewish debates—Martynova discusses her deceased husband Oleg Jurjew and asks whether it is possible to speak of a "a whole 'Jewish text' of world literature," given how Jewish culture has migrated to all four corners of the earth.[55] This 2019 essay is entitled "Das Wort Jude" (the word Jew), which recalls an extended discussion of sensitivities around naming Jews in Martynova's third novel *Der Engelherd* (Hearth of angels; 2016), a metaphysical discourse on love, home, and identity.[56]

Soviet-born writers emphasize Russianness *and* Jewishness, therefore. Alexandra Friedmann's début novel *Besserland* (Better country; 2015) depicts her family's eventful journey to Germany with "Jewish humor," as her publisher puts it.[57] Marina Frenk's *ewig her und gar nicht wahr* (a lifetime ago and not even true; 2020) has its protagonist travel to New York, Israel, and Moldova in search of her Jewish identity, including her grandparents' flight to Uzbekistan to escape the Holocaust. Dmitrij Kapitelman's *Eine Formalie in Kiew* (A formality in Kyiv)—published, in 2021, twenty-five years after his family left Ukraine—focuses on his parents' struggles to settle in Germany. Again, travel is central to the plot, as the protagonist travels to Ukraine to recover a document he needs for his application for a German passport and to excavate family history, including Jewish life stories. And—a final example—Sasha Marianna Salzmann's second novel, *Im Menschen muss alles herrlich sein* (Glorious people; 2021), focuses on life in the Soviet Union but there are references to Jewish genealogies; to the choice between America, Israel, or Germany as a destination after the family quits Russia; and—as so often in recent writing—to the Jewish writer Franz Kafka.[58]

This extended review of Soviet-born writers provides some evidence at least for Eliezer Ben-Rafael's suggestion—already cited

---

53 Isterheld, *"In der Zugluft Europas,"* 320–21. See Hoffmann, "Translator's Preface."
54 Isterheld, *"In der Zugluft Europas,"* 325.
55 Martynova, "Das Wort Jude," 81.
56 See Pörzgen, "Transgenerationale Traumatisierung."
57 See https://aviva-berlin.de/aviva/content_Literatur.php?id=14191528. Last accessed July 25, 2024.
58 Salzmann, *Im Menschen*, 144–45; 165; and 217. I am grateful to Dr. Miriam Wray for identifying these references.

in the Introduction—that, for Russian-speaking migrants, resettlement in "Germany provides the conditions to re-attach themselves to Jewishness."[59] Indeed, it might be argued that one of the most important tropes in the literary production of this cohort is precisely a protagonist's attempt to reconcile a Soviet biography with a Jewish sensibility that only emerges following exposure to German and German Jewish memory culture. In the land of the perpetrators, it seems, a Russian identity can evolve first into a Russian Jewish and then a (Russian) *German Jewish* identity.

For Jessica Ortner, the inevitable consequence of the "mnemonic migration" that takes place when Soviet-born writers introduce Russian and Russian Jewish histories into their German-language texts is "a clash between cognitive schemata in which the protagonists have been socialized and those they encounter in the host country,"[60] relating specifically to the perceived challenge that a focus on Stalinist oppression or even Soviet antisemitism appears to pose to the primacy of Holocaust memory. This framing of the interaction between Soviet, Soviet Jewish, and German Jewish histories might appear somewhat abstract, however, and may also underestimate the extent to which protagonists actively mobilize—or even fabricate—*other* kinds of memory in order to rearticulate what it means to be a Jew in Germany today. Becoming a Russian Jew and then a (Russian) German Jew, accordingly, often involves a conscious *self-positioning*—or repositioning—vis-à-vis the existing community and the occasionally coercive expectations of the non-Jewish majority.

Himmelfarb's *Sterndeutung* can be read as an auto-ethnography of Jewish migrants from the former Soviet Union and their efforts to create a new life in Germany. In a highly personal narrative that is at the same time self-consciously aware of how it is more broadly representative, the fifty-one-year-old Arthur depicts his mother's hankering for her old life in Russia, his own endeavors to achieve a prosperous future for his family, his wife Julia's difficulties in finding a job (she is a qualified teacher of Russian but her German is poor), and his daughter Anna's success in gaining a place at Business School and her relationship with Max, a German fellow student. To an extent, Arthur's account plays to stereotypes of "the Russian." In the Soviet Union, he had been a translator of German newspapers but now he renders official documents from Russian for other newcomers hoping—in fulfillment of the cliché—to access state benefits.[61] He also partners with his friend Igor in a dubious used car

---

59   Ben-Rafael, "Germany's Russian-speaking Jews," 78–79.
60   Ortner, *Transcultural Memory*, 12.
61   There are comparisons to be drawn between Soviet-born Jewish writers in Germany and Russian-speaking Jewish authors who immigrated to the United States, such as Yelena Akhtiorskaya, Masha Gessen, Nadia Kalman, Sana Krasikov,

export business, while Igor drives pizzas to ungrateful customers, his wife Ina cleans apartments, and a mutual friend Sergei heaves sacks of coal: "Aber sie werden dadurch nicht wieder zu Ärzten und Ingenieuren. Die Selbstachtung Neueingewanderter leidet fast immer."[62] (That doesn't help them become doctors or engineers again. The self-respect of new immigrants almost always suffers.) Financial need and loss of status lead the newly arrived Russian Jews to engage in insecure, off-the-books, and potentially illegal work.

Yet Arthur goes beyond a simple description of the struggles of Soviet-born migrants to find work commensurate with their qualifications and aspirations, or of how integration is of course easier for the younger generation. He also introduces three further plot strands, each narrated in a quite different mode. First, lengthy factual passages interspersed throughout the novel summarize what Arthur has learned about the Nazi genocide from standard scholarly works, including—perhaps less familiar to the reader than the death camps—the mass shootings of Jews that took place across eastern Europe as the Germans rapidly advanced in 1940 and 1941 (the "Holocaust by bullets").[63] Second, this terse historiographical narration contrasts sharply with Arthur's self-evidently implausible fabulation of the circumstances of his birth in December 1941 on a train evacuating Soviet citizens—including Jews—from the Ukrainian city of Kharkiv before the German forces arrived. Arthur claims to recall the precise moment of his entry into the world, along with details such as the train's blacked-out windows, as well as his onward journey to Stalingrad, Tashkent, and Kazakhstan, where he, his mother, and his grandmother spent the war. Finally, Arthur relates his friendship with the German Jew Roth, who survived the war in hiding in Berlin.[64] Here, Arthur strikes an intimate but measured tone, contrasting with both the evident embellishment of his birth story and the restrained emotion of his restatement of the horror. In what follows, the relationship between these three strands is explored, and specifically how they interact to position—and reposition—the Soviet-born newcomer in relation to both Jewish and non-Jewish Germans.

Arthur's extensive recital of what he has read about the phases and sites of the Holocaust includes detailed accounts of the deportation of Berlin Jews from the Grunewald railway station and their later extraction from the ghetto in Riga and mass shooting into pits they had been forced

---

Ellen Litman, Irina Reyn, Anya Ulinich, Lara Vapnyar, Anya von Bremzen, David Bezmozgis, Gary Shteyngart, Boris Fishman, and Michael Idov. See Katsnelson, "Introduction." See also Krasuska, *Soviet-born*.

62 Himmelfarb, *Sterndeutung*, 42. Hereafter *S*.
63 See Desbois, *The Holocaust by Bullets*.
64 See Lutjens Jr., *Submerged*.

to dig (*S*, 66–77); the murder of 100,000 using three gas vans at Kulmhof (*S*, 83–84); 23,000 killed at Kamenez-Podolsk (*S*, 15–16)—including his maternal grandparents—and the killing of the Jews of Kharkiv (*S*, 104–7), with whom he would have died in the womb if his uncle Naum had not been able to help his pregnant mother to board the train, along with her own mother. Elsewhere in the text, Arthur also relays historical knowledge he has acquired about the Warsaw Ghetto (*S*, 135–36); Treblinka (*S*, 147–48) and the Treblinka uprising (*S*, 241–44); the extermination of Hungarian Jews (*S*, 304–7); and the death marches (*S*, 347–50), as well as his own encounters with Germans who still cannot accept that the population as a whole was complicit (*S*, 327–39). During a visit to Auschwitz with Julia, then, Arthur overhears a young woman explaining that ordinary Germans did not know, that the leadership hid the crime, that there was resistance, and so on and so forth (*S*, 338).

In reproducing what is effectively a compressed history of the Holocaust—deportations; *Einsatzgruppen* (mobile killing units); the first use of gas; the heroic uprisings in Warsaw and Treblinka; the killing of more than 400,000 Hungarian Jews in Auschwitz in mid-1944; and the death marches of late 1944 and 1945—the Soviet-born protagonist claims his place in German and German Jewish memory culture. He has done his homework and has transformed himself from the (stereotypically) ill-informed Soviet-born migrant, with little understanding (supposedly) of the genocide, into a worthy candidate for membership of the established Jewish community of his adopted country, for which the obligation to remember is paramount. Indeed, Arthur's remedial work is impressive. In the Soviet Union, he notes, state propaganda tended to erase the Jewish specificity of the Holocaust by emphasizing the victimhood of Soviet citizens in general (*S*, 270), and it was only after his arrival in Germany that he gained access to the books that he needed in order to fully comprehend the Nazis' racial madness. Here, the Austrian-born American historian Raul Hilberg is mentioned by name. In his *The Destruction of the European Jews* (1961), Hilberg was one of the first scholars to focus on the Holocaust as a crime perpetrated against Jews *as* Jews (*S*, 373).

Arthur's internalization of Holocaust history following his arrival in Germany leads him to reassess his Jewish heritage. In Russia, he had been a Jew only because all of his ancestors were Jews: "Meine Eltern, vier Großeltern, meine acht Urgroßeltern und meine sechzehn Ururgroßeltern waren Juden." (My parents, four grandparents, my eight great-grandparents, and my sixteen great-great-grandparents were Jews; *S*, 7). Unlike many post-Soviet migrants to Germany, therefore, his *halachic* credentials are unimpeachable. Now, however, he grasps that he too was "mitgemeint" (intended too; *S*, 347; *S*, 349), as he puts it several times, and that his pregnant mother and grandmother could just as easily have ended up on a cattle wagon to the death camps, with other Jews destined for extermination. In Germany of all places, it seems, Arthur truly *becomes* Jewish.[65] This is a determinedly secular understanding of Jewish identity, of course—Arthur has no interest in the founder of Hasidism, the Baal Shem Tov (*S*, 325), for example—but it is one that would be immediately recognizable to, and accepted by, the established community in his adopted country.

Arthur's rehearsal of what he has gleaned from books about the Holocaust eases his entry into German and German Jewish memory culture. It does not, however, establish the Soviet-born narrator's personal, emotional investment in Holocaust history, or counter the presumption more generally that Russian Jews were less directly impacted by the genocide and thus cannot properly relate to commemorative practices in Germany. Arthur's *fabulation* of the circumstances of his birth is not entirely fanciful, therefore, insofar as it positions the Soviet-born migrant not simply as newcomer to Holocaust memory regurgitating what he has learned from books but as someone who is directly implicated in that traumatic past. Soviet Jews too were also forced to flee, and they were murdered if they stayed—just as happened to his maternal grandparents (*S*, 115–16). More generally, Arthur goes on to hint that for Russian Jews the genocide and the German invasion were two sides of the same coin. In a reference to the siege of Stalingrad, the narrator associates a relative's report of the heavy smoke from German bombing and the Volga in flames with the gas chambers at Treblinka (*S*, 155).

What is perhaps most significant about Arthur's switch from historiographical narration to invention, however, is the implication that it is necessary to *extemporize* a Soviet Jewish proximity to the Holocaust that is otherwise barely present in German and German Jewish memory culture. In an essay for the weekly magazine *Der Freitag*, the sociologist, historian, and curator Dmitrij Belkin describes this gap:

> But what about the families in Belarusian and Ukrainian villages who were almost entirely wiped out? The tens of thousands who were shot in the parks and woods of Ukrainian towns? The ghettos in occupied cities? The evacuations of the lucky ones, who survived, but lost everything?[66]

For Belkin, it is imperative to recognize the experience of Soviet Jews— the Holocaust by bullets that killed hundreds of thousands in their towns and villages—in addition to the horrors endured in the death camps by

---

65   This is a process that sociologist Dmitrij Belkin describes for himself in his aptly named *Germanija: Wie ich in Deutschland jüdisch und erwachsen wurde* (Germanija: How I become Jewish and grown-up in Germany; 2016). See Panagiotidis, *The Unchosen Ones*, 321.

66   Belkin, "Wir könnten Avantgarde sein."

the survivors who reestablished the community. What Arthur does is to imaginatively reconstruct this Soviet Jewish past, so that it can contribute to what Belkin describes as an emerging "Patchwork-Judentum" (patchwork Judaism),[67] characterized by overlapping identities and plural memories. Here, Arthur is typical of the protagonists of novels by Soviet-born writers. In Katja Petrowskaja's *Vielleicht Esther* (Maybe Esther; 2014), for example, the Russian Jewish protagonist re-narrates the shooting of 34,000 Jews at Babi Yar, in Kyiv, in September 1941. This text is examined in chapter 2.

Arthur's outrageous, even scandalous, suggestion that he was preternaturally cognizant of the exact moment of his birth also has a more specific resonance, however—and one that succinctly expresses how arduous it is to write the Soviet Jewish experience of the genocide into the literary canon, to say nothing of memory culture more broadly. Many, if not most, readers of *Sterndeutung*, accordingly, will recognize Arthur's narration of his birth in a train hurtling away from the advancing German army as an obvious intertextual allusion to Günter Grass's *Die Blechtrommel* (The tin drum; 1959), whose protagonist Oskar is also born fully aware of his surroundings, including the depravity of his "three" parents (his mother, his father, and his mother's lover) and the growing appeal of fascism from the early 1920s. Oskar, as is well known, refuses to grow after age three, disrupts Nazi parades but also joins the Party and entertains German troops in France, and testifies—beating his drum or shattering glass with his high-pitched screams—to the atrocities taking place around him, including the deportation of the Jews of Danzig. In sum, *Die Blechtrommel* is considered to be a landmark in West Germany's confrontation with its Nazi past, relentlessly exposing the complicity of ordinary Germans, their self-serving indulgence of the regime, and the morally ambivalent artist who is both repulsed by Nazi brutality but also drawn to its spectacle.[68] A key theme is the novel's unreliable narrator,[69] which is where Arthur's tribute begins, of course.

The invocation of *Die Blechtrommel* is even more flagrant than this. Just in case the reader fails to notice the parallel between two infants precociously alert to the chaos into which they are born, Arthur directly references a key motif in Grass's 1959 classic, namely the moth that is drumming on a lightbulb at the exact moment of Oskar's arrival. In *Die Blechtrommel*, the moth recalls German Romanticism, where it is a symbol of precarious fragility and hubris, while predicting Oskar's own percussive accompaniment to the absurdities and horrors of the Nazi period. In *Sterndeutung*, however, Arthur claims to remember that there was no

---

67   Belkin, "Wir könnten Avantgarde sein."
68   See Michaels, "Confronting the Nazi Past."
69   See Demetz, *After the Fires*.

moth drumming against a lightbulb, since the entire train was blacked-out to evade German air attacks: "Bei meiner Geburt schlug keine Falter gegen eine Glühbirne." (At the time of my birth, there was no moth beating against a light bulb; *S*, 20.) Outside the train too there is nothing but pitch-black emptiness. Arthur's birth—as he claims to recall it—was not distinguished by intimations of exceptionality (however ambivalent), by any auspicious constellation of planets, or even by the presence of stars in the night sky.

On the face of it, Arthur's allusion to this foundational literary contribution to Germany's confrontation with its Nazi past confirms his desire to integrate into the memory culture of his adopted country. Many—Jewish and non-Jewish—German readers will immediately recognize the allusion to Grass. At the same time, Arthur's emphasis that there was *no* moth drumming against a lightbulb draws attention to fundamental distinctions between the reception of his story and how Oskar's idiosyncratically representative tale has been absorbed into German memory culture. First, the absence of a drum-beating moth implies the absence of Jewish voices in the literary canon of coming-to-terms with the past. Indeed, Grass has been criticized for his privileging of German perspectives, including by the Holocaust survivor and scholar Ruth Klüger.[70] Second, in drawing attention to how Soviet Jewish voices specifically are even more marginal, Arthur is most likely making a point not only to the non-Jewish majority but also to the established German Jewish community. And third, the non-appearance of a propitious constellation of planets extends and repurposes the allusion to Goethe that was the basis for the relevant passages in *Die Blechtrommel*. Grass's use of the moth motif recalls Goethe's famous poem about longing, "Selige Sehnsucht" (blessed longing; 1814), and his references to Saturn and Mars at the time of Oskar's birth suggests Goethe's own rather self-aggrandizing and overwhelmingly optimistic account of his own entry into the world in volume 1 of his *Aus meinem Leben: Dichtung und Wahrheit* (From my life: Poetry and truth; 1811).[71] Oskar is an inheritor of the German literary tradition—even if the legacy itself and his continuation of it are ambivalent, even potentially malevolent—whereas Arthur is doubly excluded, as a Jew and a Soviet Jew.

Arthur's narration of Soviet Jewish history, therefore, is an attempt at *Sterndeutung*—interpreting the stars—where the star motif refers throughout not only to celestial objects but also to Jews, especially dead Jews, murdered in their towns and villages: "Keine Sterne mehr in Kamenz-Podolsk, in dessen Nähe doch der Baal Schem in einem

---

70 See Preece, "Günter Grass."
71 Goethe, *Aus meinem Leben*, 10. For the Goethe references in Grass, see Arnds, *Representation*, 138–41.

vergangenen Jahrhundert geboren worden war." (No stars any more in Karenz-Podolsk, near to which the Baal Schem was born in the last century, though; *S*, 325.) In composing—fabulating—this Soviet Jewish experience he claims a place for it in the memory culture of his adopted country.

Significantly, the impetus for the narrator to write the manuscript that, in due course, will be published as *Sterndeutung*—thus the novel's literary conceit—comes from his German Jewish friend Roth. (As in Martynova's *Sogar Papageien überleben uns*, discussed above, there may be an allusion here to Joseph Roth and his essay "Juden auf Wanderschaft" about encounters between German Jews and Jewish immigrants from eastern Europe after the First World War.) Roth, then, gifts Arthur a book for his birthday—perhaps this is one of the Holocaust textbooks that Arthur devours—and urges the Soviet-born newcomer to write about his own experiences. With self-reflexive irony, Arthur wonders whether this would be "ein jüdisches Buch auf Deutsch?" (a Jewish book in German), a "jüdisch-deutsches Buch" (a Jewish-German book), a "Buch auf Deutsch über Juden. Und über Deutsche" (a book in German about Jews. And about Germans), or quite simply a "Judenbuch" (Jew-book; *S*, 258). Each of these suggests a different degree of both Jewishness and integration, and the final formulation may even recall—in the similarity between the sounds Buch/Buche if not in the exact meaning of the words—Annette von Droste-Hülshoff's *Die Judenbuche* (The Jews's beech, 1842). This nineteenth-century novella famously revolves around the unsolved murder of a local Jew.[72]

In any case, it seems likely that Roth is hoping for a book confirming the Russian immigrant's willingness to conform to the expectations of the existing Jewish community, and his "successful" integration. His primary concerns, therefore, are whether Arthur had two Jewish parents—that is, whether he is *halachically* Jewish (*S*, 226)—and why Arthur takes money from the German state to pay for his mother's upkeep (*S*, 281). More specifically, Roth's injunction to write follows a gathering at Arthur's house with recently immigrated Russian friends that includes nostalgic anecdotes about home, wonderment at the German state's generosity in disbursing large sums to post-Soviet Jews, and a vision of their adopted country as a land of opportunities. "Auch aus den Nachkommen kann etwas werden, erklärte ich Roth" (*S*, 257), Arthur suggests, perhaps with ironic deference. (These later arrivals might be able to make something of themselves, I explained to Roth.) "The Russians," Arthur seems to want to reassure his native-born friend, can become proper Jews, and even *German* Jews.

Yet Arthur's account is more than simply a fulfillment of the established community's insistence that the newcomers adapt to its norms, and

---

72 See Chase, "Part of the Story."

more than simply an expansion of its existing commemorative practices to include the Soviet Jewish experience of the Holocaust. In the third of his subplots, delivered in a deceptively low-key style, Arthur thus positions himself not only as a worthy member of the community and respecter of Holocaust memory but also as a more consistent *guardian* of that memory even than the German-born Jew who survived the genocide. This bold self-styling, it can be argued, relies upon three startling assertions: the Russian Jewish immigrant's prior immersion in German and German Jewish culture; his familiarity with the international canon of Holocaust literature; and his vigilance with regard to Germany's still incomplete reckoning with its past in the present day.

After Roth gives him the book, then, Arthur shows him his existing collection: Goethe, Rilke, and Kafka. The implication is clear—the Russian-speaking newcomer had already imbibed German culture before his arrival and is well-versed in his adopted country's humanist heritage and the Jewish contribution to this heritage, before the Nazi genocide. Goethe was widely admired by German and European Jews;[73] Rilke had a Jewish mother and was fascinated by the concept of diaspora; and the German-speaking Prague Jew Kafka, of course, thematized Jewish non-belonging throughout his work.[74] Indeed, as Dmitrij Belkin notes in an essay of 2010, familiarity with German and especially German Jewish literature was common among Russian-speaking Jews: "The collected works of Goethe and Heine, Thomas Mann's *Joseph* trilogy, the novels of Kafka and Hesse accompanied hundreds of thousands of Soviet Jews to Germany, as a key component of their identity."[75] What Arthur seems to be suggesting to his German Jewish friend, accordingly, is that he is *already* part of the community—and even that fellow Soviet-born Jews are reimporting a tradition of reflection on Jewish belonging and even Jewish worldliness. More generally, the hidden and less hidden references to German and German Jewish literature throughout the text—e.g., Grass, Joseph Roth, possibly Droste-Hülshoff—reinforces this point.

More than this, however, Arthur's bookshelf also contains important works of Holocaust literature from beyond Germany, specifically Tadeusz Borowski, the Polish poet and writer best known for his short stories *Pożegnanie z Marią* (1946; This way for the gas, ladies and gentlemen) and *Roman eines Schicksallosen*, the German translation of Hungarian

---

73 See Berghahn and Hermand, eds., Goethe in German-Jewish Culture. Goethe's own attitude toward Jews was more ambivalent. See Wilson, *Goethe*.

74 See Robertson, *Kafka*.

75 Belkin, "Mögliche Heimat," 28. More generally, Marat Grinberg argues that the "Soviet Jewish bookshelf" of literary works translated from Yiddish, Hebrew, and German afforded a subterranean way of connection to a Jewish heritage that had been suppressed by the authorities and a vision of "worldliness." See Grinberg, *The Soviet Jewish Bookshelf*.

Nobel prize-winner Imre Kertész's *Sorstalanság* (Fatelessness; 1975), a semi-autobiographical account of a young Hungarian Jew's experiences in Auschwitz and Buchenwald. The point here is most likely that Arthur is better informed about German and German Jewish culture and Holocaust memory than his German hosts—whether Jewish or non-Jewish—and that his Soviet Jewish narrative should also be considered to belong to this global canon. Elsewhere Arthur mentions Primo Levi, specifically in relation to the Treblinka uprising and the Italian survivor's formulation of the imperative to stand up for humanity: "Wenn nicht jetzt, wann dann?" (If not now, when?; *S*, 242). In Levi's 1982 novel with that title, *Se non ora, quando?*, Russian-Jewish partisans try to fight their way to a Jewish homeland in Palestine. Variations of the same refrain appear on several occasions throughout Arthur's account (e.g., *S*, 196; *S*, 203), including during a brief discussion of the 1994 genocide in Rwanda, which is taking place in the narrative present (*S*, 205). This episode is discussed in greater detail below.

The most striking way Arthur asserts his more thorough internalization of the norms of contemporary memory culture, however, is his—entirely inconsequential—refusal to stand and applaud at his daughter's graduation ceremony following a speech delivered by a wealthy donor who, the press had recently revealed, has a Waffen SS past (*S*, 377–88). Once again, the allusion to Günter Grass is obvious. In 2006, Grass belatedly revealed that he had been a member of the notoriously fanatical elite unit at the end of the war, and an earlier mention that the individual under discussion had been fifteen at the outbreak of war and eighteen when he was conscripted confirms the match with the biography of Germany's most prominent postwar author (*S*, 323). What's most significant here is that Arthur's refusal to honor a public figure with a tainted past contrasts sharply with Roth's apparent indifference (e.g., *S*, 258–60) and even willingness to overlook and even indulge youthful indiscretions. When Arthur tells Roth about the patron, the latter replies with a story about his aunt, who died in hospital following the withdrawal of treatment by her doctors—a decision that he had agreed to. Only after her death was he able to cry, he relates, but he now views his tears more as an acknowledgment, after the fact, of his part in her demise than as genuine mourning. Roth concludes that he does not know what his aunt has to do with Arthur's account of his daughter's graduation (*S*, 227–33), yet the juxtaposition implies that Roth sees the donor's belated regret for his proximity to Nazi crimes as comparable to the remorse he feels for easing his aunt's pain, that is, as an act of good faith notwithstanding its distressing outcome. Here, it falls to Arthur to voice the objection that would normally be expected of the German Jew, ever vigilant against the hypocrisy of the non-Jewish majority. He treats his native-born coreligionist to a brief but uncompromising monologue on Jewish writing and Jewish memory, the impossibility of narrating the individual deaths of the millions of victims, the sacred obligation to preserve the testimony of those who were actually there, and the constant risk of German backsliding.

Himmelfarb's *Sterndeutung* juxtaposes fact, fabulation, and self-reflection to exemplify its Soviet-born protagonist's emergence as a (Russian) German Jew. Yet Arthur's self-positioning vis-à-vis the non-Jewish majority and the established community may, in the end, *limit* his Jewish identity as much as it first enables and then ratifies his claim to belong. Indeed, in migrating into the norms and expectations of his adopted country and his adopted community, it may be that Arthur sacrifices Jewish *worldliness* for Jewish *parochialism*.

Interspersed throughout Arthur's retelling of Holocaust history, the fate of Soviet Jews, and postwar antisemitism, therefore, are brief but striking references to events taking place in the narrative present, namely the burning of migrant hostels in Solingen in 1993 and the 1994 genocide in Rwanda, when around 800,000 Tutsi were murdered by their Hutu neighbors. These allusions initially appear to indicate a willingness to universalize the Jewish experience as a basis for solidarity with others—Arthur cites the famous quotation by Rabbi Hillel the Elder: "If I am not for me, who will be for me? And when I am for myself alone, what am I?" (*S*, 209). (The quotation continues with the line also used by Levi as a book title and cited elsewhere in the novel: "And if not now, then when?"; *S*, 296, 203; 252.) Following a lengthy summary of the media's reporting of incitements to kill Tutsis broadcast on Rwandan radio, the massacre of hundreds of thousands in churches, and the world's inaction, however, Arthur admits the inadequacy of his own words: "Lange genug sah, hörte und las ich. Was blieb mir übrig, als es niederzuschreiben, da es vorbei war?" (I watched, listened, and read for long enough. What else could I do but write it down, since it was over anyway?; *S*, 209.) At the end of the day, Arthur is too fixated on his own past to intervene on behalf of people thousands of miles away. "Aber in Ruanda gibt es keine Züge," he remarks (there are no trains in Rwanda; *S*, 205) on the same page as he indirectly references Levi as an "Italian Jew" always ready to use his camp experiences to call for solidarity with others. Likewise, when Arthur reads about the asylum-seekers' hostels in Solingen he notes the inconvenient train connections that a visit to join others in expressing outrage would involve: "Nur hätte ich viermal umsteigen müssen" (Only, I would have had to change four times; *S*, 124).

Chapters 2 and 3 of this book explore in detail the tension between a German Jewish identity primarily—and parochially—focused on life in the land of the perpetrators and a globally oriented Jewish sensibility that defines itself through solidarity with others. In *Sterndeutung*, Arthur's Soviet Jewish experience, of course, will recede ever further into the past. His narration begins just before his fifty-first birthday and ends shortly after his fifty-fourth, and it is clear that he is fighting a losing battle to demonstrate the relevance of what he claims to remember about his birth, or even of his more factual recounting of Holocaust history. His wife Julia, as already noted, is keen to travel to the European capitals that were inaccessible to her in Soviet times, and their daughter Anna is solely interested in getting good grades and securing a high-paying job—just like her non-Jewish German boyfriend. For this (Russian) German Jewish family at least, integration—and conformity within the German mainstream—seems to be the future.

An Unorthodox Orthodox Judaism: Benjamin Stein's *Rabbi Löw*

Benjamin Stein was born Matthias Albrecht in 1970 in East Berlin, the grandson of a returned exile and then high-ranking functionary in communist East Germany (the GDR). Unlike Altaras and Himmelfarb, consequently, Stein is a German-born Jew, although his identity is complicated by the fact that his grandparents had abjured Judaism in favor of communism in the GDR and—perhaps more important—by the fact that his Jewish lineage is unambiguous only on his father's side. The author reflects at length on this biographical uncertainty on his website, https://turmsegler.net, especially "Der Autor als Seelenstripper" (The author as soul stripper; June 3, 2010) and "Familiengeschichte" (family history; June 14, 2010) in which he responds with frustration and hurt to tactless enquiries about his Jewishness. He has formally converted not once but on three occasions, he divulges, first within a Reform congregation, then a second and third time as Orthodox. No one should be surprised, then, that he feels the "heftigste Wut" (greatest anger) when he thinks back to what he and his wife went through in order to establish their legitimacy—and their children's legitimacy—as Jews.[76]

In public appearances and interviews, Stein thus presents himself as a strictly observant Jew. On the one hand, this aligns the author with the long tradition of Orthodox Judaism in Germany before the Holocaust, including the neo-Orthodox revival of the late nineteenth century,[77] with the largely Orthodox survivors who refounded the community after 1945[78] and dominated it until relatively recently,[79] and with the growing presence once again of Orthodox and ultra-Orthodox Jews today, including many new arrivals from the United States.[80] On the other hand, it

---

76 Stein, "Der Autor als Seelenstripper." See also Stein, "Familiengeschichte."
77 See Breuer, *Modernity within Tradition*.
78 See Cohen-Weisz, *Jewish Life*, especially 181–88.
79 See Wolffsohn, "Jews in Divided Germany and Beyond," especially 28.
80 See Brenner, "A New German Jewry?," especially 425.

positions him against the more liberal and even secular versions of Jewish practice that have emerged with large-scale immigration from the former Soviet Union but also from the United States and Israel, and following the recent revival of Reform Judaism in the country where it originated in the mid-nineteenth century.[81]

Stein's self-staging as an Orthodox Jew very obviously intervenes in key debates—and controversies—animating the community in Germany and Jews across the diaspora more generally, namely whether a patrilineal heritage is "sufficient" to count as a Jew, how and by which branch of Judaism conversion is recognized, and to what extent *halachic* conformity defines Jewish identity. (The history of the small Jewish community in the GDR, and of the Jews who opted for the Soviet zone after 1945, is a more marginal discourse.[82] It features in Mirna Funk's 2015 novel *Winternähe*/Near winter, which is discussed in chapter 2.) Stein's response to these fundamental questions dividing the community seems to be that a Jewish identity is expressed through *Jewish actions* rather than simply inherited and inhabited. In an interview with the German-Nigerian journalist Iljoma Mangold about his 2010 novel *Die Leinwand* (The canvas)—a postmodern metafiction that references Binjamin Wilkomirski's fake Holocaust memoirs[83]—the author comments:

> "Für mein Judentum," sagt Stein, "brauche ich keinen Zionismus und keinen Holocaust. Das spielt zwar eine Rolle, kommt aber von außen. Wenn sich jemand an mich wendet, weil er seine jüdische Identität sucht, dann sage ich ihm: Versuche doch mal, Schabbes-Kerzen anzuzünden, und schau, was das mit dir macht."[84]

> ["For my Jewishness," Stein says, "I don't need Zionism and I don't need the Holocaust. That plays a part, of course, but is imposed from outside. Whenever people turn to me, in search of their Jewish identity, I say: Just try lighting some Shabbat candles, and see, what that makes of you."]

To live as a Jew is not (only) about defending Israel or commemorating the Holocaust, although these are important, of course. It is about *performing* a Jewish identity, through ritual acts and declarations of faith. In essence, Stein is a Jew because he wills a Jewish identity for himself.

As Katja Garloff notes, Stein's project is to "broaden the range of Jewish identities, and especially religious identities, that can be expressed in German-language literature," with "an emphasis on the ways that

---

81 See Cohen-Weisz, *Jewish Life*, especially 181–88.
82 See Wolffsohn, "Jews in Divided Germany."
83 See Maechler, *The Wilkomirski Affair*.
84 Mangold, "Religion."

Jewish law structures the everyday life of observant Jews and sets them apart from non-Jews."[85] As will become evident from the analysis of *Das Alphabet des Rabbi Löw* (2014) that follows, however, Stein's enterprise is radical not only because it inserts a religious and even Orthodox voice into a secular literary tradition. In declaring that Jewishness is derived not from *halachic* principles and not even from Holocaust memory but rather from a gesture of self-enactment, the author implies a rearticulation of Jewish identity that is as transgressive as it is pragmatic. *Rabbi Löw*'s kabbalistic rewriting of family history, then, elaborates an *unorthodox* Orthodox Judaism that—precisely through its scandalous inversion of religious and cultural injunctions—reinvigorates and reinvents Jewish identity to respond to the modern-day reality of assimilation, intermarriage, and near-extermination.

In 2014, Stein reissued *Das Alphabet des Juda Liva*, first published in 1995, as *Das Alphabet des Rabbi Löw*.[86] A side-by-side comparison of the two versions confirms his assertion in an editorial notice at the conclusion of the 2014 version that the changes are chiefly "shortenings and corrections" of an unwieldy, even overwritten debut novel.[87] It is likely that both publisher and author were keen to insert an out-of-print novel that had been largely overlooked into what, by then, had become a significant revival of German Jewish literature. At the same time, *Rabbi Löw* stands out on account of its unusually intense exploration of the intricacies of Jewish faith, theological debate, and ritual practice.

Stein's novel tells of its protagonist Rottenstein's self-transformation from a regular German student with distant Jewish roots into a model of strict religious observance, via a crash course in Kabbalah and Hebrew numerology in Prague and Budapest.[88] Most conspicuously, this involves a series of literally incredible encounters with the resurrected sixteenth-century Talmudic scholar Rabbi Löw and his adolescent son, who doubles as the wildly eccentric Jewish mystic's Golem. (According to legend, Rabbi Löw fashioned the original Golem from clay to protect Prague's Jews from the attacks of gentiles.)[89] At the same time, Rottenstein's emergence as an Orthodox Jew also requires a confrontation with family history. This is recounted in a disjointed, episodic manner by the novel's two narrators, Jacoby and Bergcowicz, who may or may not be one and the same person.

---

85   Garloff, "The Power of Paratext," 141.
86   What follows is an extensive rewriting of my article in *The Modern Language Review*, from 2021. See Taberner, "Redemption."
87   Stein, *Rabbi Löw*, 285. Hereafter *RL*.
88   For Kabbalah in contemporary popular culture, see Myers, "Kabbalah in the Modern Era."
89   See Idel, *Golem*.

Liva/Rabbi Löw begins with a framing narrative involving two non-Jewish Germans, Bergcowicz and his girlfriend Sheary, who pay Jacoby a bottle of vodka to appear each Tuesday evening at their Berlin flat and to relate the adventures of his friend Rottenstein, specifically Rottenstein's journey to Prague and Budapest to "become" an Orthodox Jew. Bergcowicz speculates that Jacoby's choice of alcohol could identify him as a Russian: "Seinen Trinkgewohnheiten nach hätte er Russe sein müssen" (given his drinking habits, he must have been a Russian; *RL*, 13). His accent, however, marks him as Berlin-born. Nevertheless, the reader is likely to make a connection to the mass arrival of Jews from the former Soviet Union, which had just got underway as the novel was first published in 1995 and which by the time of its rerelease in 2014 had transformed Jewish demography in today's Germany. As in Altaras's *titos brille*, the implication may be that Russian Jews have appropriated the legacy of the postwar community. After only a few weeks, however, Jacoby self-ignites in the mental asylum of the Charité hospital. This story-before-the story is related retrospectively, following the opening lines of the novel, which tell of the arrival of a telegram notifying Bergcowicz and Sheary of Jacoby's combustion and instructing them to contact his lawyer. This they do, and Bergcowicz takes over the narration, drawing on newspaper cuttings, video cassettes, and voice recordings that Jacoby has purportedly bequeathed to him. What follows is a labyrinth of intersecting narratives set in Berlin, Prague, and Budapest, extracts from the Kabbalah and the Aggadah, and allusions to the false messiah Sabbatai Zevi and the prophet Elijah. In essence, however, the underlying theme is Alex Rottenstein's family history, though frequent shifts across time and place mean that it is for the reader to reconstruct the relationships and the chronology set out below.[90]

Rottenstein's grandfather Max Regensburger flees Nazi Germany in 1933 with his mother Anna after his communist father is murdered by brownshirts. In Prague, Max is briefly taken in by an adolescent Czech girl, Lydia, and her father, before he travels on to meet Anna in Moscow. He returns twelve years later in 1945, now a young man, and impregnates Lydia, after which he settles in East Germany, where he becomes a high-ranking official. (Anna's family history is told in a lengthy excursus. Her father is a "circus Jew"[91] while she joins the Jewish middle class by marrying the son of an undertaker.) Lydia, it transpires, is a seraph—angel—as is her daughter Mirijam, conceived with Max, and as is Eva,

---

90 Stein includes a family tree on his website: https://turmsegler.net/alphabet/languages/en/index.html. Last accessed July 25, 2024.

91 In the nineteenth and early twentieth centuries, Jews—and Romani people—were often involved as owners of or artists in circuses. See Hödl, *Entangled Entertainers*.

who is born half a year after Mirijam's tryst with Jaroslav Vonka, the non-Jewish son of a local innkeeper. (Angels, apparently, are born at six months; *RL*, 102–3.) Jaroslav flees to avoid the fate that befalls men who abandon female angels—combustion—but he later turns up in Berlin, now named Slosil, with an axe in his head. On cremation, he sits upright, his body bursts into flame, and his soul escapes into Alex Rottenstein, aged twelve (the age Jewish boys enter adulthood) and living with his great-uncle Franz, Max's older brother, who had survived the war in Paris. The young Rottenstein subsequently develops an interest in the Jewish texts in Franz's library. (His grandmother Inge, whom Max married in the GDR, was not Jewish and therefore—*halachically*—neither is his mother Marianne nor Rottenstein himself.) Years later, Rottenstein travels to Prague, where he meets his distant cousin Eva in the corner shop owned by her uncle, Jiri Procházka. Predictably, Rottenstein sleeps with Eva, abandons her, and is burned to death. Except that he is also a witness to his own immolation, levitated outside his blazing apartment by the very same Procházka, a.k.a. Rabbi Löw of Prague. (Procházka also features as the Ein Sof, the infinity that is G-D, just as most other characters appear in different guises, and with different names.) Rottenstein studies the Talmud in Budapest, makes *aliyah* to Jerusalem, and here his story, as assembled by Jacoby, ends. Bergcowicz, however, continues to narrate on his own account. He has Rottenstein return to Berlin on Pesach (Passover) with the prophet Elijah—Jacoby—to prove the "truth" of the Jewish ritual to the woefully non-observant Jewish community. In a final twist, Bergcowicz insinuates that he is in fact Rottenstein, and the Messiah, even as the ambulance pulls up, presumably to transport him to the mental hospital at the Charité (*RL*, 279).

The (relatively scant) scholarly literature on the novel's 1995 iteration as *Das Alphabet des Juda Liva* largely follows the contours of the plot summary given above and frames Stein's first work as an indictment of assimilation and as an injunction to return to a more authentic Jewish practice. Cathy Gelbin, for example, argues that "Stein configures assimilation as a false ideal ultimately leading to the fires of the Shoah" even as "the consumerism brought to post-socialist Prague by fun-seeking Western youths merely appears as the last manifestation of the 'real' world."[92] Dorothee Gelhard, similarly, explores the allusions to Jewish mysticism—including the power of the Hebrew alphabet to instigate *tikkun olam* ("repair of the world")—and argues that the novel presents a kabbalistic critique of Enlightenment reason.[93] More generally, critics emphasize the abstruse plotline and complex form, including the lack of punctuation to mark direct speech; uncertainty as to who is speaking;

---

92 Gelbin, "The Monster Returns," 23.
93 Gelhard, *Mit dem Gesicht nach vorne gewandt*, 179.

multiple retellings of the same episode; characters who are in two places at once or in the wrong time entirely; the power of storytelling to create reality; and how the framing narrative finally collapses into the story within a story that it is supposed to enable.[94]

Yet Gelhard also points to the overblown irony that suffuses and even drives the novel's fabulistic exuberance, and specifically to how this throws into doubt its ostensible purpose of resurrecting an authentic—Orthodox—Jewish tradition.[95] Certainly, the appearance of a resurrected Rabbi Löw in felt slippers (throughout), his Golem-son adorned with a red headband (throughout), and a self-combusting narrator, Jacoby, who dons a beret with the emblem of the elite Givati brigade of the Israeli Defense Forces and turns out to be the prophet Elijah (*RL*, 11, 263, 270)—all this provokes skepticism about how seriously the reader is expected to take Stein's Jewish mysticism. Hardly mentioned in the existing scholarship, moreover, is the disclosure that Jacoby completed four semesters of Jewish Studies in Berlin (*RL*, 212). Benjamin Stein also read Jewish Studies in Berlin, and it is possible, and indeed probable, that the author is playing with what he has learned.

Irony is strongly associated with modernity, and indeed with the secular challenge to religious faith.[96] Within *Rabbi Löw*'s no doubt sincere commitment to Jewish beliefs, therefore, it is also possible to glimpse more worldly, even profane concerns that certainly disrupt the novel's kabbalistic esotericism, as Gelhard puts it, but which are also expressed through it, as we shall see. In what follows, we examine how *Rabbi Löw* offers an unexpectedly pragmatic response to the fundamental dilemmas of German Jewish identity today: how to assert the continuity of Jewish faith and tradition when so much has been destroyed; how to be at home in Germany, and in German culture; and how to revive an authentic Judaism in a country where—for understandable reasons—Holocaust memory is more definitive than religious conviction and ritual practice. Even more than in *titos brille* and *Sterndeutung*, moreover, transgression is indispensable. Allusions to the false messiah Sabbatai Zevi invoke a subterranean tradition of deliberate sinfulness that, historically, has proliferated new Jewish life-worlds. In *Rabbi Löw*, it is argued, the impulse to defy authority and reinvent Jewish identity even appears, paradoxically, as quintessentially and even conventionally Jewish. Indeed, insofar as it frames transgression as the prerequisite for the reinvigoration of Jewish identity, the unorthodox Orthodox Judaism of *Rabbi Löw* may even anticipate the abundance of pluralistic and certainly

---

94   See Bock-Lindenbeck, *Letzte Welten*, 231–49. See Oberwalleney, *Heterogenes Schreiben*.
95   Gelhard, *Mit dem Gesicht nach vorne gewandt*, 184.
96   See Behler, *Irony and the Discourse of Modernity*.

non-halachic—patrilineal, Russian, queer, cosmopolitan, and even non-Jewish—Jewish practices in Germany today.

It is Kabbalah that enables, as it were, the telling of what is in essence a tragically familiar story of assimilation, the horrors of the Holocaust, a survivor's embrace of communism in the avowedly anti-fascist German Democratic Republic, and the third generation's attempts to make sense of this history and to reconnect with its Jewish heritage. The magical realism of Kabbalah, therefore, provides a set of narrative devices that permit the novel's various storytellers to initiate movements across time and place, to suggest connections between disparate events, and to justify the occasional "jähe Wendung" (abrupt turn; *RL*, 122) in the plot—and to entertain, even as what is being told is a tale of dislocation, mass murder, and trauma transmitted through the generations. Kabbalistic motifs such as the number twelve, for example, link the twelve simple letters of the Hebrew alphabet[97] to Anna's age when she was first kissed—by a twenty-year-old Italian, who introduces her, also with his roasted chestnuts, to the temptations of an assimilated life (*RL*, 165)—to Rottenstein's age when he was impacted by Jaroslav's spirit and began to be interested in his Jewish roots (RL, 251), to the adolescent Golem (*RL*, 252), and to the twelve years of National Socialism (*RL*, 196). Most important of all, however, is the kabbalistic notion of predetermination. Jacoby thus relates Rottenstein's explanation of his witnessing of his own death: "Du glaubst nicht, dass es möglich ist, zur selben Zeit an verschiedenen Orten zu sein, aber sobald Bestimmung ins Spiel kommt, gibt es kein Jetzt, kein Später und kein Zuvor mehr." (You don't think that it's possible to be in different places at the same time, but as soon as predetermination comes into play, there is no now, no later, and time before; *RL*, 88.) Predetermination, of course, both confirms the proposition that assimilation inevitably led to the crematoria of the Nazi death camps—also implied by the characters' tendency to combust—and gives the novel's various narrators significant latitude to collapse time and place, to their own advantage.

At the same time, the novel's unabashed self-referentiality ensures that the reader cannot be ignorant of its artifice. Frequent interjections such as "Doch das wissen wir bereits" (we know that already, of course; *RL*, 114); irony-laden direct addresses to Bergcowicz and thus the reader: "Auch mir kam die Einsicht in die Zusammenhänge erst reichlich spät" (even I didn't grasp how everything fitted together until much later; *RL*, 87); and insights into the intrinsic fictionality of the narrative—"Was ich erzähle, geschieht, nicht umgekehrt" (what I narrate, happens, and not the other way around; *RL*, 17)—all focus attention on the constructedness of the story, and storytelling more generally. As significant, however, are kabbalistic inconsistencies that are not functions of its time- and

---

97 See Mordell, "The Origin of Letters and Numerals," especially 560.

space-bending logic but rather hint that the reader should not overinterpret. For example, the anarchist "circle A" graffitied on a building is claimed to be the Hebrew letter Aleph (א) but is in truth only superficially similar (*RL*, 44). Similarly, Rabbi Löw asserts that he wrote the *Sefer Yetsir* and owns the only copy in existence, but the book of creation actually dates from around two centuries before Christ, with many versions since.[98] Above all, it is an extended citation from the Aggadah—the body of rabbinical texts that explore the meanings, values, and ideas of religious life—that sounds a warning. Rabbi Löw introduces the story of the four rabbis who ascend into Pardes (heavenly orchard), the first of whom died from looking at the Divine Presence, the second lost his sanity, the third became a heretic, and the fourth the leading rabbinical figure of the era. No exposition is given, but the reader who seeks one in the academic literature will discover that most scholars agree that the legend is a warning not to deviate into mysticism.[99] For readers less well-versed in Jewish spirituality, the words of Jiri Procházka a.k.a. Rabbi Löw a.k.a. Ein Sof may serve as a more explicit caution: "Wo stehen wir? Vor oder hinter dem Spiegel? Neben oder mitten in der Geschichte? Ich rate Ihnen, sich vorzusehen. Am Ende geraten auch Sie in den Strudel." (Where do we stand? In front of or behind the mirror? Next to or in the middle of the story/history. I would advise you to be careful. In the end, you too will end up being pulled into the vortex; *RL*, 88.)

None of the above should be taken to dismiss the central importance of Stein's allusions to Jewish mysticism. First and foremost, kabbalistic motifs suggest correspondences across historical disruptions, geographical dislocations, and other breaks in the real, e.g., assimilation, intermarriage, displacement, and genocide. This is what Elliot Wolfson describes as Kabbalah's elaboration of time as "the repetition of the same as different in the renewal of the different as same."[100] Kabbalah appeals, then, insofar as it shapes a Jewish identity across disparate epochs and locations, and in spite of all the harms inflicted.[101] Its deployment in *Rabbi Löw* intimates repair—albeit of a purely symbolic kind.

At the same time, Kabbalah also predicts *Rabbi Löw*'s marked self-referentiality, foregrounding narrative uncertainty, the duplicity of the narrator/artist, and how storytelling itself may be morally suspect. This literariness frames a more specific and localized effort to restore what has been lost, even as it also highlights the ambivalence of both what was there before and what might be resurrected in the present. The novel not only describes a process of disentanglement and detachment,

---

98 See Kaplan, *Sefer Yetzirah*.
99 See Sweeney, "Pardes."
100 Wolfson, "Structure," 156.
101 See Samuelson, "Kabbalah."

therefore—Rottenstein's turning away from the secular and toward religious observance. It also intimates that its protagonist's efforts to fathom "Wer ich bin" (who I am; *RL*, 73) necessarily involve a reiteration of the often painful but in some periods also productive German–Jewish encounter. In the end, *Rabbi Löw*'s allusions to the German and German Jewish literary traditions—and to their dynamic if always precarious mutual imbrication—may be a more concrete and indeed more radical rearticulation of modern-day German Jewish identity even than its advocacy of Orthodox Judaism.

Writing in 2008 on his blog *Turmsegler*, Stein reports how he had happened across an analysis of *Juda Liva* by the American Germanist Sander Gilman—and unceremoniously dismisses as "reiner Quatsch"[102] (absolute nonsense) Gilman's claim to see echoes of an East German literary tradition with "a massive dose of Jewish mysticism."[103] Certainly, such is the capaciousness of *Juda Liva/Rabbi Löw* that it might be possible to impute all manner of resonances. Yet the novel's invitation to seek intertextual references may be precisely the point, notwithstanding its author's likely staged refusal to admit any influences apart from Kabbalah. Where Gilman detects hints of the formally complex, highly self-referential *Levins Mühle* (Levin's windmill; 1964) by the East German Lutheran author Johannes Bobrowski, and of Jurek Becker's *Jakob der Lügner* (Jakob the liar; 1969)—the GDR's "first Jewish novel"[104]—other readers will intuit other forebears. With its concern with the pitfalls of assimilation, for example, Rabbi Löw recalls the nineteenth-century German Jewish family novel,[105] as does its depiction of colorful relatives whose intrusions evidence that entry to the bourgeoisie is uncomfortably recent. Elsewhere, the tone of a melancholically inflected thriller harks back to the exile literature of German and German Jewish writers who fled Nazism, such as Anna Seghers, whose name and best-known theme may even be invoked: "Dann kam das Signal des Schaffners, ein schrilles Pfeifen. Anna stieg in den Zug und fuhr ab. Was für ein Wort war das eigentlich? fragte sie sich, als der Zug den Bahnhof verließ. Ein Nichtsnirgends, ein Keinwort: Exil" (*RL*, 196). (Then came the conductor's signal, a shrill whistle. Anna climbed into the train and set off. What kind of word was that actually, she asked herself, as the train left the station. A notnowhere, a non-word: exile.) At the same time, premonitions of "Aschenwege: grauweiß und übersät mit Knochen" (paths formed of ashes: gray-white and littered with bones; *RL*, 191), and of how Anna's husband Hans was tortured and killed in a police cell (*RL*,

---

102 Stein, "Erstaunlicher Zufallsfund."
103 Gilman, *Multiculturalism*, 193.
104 Gilman, *Multiculturalism*, 193.
105 See Robertson, *The "Jewish Question,"* 273–85.

193), unmistakably recall the graphically disturbing Holocaust fiction of postwar writers such as Jean Améry or Edgar Hilsenrath.

Reaching further back, there are echoes throughout *Rabbi Löw* of the German intellectual and literary tradition of the eighteenth and nineteenth centuries, and especially the contest between reason and feeling. It may be too much to suppose that Jacoby is a latter-day Friedrich Heinrich Jacobi—the proponent of "philosophy of feeling" who rejected the proto-Enlightenment rationalism of the seventeenth-century Dutch-Jewish thinker Spinoza[106]—but *Rabbi Löw* consistently encourages its reader to look for more or less concealed parallels. (Spinoza's questioning of the Hebrew Bible caused him to be expelled from the community. The "other" seventeenth-century heresy was Sabbateanism, which undermined rabbinical authority through mystical transgression rather than reason—of which more later).[107] The framing narrative, for example, reminds of a realist tradition in which this device exposes the subjectivity of a protagonist's perspective and the gap between knowledge and superstition, as in Storm's *Der Schimmelreiter* (The rider on the white horse; 1888).[108] In Stein's novel, however, this distancing effect is undone once Bergcowicz takes over the storytelling and declares himself to be the Messiah. Elsewhere, German Romanticism's rejection of the Enlightenment is suggested by the story of the young man on his journey to becoming a poet, in which a mundane reality is juxtaposed with allegorical insets gesturing toward higher meaning, such as in Novalis's *Heinrich von Ofterdingen*, from 1802.[109] Again, the irony is palpable, as *Rabbi Löw* overdoes Romantic tropes such as medievalism, the female muse, and the male artist-genius.[110] Finally, the inclusion of an adolescent Golem no doubt sardonically references the long history of the German tradition's appropriation of Jewish motifs. In her *The Golem Returns* (2011), Cathy Gelbin describes how Jewish and non-Jewish writers have turned to this figure in order to reflect on reason and unreason but also Jews' "otherness."[111]

Above all, *Rabbi Löw* seems to allude to German literature of the early twentieth century, including a fascination with the city's underworld—in the final section, Rottenstein descends into Berlin's depths—and with

---

106 This was the famous *Spinoza-Streit* of 1781, which pitted Jacobi against Moses Mendelsohn, the foremost proponent of the "Jewish Enlightenment" and an advocate of Spinoza's thought. See Sutcliffe, "Quarreling over Spinoza," especially 175–81.
107 See Popkin, "Two Jewish Heresies."
108 See Heine, "*Der Schimmelreiter*."
109 See Stone, "Being, Knowledge, and Nature in Novalis."
110 See Helfer, "The Male Muses of Romanticism."
111 See Gelbin, *The Golem Returns*.

the exotic, the erotic, and the unconscious.[112] More specifically, a direct mention of Thomas Mann's *Tonio Kröger* (1903) demonstrates that the novel's scope extends beyond Jewish mysticism or even Jewish ritual. The twelve-year-old Rottenstein begins reading *Tonio Kröger* just after Jaroslav's soul enters into him, and around the time that he begins to lust after his female classmates (*RL*, 203). Mann's wife Katja Pringsheim was from an assimilated Jewish family, and Jewish characters feature in many of his works, often ambivalently.[113] More specifically, Tonio Kröger's dilemma—he is split between the poetic fantasy of his South American mother and the austere rationalism of his German father—clearly resonates with Rottenstein, as he navigates his family's Jewish roots and fragile assimilation. (Rottenstein also devours stories of the Hindu deity Vishnu, just as Hermann Hesse and other early twentieth-century writers sought inspiration in the East.)[114] Yet *Tonio Kröger*, like much of Mann's oeuvre,[115] is also about an artist figure, particularly the conflict between bourgeois self-restraint and the freedom to fantasize and even fabulate.

Stein's allusions to Franz Kafka are more oblique, but they are perceptible nonetheless. Kafka, of course, became increasingly interested in his Jewish heritage and in Jewish mysticism over the course of his short life but he was also plagued by anxiety about his vocation as a writer in the face of the demands of bourgeois conformity.[116] (He was also a German-speaking Jew from Prague, a center of European Jewry[117] and one of the settings for *Rabbi Löw*.) Cathy Gelbin argues that Stein invokes but also inverts Kafka's most famous story, *Die Verwandlung* (Metamorphosis; 1915), by acclaiming Jewish disassimilation rather than lamenting the "disintegration of the assimilating Western Jew,"[118] but there may be a more intimate connection to another of Kafka's texts. In the "Epilog" that concludes *Rabbi Löw*, therefore, Bergcowicz—the non-Jewish addressee of Jacoby's account who takes over the narration, and later claims to be Rottenstein—describes his own nightmare in a manner that reminds of *Der Prozess* (The trial; 1925), with its themes of law, punishment, and internalized guilt. Bergcowicz receives notice that he should collect a package; he surmises that this will be his corrected manuscript for *Rabbi Löw*. At the post office, however, he is rebuffed by

---

112 See Gay, *Weimar Culture*.

113 There has long been a debate on whether Mann was antisemitic, especially in his early texts. See, for example, Gelber, "Thomas Mann and Anti-semitism" and Levesque, "The Double-Edged Sword." For a more extensive discussion, see Kontje, *Thomas Mann's World*.

114 See Brown, "Toward a Perspective."

115 See Meyers, *Thomas Mann's Artist-Heroes*.

116 See Robertson, *Kafka*.

117 See Nekula, *Kafka*.

118 Gelbin, *The Golem Returns*, 162.

an unfamiliar official who claims that he is not in fact Bergcowicz. This seems to be confirmed when he checks his identity card and sees a different name. The next day he confronts the same official, who now has a second star on his epaulette, but this time Bergcowicz's name is correct, and he wonders why he fled before. That same night, the official—with three stars—bursts into his bedroom with a group of officials and accuses him of falsifying his identity and trying to escape his just punishment (*RL*, 277). Bergcowicz is deposited in a prison cell and his book is burned, whereupon he alludes laconically to historical precedents: "He! Romane zu verbrennen, ist unmodern, sage ich." (Hey. Burning novels is not at all modern; I said; *RL*, 277). Clearly, the epilogue mimics both Kafka's technique—allegory, the protagonist's limited perspective, and narrative uncertainty—and the Prague author's themes: self-doubt, vulnerability, and the ambivalence of Jewish identity.

The fact that *Rabbi Löw* remains so profoundly inflected by German and German Jewish traditions until its very end suggests that, far from transcending these traditions, the novel instead incorporates and continues them. Certainly, the epilogue reinscribes a history of artistic self-reflection that reaches back at least to German Romanticism,[119] and it is telling that the novel does not dwell on Mann's supposed antisemitism, or indeed on antisemitism more generally in the German literary tradition—including Romanticism.[120] Instead, it is the mutual, if frequently uncomfortable imbrication of German and Jewish identities that Rottenstein surely reclaims when, toward the close of the novel, he reverses his *aliyah* to the Land of Israel and returns to Berlin. As the descendent of a gentile mother and grandmother, his highly unorthodox Orthodox Judaism simply acknowledges the reality that Jewish genealogies in Germany (and across Europe) were forever altered by assimilation and then almost destroyed by the Holocaust, and that repair requires definitional flexibility. Indeed, as is implied when he scolds the Jewish congregation for not crediting the prophet Elijah (who is always expected on Passover), it is belief that defines Jewishness rather than bloodline, and adherence to ritual should not erase German Jewish identity but become its foundation (*RL*, 265–70). Once he has delivered his message, Rottenstein self-combusts on the Holocaust memorial that (in real life too) is placed in front of the community center in the Fasanenstraße (*RL*, 265–70). However, a young boy, Simon, is prepared to recognize what he has made out with his own ears and seen with his own eyes, offering some hope that German Jews might yet become observant. The name Simon derives from the Hebrew for "to hear" or "listener."

---

119 See Schmitz-Emans, "Der Roman."
120 See Beiser, "Romantic Anti-semitism."

Jacoby/Bergcowicz/Rottenstein's transgression is threefold. First, he re-entangles German Jewish and German literary traditions and thereby unapologetically asserts their insoluble, if uncomfortable, intimacy—German modernity, to cite Todd Presner, is "always already German/Jewish modernity."[121] Second, his return from Israel could be seen as a betrayal. Jews in the diaspora are bound to long for the promised land, and they certainly should not feel at home in Germany. Third, his self-styling as an Orthodox Jew is entirely *non-halachic*, given his lack of a Jewish mother. The contrast he implies between his "authentic Judaism" and the Berlin community is nothing less than scandalous, therefore. In fact, if Bergcowicz really is Rottenstein, then perhaps anyone can be an Orthodox Jew, even Germans. In the end, *Rabbi Löw* declines to confirm whether Bergcowicz's Kafkaesque nightmare reveals his actual fraudulent appropriation of a Jewish identity or—conversely—the characteristic ambivalence that definitively proves that he really must be Jewish.

Rottenstein is twice named as Sabbatai Zevi (*RL*, 225; *RL*, 239), the Sephardic rabbi from Symrna (now İzmir, Turkey), who in the late seventeenth century defied Jewish authorities, declared himself to be the Messiah, convulsed the Jewish world with the promise of redemption, was imprisoned by the Ottoman Sultan Mehmed IV, and finally committed apostasy by converting to Islam. (Rottenstein is referred to as Sabbatai Zevi Beth—Sabbatai Zevi Two). Yet the allusion to perhaps the most famous—or infamous—of Jewish heretics is sustained throughout. In the opening paragraphs, it is reported that Jacoby, the first narrator, prefers to be known as Nathan ben Gaza (*RL*, 9), and this is reiterated some 240 pages later (*RL*, 246). Nathan ben Gaza enthusiastically supported Sabbatai Zevi following his arrival in Jerusalem in 1663,[122] taking on the role of the prophet Elijah in confirming the imminent appearance of the Messiah for 1666—a pivotal year for millenarian movements of the time, including Christians[123]—who would then usher in the restoration of Israel and the salvation of the world. Later, Nathan ben Gaza would propagate that Sabbatai Zevi's conversion to Islam assisted in the messianic project of *tikkun olam*, whereby sparks of creation were spread as widely as possible in order to redeem the fallen world.[124]

What Jacoby and Bergcowicz narrate, therefore, is not simply Rottenstein's emergence as an Orthodox Jew. Rather—following Gershom Scholem's groundbreaking article "Redemption through

---

121 See Presner, *Mobile Modernity*.
122 Goldish, "Sabbatai Zevi."
123 See Popkin, "Jewish Messianism."
124 See Dweck, *Dissident Rabbi*, especially 227.

Sin"[125] (1937)—what is more fundamentally at stake is the transgression of social and religious norms, and the emergence of new potentialities of Jewish identity as a result of transgression.[126] (Stein will have read Scholem's essay in the course of his Jewish Studies program in Berlin.) For Scholem, the challenge to rabbinical authority initiated by the most likely bipolar Sabbatai Zevi opened the way to the orgiastic outrages of the eighteenth-century Frankist sect (including many converts to Catholicism)[127] and to the emergence of Hasidism in Eastern Europe, as well as Reform Judaism.[128] Subsequently, Sabbateanism would be influential in secular reinterpretations of Jewish belief and practice too, including the Jewish Enlightenment (Haskalah),[129] nineteenth- and twentieth-century Zionism,[130] and revolutionary, socialist, and anarchist impulses.[131] In the Ottoman Empire, Sabbatean families—*Dönme*, or hidden Jews—contributed significantly to the modernizing movements that prepared the way for Atatürk's creation of the Republic of Turkey.[132]

In its reinvention of Orthodox Judaism for the modern day, Stein's *Rabbi Löw* belongs to an established Jewish tradition of the transgression of norms for the sake of reconfirming and reinvigorating Judaism itself. As intellectual historian Benjamin Lazier argues, the dialectic of heresy means that "the freedom of transgression is made possible by the enduring force of the norms it disputes."[133] Even as it disrupts the conventions of Jewish life in Germany and across the diaspora, consequently, *Rabbi Löw* reimagines its future.[134]

125 Scholem, "Redemption through Sin." See Scholem, *Sabbatai Sevi*. Scholem was also fascinated by Franz Kafka. See Moses and Wiskind-Elper, "Gershom Scholem's Reading of Kafka." According to Paul Mendes-Flohr, Scholem considered Kafka to be "a secularized kabbalist." See Mendes-Flohr, *Gershom Scholem*, 16–20.
126 See Biale, *Gershom Scholem*.
127 Mandel, *The Militant Messiah*.
128 See Rapoport-Albert, ed., *Hasidism Reappraised*.
129 See Maciejko, ed., *Sabbatian Heresy*.
130 See Shavit, "Realism and Messianism."
131 See Millet, "Our Sabbatian Future."
132 See Baer, *The Dönme*.
133 Lazier, *God Interrupted*, 198.
134 Of course, *Rabbi Löw* can be read quite differently. It is even possible to interpret the novel as a warning not to rely on innovators of new German Jewish identities whose motives may be less than pure. Jacoby delivers Jewish stories in weekly installments in exchange for a bottle of vodka. Rottenstein is driven by the fantasist's delight in pure invention. And the non-Jewish German Bergcowicz takes over the narration once Jacoby has self-ignited and even suggests that it is his story. Jewish tales, Bergcowicz confesses, have an aphrodisiacal impact on his German girlfriend (*RL*, 12), and it may be that they both crave the release from inherited German guilt that could possibly be gained from "becoming a Jew."

German Jewish Parochialism or Solidarity with Others?

Each of the three novels discussed in this chapter are transgressive in one way or another. Altaras's *titos brille*, then, emphasizes reconciliation with the non-Jewish German majority even as it seems to suggest that the secular and avowedly liberal Judaism that it espouses is superior to both the Orthodox tradition of the survivors who refounded the community after 1945 and the "Russians" who arrived after the collapse of the Soviet Union and whose Jewish commitment—and even provenance—is suspect. Most scandalous of all, Altaras's literary alter ego seems to suggest that her Sephardic, *yekke* heritage embodies a greater degree of continuity with the largely assimilated, even patriotic Judaism that existed in Germany before the genocide. In Himmelfarb's *Sterndeutung*, in contrast, it is a Soviet-born protagonist who claims to be the more authentic German Jew, once he has internalized the commemorative practices of his adopted country, and indeed expanded their scope. The transgression in this novel is Arthur's assumption of the role—formerly reserved to the established community—of custodian of Holocaust memory. Finally, Stein's heretically fanciful *Rabbi Löw* rewrites *halachic* principles to assert a modern Orthodox Judaism defined not by descent but by self-ascription and devotion and even suggests that this unashamedly performative Jewishness might be a more genuine expression of Jewish identity than the established community.

Transgression, in summary, is the means by which Jewish protagonists position themselves in relation to other Jews. (Their self-positioning in relation to the non-Jewish majority is generally less pointed—ironic affection in *titos brille*; a relatively conventional critique of German hypocrisy in *Sterndeutung*; and a melancholic reverence for the German and German Jewish literary tradition in *Rabbi Löw*.) It is through challenges to established hierarchies, religious and cultural norms, and ways of relating to the majority, therefore, that the recent pluralization of Jewish life in Germany is negotiated. On the one hand, German-born Jews of the second and third generations assert their prior "belonging" as members of the established community while also referencing Jewish traditions and geographies that had previously been marginalized and even broadening the definition of who counts as a Jew. On the other hand, newcomers from the former Soviet Union seek integration into the existing memory culture while also insisting upon the salience of *their* history, and especially their proximity to the Holocaust. Indeed, Holocaust memory is the focal point of this mediation of plural Jewish identities in all three novels—whether expanding its scope to include the Sephardic experience in the Balkans, or the Holocaust by bullets in Belarus, Ukraine, and the Baltic states, or the flight of Soviet Jews to Central Asia, or even suggesting that faith and religious ritual and practice might be more essential than commemorating the genocide.

Transgression, of course, is also evidence of a fixation—the protagonists of *titos brille*, *Sterndeutung*, and *Rabbi Löw* disrupt the norms of the established community because they want to claim a role, even a leading role, *within* it. Self-positioning might seem parochial, then, suggesting a maneuvering for acceptance, status, or advantage in relation to a specific social and political context rather than, say, a more visionary, globally engaged enterprise to rearticulate Jewish values or what interventions Jews could or should make in issues that do not directly concern them, but which resonate with their historical experience. In *Sterndeutung*, Arthur shies away from engaging with the genocide in Rwanda and with the burning of asylum hostels in Solingen, as discussed above (*S*, 209; 124). In *titos brille*, when violence breaks out in the West Bank between Israeli settlers and Palestinians, Adriana's first instinct is to worry about the security around Berlin's Jewish institutions, including her sons' school, and not to ponder the potential rights and wrongs of the decades-old conflict in the Middle East (*tb*, 209). And in *Rabbi Löw*, there is almost no mention of the world beyond the Jewish esotericism and German framing narrative that the text fabulates for its reader.

Chapter 2 examines three novels that focus more specifically on the tension between an inwardly-focused identity—fixated on demarcation, integration, and self-assertion—and a more worldly self-positioning that draws on the Jewish past to mobilize on behalf of others. In Mirna Funk's *Winternähe* (Near winter; 2015), Kat Kaufmann's *Superposition* (2015), and Katja Petrowskaja's *Vielleicht Esther* (Maybe Esther; 2014), it is argued, the centuries-old debate on Jewish particularism versus Jewish universalism is rehearsed once again. In each novel, there is ambivalence about whether solidarity with others comes at the cost of Jewish specificity, especially when this specificity has only just been recovered, by the Soviet-born leads of *Superposition* and *Vielleicht Esther*, or is at risk of being relativized in current cultural and political discourses on Israel, as Funk's Lola sees it. How much detail from family history is required to confirm Jewish identity? To what extent does the generality of the Jewish experience make it possible to connect to—and even form alliances with—others?

2: Solidarity: Mirna Funk, Kat Kaufmann, and Katja Petrowskaja

In a book published in 2002, just as the full extent of the generational and demographic transformation of the Jewish presence was becoming clear, sociologist Y. Michal Bodemann asked how "cosmopolitanism and globalization" might be mirrored in the "character of a particular ethnic group, namely the Jewish community in Germany."[1] A few years earlier, the historian Michael Wolffsohn—also a prominent Jewish voice in the media and public discourse—had predicted the emergence of "a community of Jews without Judaism."[2] For both scholars, a trend toward secularization and toward a more global perspective was reshaping German Jewry to become "less Jewish." The arrival of several hundred thousand Soviet-born Jews in the 1990s would lead to an acceleration of this development.

Yet a "community of Jews without Judaism" need not mean a community of Jews without Jewish values, or at least a *Jewish sensibility*—however that is defined. Indeed, while Bodemann and Wolffsohn seem to equate cosmopolitanism and globalization with a decline in Jewish faith and knowledge of ritual and practice, it is still possible to glimpse Jewish elements within a thoroughly secularized outlook, including how Jewish memory, thought, and even theological commentary might actually *inspire* worldly engagement. Writing about young Russian Jews in Germany, for example, Alina Gromova argues that many view their "political and social engagement as a central component of their identity as Jews."[3]

Contemporary novels by German Jewish writers from all backgrounds suggest solidarity with migrants, refugees, and other marginalized groups. In Julya Rabinowich's *Erdfresserin* (Eater of earth; 2012), for example, the Holocaust is invoked as a historical foil to a story about a woman from Dagestan who now works in Vienna as a prostitute, and reworkings of the golem figure suggest a more generally Jewish framing for the novel's indictment of the trafficking of women after the collapse of

---

1 Y. Michal Bodemann, *In den Wogen*, 169.
2 Michael Wolffsohn, "Jews in Divided Germany," 28.
3 Gromova, "Eine heterogene Gruppe," 55.

communism.[4] Lana Lux's 2017 début *Kukolka* tells a similar tale about a trafficked Ukrainian orphan who ends up in Berlin, where she suffers more abuse. (Lux arrived from Ukraine in 1996.) And Vertlib's *Viktor hilft* (Viktor helps; 2018) prompts empathy with Muslims arriving from North Africa and the Middle East in the summer of 2015,[5] as does Olga Grjasnowa's *Gott ist nicht Schüchtern* (God is not shy; 2017). In fact, solidarity with Muslims in particular is especially common, whether refugees or residents. Esther Dischereit's opera libretto *Blumen für Otello* (2014) is a well-known example, which exposes the structural racism of German society with specific reference to the murders committed by the National Socialist Underground between 1998 and 2001. Haunting the text is the legacy of the Holocaust, although the present-day victims were almost entirely Muslim. Likewise, in Olga Martynova's 2013 novel *Mörikes Schlüsselbein* (Mörike's collarbone), a secondary character compares anti-Muslim rhetoric with Nazi antisemitism: "er erzählt, dass in Deutschland momentan anti-muslimische Propaganda herrscht, damit vergleichbar, wie in der Nazizeit die Juden behandelt wurden."[6] (He says that anti-Muslim propaganda is everywhere in Germany right now, comparable to how the Jews were treated in the Nazi period.) Here, it is important to note that Muslim writers such as Sevgi Özdamar and Navid Kermani as well as Islamic organizations in Germany have long been active in opposing antisemitism and in engaging in Holocaust remembrance.[7]

Recent German Jewish literary fiction thus provides some evidence for the emergence—or rather reemergence—of what Andreas Kilcher, in a discussion of early twentieth-century German Jewish authors including Joseph Roth, Lion Feuchtwanger, Alfred Döblin, Stefan Zweig, and Carl Zuckmayer, describes as a "decidedly diasporic model," that is, a self-consciously exilic mode that is "essentially universalistic, cosmopolitan, exterritorial or transnational" and also references Jews' specific "historical mission" to demonstrate the principle of solidarity with all humankind.[8] Jewish and Christian thinkers and theologians, of course, have long asked whether such a mission might derive from Jews' exemplary status as the chosen people, their dispersion around the world, and their experience of suffering.[9]

---

4   See Mayr, "Europe's Invisible Ghettos" and Nagy, "Representations of the Other."
5   See Garloff, *Making German Jewish Literature Anew*, 132–36.
6   Martynova, *Mörikes Schlüsselbein*, 59. I am grateful to Dr. Miriam Wray for drawing my attention to this scene.
7   See Kermani, "Auschwitz morgen." See also Esra Özyürek, *Subcontractors of Guilt*.
8   Kilcher, "Diasporakonzepte," 135–36.
9   See Gelbin and Gilman, *Cosmopolitanism and The Jews*.

In German Jewish writing of the 1920s and 1930s, Kilcher argues, this "universalistic, cosmopolitan, exterritorial or transnational" diasporic consciousness often implied both a refusal of complete integration into German society and a rejection of the Zionist movement that had been growing in strength since the late nineteenth century, with its goal of a Jewish national home in Palestine. Kilcher cites Roth's 1934 essay "Jedermann ohne Pass" (Anyone without a passport), therefore: "Unser Vaterland ist die ganze Erde." (Our fatherland is the whole earth.)[10] In at least some twenty-first century German Jewish novels, a similar dynamic is evident, when protagonists reject Germany and (now) Israel for a more diffuse worldliness—with worldliness associated with engagement on behalf of others. In Olga Grjasnowa's début *Der Russe ist einer, der Birken liebt* (All Russians love birch trees; 2012), for instance, the Azerbaijan-born, Russian-speaking Jewish woman Mascha is indifferent to Germany but also feels no affection for Israel once she has witnessed its treatment of Palestinians in Gaza and the West Bank. Instead, Jewish *memory*—her grandmother's narrow escape during the Holocaust—enables Mascha's reckoning with her own childhood trauma, when she witnessed the bloody clashes between ethnic Armenians and Azeris in 1992, and her empathy with Palestinians.[11] Throughout Grjasnowa's work, in fact, a worldly Jewish identity is articulated almost exclusively through solidarity with other minorities. In the Soviet-born author's other novels—notably *Gott ist nicht schüchtern* and *Der verlorene Sohn* (The lost son; 2020)—Germany and Israel hardly feature, as a globally-engaged Jewishness no longer depends on belonging to/in a nation but rather expresses "Jewish values."

To the extent that the "universalistic, cosmopolitan, exterritorial or transnational" diasporic model is fundamentally about openness to the world as opposed to the fixation on where Jews "belong," it is best understood within the larger context of the debate on Jewish universalism versus Jewish particularism. On the one hand, the Jewish experience of exile and diaspora, persecution, and, of course, genocide is understood to exemplify *all* human suffering and to imply a universal obligation to intervene to counter injustice wherever it may occur. What British historian Adam Sutcliffe terms "progressive Jewish universalism"[12] endorses this universalization of Jewish memory and inspires individual Jews to engage on behalf of others enduring prejudice, discrimination, and worse. On the other hand, the fact that Jews have for the most part been victimized *as Jews* is taken to demonstrate the necessity of insisting on the

---

10   Kilcher, "Diasporakonzepte," 147. Roth, "Jedermann," 546–47.
11   See Skolnik, "Memory without Borders?". See Taberner, "Possibilities and Pitfalls."
12   Sutcliffe, *What are Jews for?*, 257.

Jewishness of Jewish history—and especially Jewish suffering—and for Jews to remain focused on their particularistic interests, first and foremost their own survival.

An avowedly cosmopolitan outlook can also be a form of self-positioning, of course, contrasting with the established community's traditional fixation on Germany and offering the younger generation and especially younger Russian speakers a way of being Jewish that makes sense for them, given their familiarity with Moscow, Tel Aviv, and New York, and their transnational networks and global travel. More specifically, Jewish universalism may suggest a critical attitude toward Israel (again generally taboo in the established community) and a distinctly modern Jewish self-understanding, defined by anti-racism and an emphasis on intersectionality. As we shall see in chapter 3, in the novels of Grjasnowa and Salzmann, Jews and Muslims are sometimes also LBGTQ individuals or migrants, or both, and build alliances to advance their own and others' cause, though not always without tension or differentials of privilege, of course. Likewise, younger Jews and Soviet-born Jews may reframe Holocaust memory as a call to realize universal human rights, reframing it as what sociologists Levy and Sznaider call "cosmopolitan memory" or as what Michael Rothberg calls "multidirectional memory."

In fact, embracing global solidarity may offer secular Jews, Jews without a Jewish mother, and Soviet-born Jews a way of establishing a Jewish identity that does not depend on religious conviction (or even knowledge), Holocaust trauma in the family, or an unbroken, matrilineal Jewish lineage. In essence, a Jewish identity can be *asserted* with reference to the Jewish credo of engaging "to repair the world" (*tikkun olam*). This suggests a far more diffuse Jewishness, of course, as conventional classifications—Orthodox, Reform, and non-believing-but-still-avowedly-Jewish—break down and are replaced by a more fluid self-ascription as a Jew by virtue of intervening in solidarity with others. (This may be thought of as a secular variation on Stein's performance of Jewish ritual as a means of styling an unorthodox Orthodox Judaism.) This does not mean that Jewish universalism is insincere—or that only Jews without faith or *non-halachic* Jewish ancestry espouse it—but it is clear that mobilizing on behalf of other minorities also propounds a kind of *legitimacy* as a Jew.

The three close readings that follow provide further insight into the self-positioning that is implied by acting in solidarity with others, but also reveal that Jewish worldliness is by no means unequivocal or without sacrifice. In Kat Kaufmann's *Superposition* (2015), Mirna Funk's *Winternähe* (Near winter; 2015), and Katja Petrowskaja's *Vielleicht Esther* (Maybe Esther; 2014), self-identified Jewish protagonists, born in Germany or from the former Soviet Union, without a Jewish mother or with only a tenuous connection to their heritage, attempt to reconcile worldliness with their insistence on the specificity of the Jewish identity that they have only just recovered. Notwithstanding their very different literary styles—a brash pop aesthetic in *Superposition* and *Winternähe*, a formal complexity reminding of early twentieth-century modernism in *Vielleicht Esther*—all three novels address the fundamental question of what it means to be a Jew "in the world" when Jewish identity itself is inherently fragile.

Cosmopolitan Delusions: Kat Kaufmann's *Superposition*

Izy Lewin, the twenty-six-year-old Soviet-born protagonist of Kaufmann's *Superposition*, is a similar age to Arthur's daughter in Himmelfarb's *Sterndeutung* (Star reading; 2015) and seems to embody what cultural anthropologist Alina Gromova describes as the "Generation 'kosher light,'"[13] or Dmitrij Belkin more generally terms "German Judaism 2.0."[14] Certainly, in her loose attachment to Judaism and in her preference for parties, fashion, and pop music—along with a more retro affection for jazz—Izy might be taken to sum up the outlook of a cohort of young Russian-speaking Jews coming of age in Germany beginning in the early 2000s.

Izy is a more complex character than a straightforwardly ethnographic reading of the novel might imply, however. Most obviously, she is bewildered by the arbitrariness of her presence in Germany as the child of a Russian Jew who seized the opportunity to quit the collapsing Soviet Union in 1990, and she is burdened by the "Bringpflicht" (obligation to deliver)[15] that she feels she owes her parents to be a success in her new life. More generally, though, Izy is unable to reconcile her self-understanding as a Russian, a half-Jew—only her father is Jewish—and a (relatively privileged) migrant. As she puts it, her identity cannot be resolved into a single entity, much less into the superposition of the novel's title: "Ich kann mich selbst gar nicht mehr messen, so überlagert bin ich inzwischen. Und ich frage mich, wer würfelt wohl da so herum, im Multiversum, das all diese Realitäten in sich birgt?" (I cannot measure myself anymore, because I am so superimposed. And I ask myself, who is throwing all these dice, in the multiverse, which contains all these realities within itself?; *SP*, 143.)

Izy's narration, it can be argued, manifests symptoms of the disorientation and even delirium that ensues as she struggles to inhabit her multiple realities simultaneously. In some places, then, there are lengthy passages of sociological reporting, for example when she describes the

---

13 Gromova, *Generation "Koscher Light."*
14 Belkin, *Germanija*.
15 Kaufmann, *Superposition*, 128. Hereafter, *SP*.

hostility her family encountered when they first arrived in 1990 (*SP*, 32) and the bullying she experienced at school (*SP*, 65–67); or when she references the stereotyping of Russians as mafia (*SP*, 136–37); the former astronauts, physicists, and teachers who are now unemployed (*SP*, 158–59); and documents "proving" Jewish ancestry that can be bought on the black market (*SP*, 159). Elsewhere, she adopts a more contemporary pop aesthetic to relate her life in the narrative present, including sexual harassment by her boss, erotic interludes with Timur—a fellow Russian who always goes back to his German girlfriend—the parties she attends, her love of Black jazz musicians and rave music (*SP*, 22–23), and her nighttime peregrinations through Berlin. Interspersed with all this, there are also elegiac reminiscences of her Russian childhood, somber retellings of her two grandmothers' wartime traumas, and a surreal one hundred-page dream sequence set in a mansion full of Nazi, Soviet, and Jewish symbols. As if this were not enough, Izy and her friends also engage in an almost parodic academic discourse, reaching for the radical gender theorist Beatriz Preciado to debate biological sex (*SP*, 39–40) and for fringe scientific publications on "polysingularity." This esoteric concept draws on mathematical theory to posit the simultaneity of multiple potential perspectives on self and the world and the act of transcending the contingency of this multidimensionality by taking a particular path while knowing that innumerable others are equally possible.[16]

Underlying Izy's often dissonant narrative is a tension between infinite possibility and finite actuality, that is, between the lives she could have had and the one that she has in fact lived. The first suggests arbitrariness—being born a Russian and a Jew rather than something else, migrating to Germany rather than the United States or Israel, and partying with chance friends in Berlin—as well as performance: *playing* at being Russian, Jewish, etc. The second relates to the singular reality that Izy has actually known—how childhood memories resonate; how shared experience draws her to Timur; and how her grandmother's wartime suffering substantiates a Jewish identity that would otherwise appear as simply a historical accident. Notwithstanding the infinite possibilities of what could have been, then, the life lived generates an emotional investment—nostalgia, perhaps, and an attachment to a particular group and its history—that both undermines performance and places limits on a truly boundaryless "being-in-the-world."

Izy's performance is intimated through her profession as a musical director at an experimental theater, where she fends off her boss's advances, and her sideline as a jazz pianist at company functions. Jazz

---

16 The novel cites from a website run by Dmitry Paranyushkin (*SP*, 195–97), a Russian electronic musician, choreographer, and "network researcher," living in Paris. See Paranyushkin, "Polysingularity of Itself."

is improvisational, suggesting her constant adaptation, and as a space of encounter between Black artists and white consumers it is strongly associated with ethnic performance and subalternism.[17] (Izy also conducts a form of resistance by riffing on well-known lyrics: "Night and Day = White and Gay ... Bei There will never be another you das you zu Jew"; *SP*, 22). In Izy's case, two ethnic identities are staged—Russian and Jewish—causing consternation for the non-Jewish German majority and adding to her own disorientation. At a party with other Soviet-born migrants, she is Russian for Andreas, who is learning the language and gets an erection when he presses up against her at the bar and when she dances like a drunk Cossack for him (*SP*, 44–49). There may also be a sly reference to Wladimir Kaminer, the well-known writer, DJ, and consummate "Russian": "Ah, russischer DJ, war ja klar eigentlich." (Ah, Russian DJ, was actually pretty obvious; *SP*, 49.) Izy's other performance is less accomplished. Unlike her father, she fails to grow into her Jewishness in Germany. Despite his indifference in the Soviet Union, her father now wears a Star of David, speaks of the "Volk der Opfer" (people of victims) and defends customs that he himself ignores (*SP*, 159–62). (He is also accused of embezzling community funds by other Russian Jews and suffers—paradoxically—their antisemitic slurs; *SP*, 158–60.) Izy, in contrast, is indifferent, even hostile to Jewish beliefs and rituals: "Wir sind nicht mehr in der Wüste!" (We are no longer in the desert!; *SP*, 98) She seems to have more in common with Stascha, a borscht-eating colleague who arrived as one of the 2.3 million Russians of German ancestry who immigrated from the mid-1980s, than she does with other Jews, whether newly arrived or settled. In fact, she doesn't even mention the established Jewish community, and she would no doubt be a sore disappointment for a survivor like Himmelfarb's Roth.

Izy's presence in Germany is entirely accidental. Her "stellvertretendes jüdisches Blut" (representative Jewish blood; *SP*, 98) caused her to be summoned into the land of the perpetrators—ignoring the fact that she is *halachically* not Jewish at all—and now she is expected to fulfill the role that was assigned to her by her remorse-ridden hosts: "wir sind deine Wiederbesiedlung, Scheinjuden. Juden nach Schein, kommt wieder rein." (We are your repopulation. Fake Jews. Jews with a document, come back; *SP*, 69.) She could just as likely have gone to Israel, had her parents not plumped for Germany after 1991. There she might have become a solider in the Israeli Defense Forces, appearing astride a tank in a family photo, and married a fellow Russian immigrant, just like her cousin (*SP*, 69). Or, following in the footsteps of other Soviet-born Jews, she might have gone to America, to New York. In Israel, it would have been military service "in einem immerwährenden Krieg" (never-ending war). In Brooklyn,

---

17 See Sandke, *Where the Dark and Light Folks Meet.*

she would now be living among Orthodox Jews (*SP*, 69). Germany is the better destination, on the whole, although she pauses to reflect when she sees armed guards outside one of Berlin's new Jewish schools, guarding against potential terror attacks: "Vielleicht doch lieber Schläfenlocken und Brooklyn? Oder in Hollywoods Koschernostra." (Maybe better sidelocks and Brooklyn? Or in Hollywood's Koscher Nostra; *SP*, 198). The allusion to the Koscher Nostra—Jewish gangsters in late nineteenth-century America—invokes the present-day stereotyping of Soviet-born Jews in Germany, of course.[18]

Izy performs Russianness and Jewishness for the German majority, ironically and seemingly resigned to the arbitrariness of identity. Yet her self-staging is repeatedly disrupted by what appear to be more authentic behaviors and emotions. When she visits a café, for example, Izy instinctively orders a "russisches Gedeck" (Russian platter; *SP*, 9), and she cries when she watches Soviet movies or listens to war hymns with Timur (*SP*, 69), the on-off lover who embodies home for her: "Mein Stück Heimat. Und ich deins. Wenn wir Russisch miteinander reden, wie eine Geheimsprache." (My piece of home. And yours. When we speak Russian together, like a secret language; *SP*, 68.) Similarly, when Izy recalls her Jewish grandmother, her empathy and solidarity are clearly genuine. Ella saw her entire family being killed in an air raid and still insisted on being registered as Jewish in her Soviet papers, aware that Jews were being targeted for extermination by the advancing Nazis and that antisemitism was rife in her socialist motherland too (*SP*, 27). "Wegen der Familie," Ella says: "'Dabei waren alle tot [. . .] Ich bin, wer ich bin,' sagte sie, und war kaum achtzehn." (For my family. Yet they were all dead [. . .] I am who I am, she said, barely eighteen; *SP*, 27.) Izy recalls her grandmother's decision quite suddenly as she is being driven to Wannsee and in so doing she associates the Holocaust—decided in Wannsee in 1942—with what Ella said about her obligation to remember her parents' suffering: "Und du siehst an dir herunter, und alles, was du hast, ist das blutverschmierte Sommerkleid. Das Blut deiner jetzt im Graben wie Abfall verschwundenen Eltern trägst du an dir." (You look down at yourself, and all that you have is the blood-stained summer dress. You're wearing the blood of your parents, now disappeared into the pit like trash; *SP*, 27.) Trauma is *real*, and it is remembered through the generations.

Izy's fixation on her Russian Jewish past—even if the second element is "only" a Jewish grandmother who insisted on being registered as such—blocks her integration in the present day: "Im Vergangenen leben, obwohl ein neuer Anfang sich dir zu Füßen schmeißt und 'Nimm mich, nimm mich' schreit?" (Living in the past, even though a new beginning is throwing itself at your feet and screaming "take me, take me"; *SP*, 27.) In

---

18 See Metz, *Koscher Nostra*.

fact, her fixation on the finite actuality of this history—on its *particularity*—predicts her narcissistic obsession with Timur, the fellow Soviet-born Jewish migrant whose experience is identical to hers. Their sex involves Izy's willed submission, a hint of coercion—"Und du kommst hart in mir, als wäre es ein Gewaltakt" (you come inside me, hard, like an act of violence; *SP*, 142)—and love shaded with sadomasochism: "Und fickst mich wie ein Dämon. Liebesbekungungen." (And fuck me like a demon. Declarations of love; *SP*, 143.) There is even a hint of incest, as Izy continues, ironically mixing English and German in a mimicry of biological essentialism: "I'm so fucking related to you. By quality, character. And blood. And Herkunft. And I want my Herkunft to be related to you too" (Herkunft=origins; *SP*, 235). Yet Timur has moved on. With Izy he indulges his own nostalgia for the past and takes advantage of her vulnerability to satisfy an urge to dominate. For the most part, however, the Russian Jewish migrant spends his time with his independently minded German girlfriend, visiting Izy only when Astrid is in London for business (*SP*, 117) and periodically emailing to end their affair (*SP*, 171).

One way out of the paralysis that afflicts Izy might be to transcend the particularity of her Russian Jewish past and to embrace all of humanity in her German present. And indeed, the final one hundred pages or so of the novel seem to dissolve the burden of history and re-signify the formlessness of the present as a boundless, joyous communing with others, as Izy and her friends take up residence in a vast Berlin mansion where they cook, debate, and make love. In the end, however, this lengthy episode is revealed as an illusion—or delusion—elaborated by her unconscious mind as she lies in a coma following a bomb explosion in her train carriage (*SP*, 172). Islamist terrorism is implied, as is—later in the text—the West's overreaction in drone attacks from "fernen Aussichtstürmen" (distant observation towers; *SP*, 232). Rather than an embrace of the world, therefore, Izy's coma-induced fabulation of togetherness with her Russian and German-majority friends might actually signal a desire to retreat inwards.

In any case, Izy's cosmopolitan fantasy was always doomed from the start, and always limited to the privileged few. The past still intrudes, initially as a positive memory of Europe's cultural legacy but then as an adumbration of twentieth-century trauma. Describing the mansion, Izy mentions impressionist and expressionist portraits, Art Deco furniture, an extensive library, echoes of her parents' Soviet apartment that they somehow transformed into a baroque exhibition, a table from Imperial Russia, a huge mirror in the Parisian style, and a garden room that leads into a painterly landscape of tiger lilies and peonies (*SP*, 210–11). A mention of swastikas on a Moroccan carpet (*SP*, 211), however, introduces a jarring note into Izy's reporting of this pastiche of nineteenth- and early twentieth-century artistic movements, by reminding of what came next. The swastika appears in many cultures, of course, but here the allusion is as obvious as it is ominous: "Jede einzelne rote Swastika auf dem schwarzen Grund. Willkommen zu Hause." (Every single red swastika against the black backdrop. Welcome home; *SP*, 211.) Home is the Nazi emblem, antisemitism, and genocide, as much as childhood holidays or her grandmother's wartime trauma, both of which are also invoked earlier in Izy's coma (*SP*, 182), when she had imagined the swastika juxtaposed with the Star of David and the Red Star (*SP*, 186). Even in her delirium, fascism and totalitarianism infect and destroy from within the cosmopolitan potential of the pan-European flourishing of art and culture in the late nineteenth and early twentieth centuries.

Power and violence also infuse the intimate relationships between the guests in the present day. Izy's work colleague Fili kisses her on the mouth in a gesture that signals not affection or even longing but ownership, and perhaps contempt (*SP*, 217–18). Staggeringly beautiful, Fili is frequently the object of male interest (*SP*, 39), and as might be predicted, in Izy's coma-induced fabulation Fili ends up having sex with Timur in the gardens. Izy even colludes in Timur's domination of the (willing) young German woman. She stands behind him as he penetrates Fili, bites into his neck, becomes one with him—"Wir sind ein Körper, ein Blut, und wir ficken Fili" (we are one body, one blood, and we are fucking Fili; *SP*, 234)—and presses down on his back as he ejaculates. There is a cosmopolitan fantasy of sorts within Izy's hallucination, but this is undermined by the scene's suggestions of aggression and submission, and by Fili's ultimate triumph in claiming sole possession of Timur: "Sie öffnet ihre Augen, sieht dich an, greift deinen Hals, zieht dich zu sich herunter." (She opens her eyes, looks at you, grabs your neck, and pulls you down to her; *SP*, 235.) Izy walks off and consoles herself with the thought that when Timur is kissing Fili, he is actually kissing her, just as she imagines that he is making love to her when he is with Astrid (*SP*, 236).

Fili is Izy's opposite. Where Fili is endlessly fluid and mobile, Izy cannot move past her perception of the immutability of who she *is*. Fili flirts with Izy but Izy is irredeemably heterosexual; Fili's dressing-up as a man at the mansion, with a drawn-on beard, similarly fails to inspire Izy to break gender norms; and an ensuing conversation, led by Stascha, about the genetic editing-out of Y chromosomes excites Fili but provokes only skepticism on Izy's part (*SP*, 221–22). Most revealing is Izy's abrupt dismissal of Fili's utopianism during an earlier conversation about the reconfiguration of desire to eliminate power imbalances. Fili cites the theorist Beatriz Preciado, who speculates that it would be possible to focus sex on the anus so as to equalize who penetrates whom. This provokes Izy to ask whether women would then need to grow an oversized clitoris "zum da Reinpenetrieren? In den Anus? Als Penisgegenstück." (To penetrate there. In the anus. As a counterpart to the penis; *SP*, 40.) Here and more generally, Izy's point seems to be that there are limits to how far we can reinvent ourselves. At the (imagined) mansion, Izy asks Timur whether, if she were a man, he would perform oral sex on her. He politely declines—he desires Izy as a woman only—though Fili once again persists in her undifferentiated idealism: "'Ich fick alles!', sagt Fili, 'sind doch nur Quanten.'" ("I fuck everything!," Fili says; "it's just quanta"; *SP*, 245.)

In their delirium, Izy's friends imagine a new world order in which there is no hate, desire is ever-changing and gender mutable, genes mix, languages merge, and human beings have no limits: "In der neuen Weltordnung ist der Mensch grenzenlos!" (In the new world order humankind is without boundaries!; *SP*, 239–41.) In reality, however, the polysingularity that they aspire to—a "Multiversum" of parallel possibilities, as her German friend Len describes it (*SP*, 242–43)—is an abstraction that is contradicted by the particularities of biography and personality. Fili has a penchant for mutilating the corpses of dead animals (an activity that Izy joins her in), in Izy's dream sequence at least, and she enjoys staging a photograph in the mansion's drawing room in which Izy lies mortally wounded by a knife in a pool of her own blood on the swastika-adorned carpet (*SP*, 251). At best, Fili's norm-breaking is a pose, or a work of art, like a second, equally stylized image featuring the entire group naked in the garden, with Len and Timur hiding their penises with commedia dell'arte masks (*SP*, 251). At worst, it masks a perverse fascination with death and violence that—especially when it involves a German, a Jew, and a "Hitlerteppich" (Hitler carpet)—may even suggest an urge to eradicate "otherness." One version of the new world order would be a forced uniformity in which difference, specificity, and even memory had been erased.

Izy, in sum, is unable to transcend the finite actuality of the life she has lived and inhabit the cosmopolitan delusion that her German-majority friends embrace. At the same time, her fixation on her Russian Jewish past, and on the suffering visited on her grandmother by Nazi and Soviet regimes, may immunize her against utopian fantasies, and worse. Certainly, Izy's focus on the *real*—on history, trauma, and memory—deflates a universalism that is entirely performative, self-indulgent, and even totalitarian. Arguably, this is the worldly self-possession of the white, Western elite, as elaborated in a mansion in Berlin filled with the detritus of European civilization and its phantasmagoria of global domination.

Yet Izy also seems unable to demonstrate a more authentic solidarity with the foreigners, refugees, homeless people, and gypsies that might be expected of the Russian Jewish migrant as she wanders through Berlin. These minorities inhabit the margins of a narrative that is primarily focused on Izy, other Russians, and their German-majority fellow partygoers, and it is striking that Izy refuses their attempts to make common cause with her and even descends into racist stereotypes. For example, she rails against a Turkish (or Iranian . . .) waiter's use of the informal form of address, objecting to the implication that they are "Verbündete" (allies;

SP, 15). Later, she imagines advising her future child not to confess to being Jewish in front of Muslim classmates (*SP*, 77); and, in a café in the Turkish district of Kreuzberg, Izy and Timur declare: "Wir sind hier nicht im Orient, Liebster, auch wenn es so aussieht manchmal." (We're not in the orient, dearest, even if it looks like it sometimes; *SP*, 125.) Finally, at the same party at which she dances "like a Russian" for the German Andreas, she imagines touching an enticingly slim Iranian girl between the legs. "Du kleines geiles Ding" (you horny little thing; *SP*, 51), she murmurs, with orientalizing prejudice. Even when Izy *does* attempt solidarity, in fact, she either fails to connect or is refused. She watches a gypsy family playing ethnic music, for instance, and declares (to herself) that she is one of them—"Ich bin auch ein Zigeuner, eine Heimatlose, Zugezogene" (I am also a gypsy, without a home, an immigrant; *SP*, 69)—but the child collecting tips ignores her offering. Likewise, she walks past homeless people but is unable to speak to them, and she rues the fact that the food she eats mostly likely comes from the same countries as the refugees struggling to reach Europe and Germany but, again, fails to act (*SP*, 71). Izy's situation is quite different, of course. She is "quotenjüdisch" (a quota Jew; *SP*, 69), as she puts it, and as such relatively welcome in Germany, fluent in the language, and, above all, *white*.

In the end, Izy is too fixated on her Russian Jewish past to fully align with the German majority but also too privileged to relate to other minorities, or even to refrain from racism. In any case, she seems unable to adopt a universalist perspective: having a single Jewish grandmother who fled the Nazis and endured Soviet antisemitism is enough to prompt Izy to position herself as Jewish—even with "only" a Jewish father and notwithstanding the arbitrariness of her presence in Germany—but insufficient to generate solidarity with those who are victimized in the present day. A similar parochialism characterizes Arthur in Himmelfarb's *Sterndeutung*, of course, as discussed in chapter 1. In chapter 3, Salzmann's *Außer sich* (Besides oneself; 2017) and Grjasnowa's *Der verlorene Sohn* are analyzed as attempts to resolve this tension between Jewish particularism (and privilege) and Jewish universalism, although at the risk of dissolving Jewishness altogether. For now, however, we turn to Mirna Funk's *Winternähe*, in which another—this time German-born—protagonist with "only" a Jewish father appears to succeed where Izy fails and articulates not one but two versions of Jewish worldliness. Neither, however, fully resolves her fragile identity.

First-World Privilege: Mirna Funk's *Winternähe*

Beyond her attachment to her grandmother and her traumatic experience, it is clear that the Soviet-born migrant Izy struggles to articulate what her Jewishness is *for*. She remains stuck, therefore, between her Russian Jewish past and her German present, and between the self-congratulatory, entirely hypocritical cosmopolitanism of her German-majority friends and genuine solidarity with minorities. She ends her narrative as disoriented and nihilistic as she began it: "Das Logbuch schreibt das Jahr Fuck off." (Ship's log, the year fuck off; *SP*, 269.)[19]

Lola, the German-born protagonist of Mirna Funk's *Winternähe*, seems to have a much firmer sense of her Jewish identity—at least initially. Her close relationship with her father's parents, both survivors, motivates her protest against resurgent antisemitism in Germany and her empathy with Israelis *and* Palestinians in Tel Aviv, and the progression from Jewish suffering to Lola's solidarity with others is even explicitly framed as Jewish universalism. As we shall see, however, Lola's efforts to articulate a Jewish identity that does not require faith or even two Jewish parents are overwhelmed by contemporary controversies, including the bitter wrangling about who "counts" as a Jew and European and diasporic Jewish responses to Israel's treatment of the Palestinians. In its final third, set in Thailand, the novel poses the question of whether Jewish worldliness is actually just first-world privilege.

Winternähe opens with a shocking affront to German memory culture, which—the novel's protagonist suggests—prescribes just how the Nazi past is to be remembered while overlooking the persistence of antisemitism in the present day. Lola returns to the Berlin courtroom where two coworkers are about to be acquitted of racially abusing her in several Facebook posts, having drawn a Hitler moustache on her upper lip while in the bathroom. She is ejected from the proceedings, but not before she mimics a Hitler salute from her hip.[20] Subsequently, Lola spirals into despair, quitting her job, engaging in casual sex, and doubting all her relationships with her non-Jewish compatriots, before she leaves for Tel Aviv to spend time with her grandfather Gershom—he later dies—and to pursue her affair with Shlomo, a traumatized former Israeli soldier whom she met through Tinder when she was still in Berlin. Disillusioned with Israel, and with Shlomo, Lola travels to Thailand, where she composes letters to her estranged father in Australia. At the end of the novel, she goes back to Germany.

Lola's taboo-breaking self-adornment with a Hitler moustache in the first few pages of the novel suggests a thematic focus on the righteousness of Jewish resentment in the face of the persistence of antisemitism despite the formal—and formulaic—abhorrence of anti-Jewish sentiment in contemporary German memory culture. To this extent, and as often in the work of younger self-identified Jewish writers, comparisons can be drawn with Maxim Biller as well as with a tradition of "ugly feelings"[21]

---

19 There may be an allusion here to the opening of *Star Trek: Enterprise*.
20 Funk, *Winternähe*, 9–11. Hereafter *W*.
21 See Ngai, *Ugly Feelings*.

reaching back to Holocaust survivors such as Jean Améry.²² As Lola exclaims some way into the narrative: "Ich verstehe nicht, wieso man immer alles verzeihen muss." (I don't understand why we always have to forgive everything; *W*, 183.) Her courtroom protest, then, is aimed at the judge and the police—for their self-serving attempts to mollify her—but it is also intended to disrupt the expectation that Jews should affirm Germany's smug self-image of successful confrontation with its dark past. Following the failed prosecution of Olaf and Manuela for posting pictures of her on social media with a Hitler moustache, Lola begins to perceive the reality of anti-Jewish prejudice all around her. Colleagues at her office invoke the trope of Jewish property mogul driven by greed (*W*, 23); a washed-up pop singer comes on to her and then racially abuses her (*W*, 97–100); and German filmgoers celebrate a film about a Nazi functionary directed by his granddaughter—who once delighted in telling Lola what she would have done to her during the Third Reich (*W*, 105–6). Almost as bad are the philosemitic Germans whose declarations of solidarity actually serve their own psychological needs. Her acquaintance Myrna, for example, is a fervent Zionist and hates Palestinians, but only because her mother was killed in the bombing of a bus in Jerusalem during a tourist trip in 2002 (*W*, 101–4).

German hypocrisy is most evident, Lola suggests, in the responses to the flare-up of hostilities in the summer of 2016, when Israel sent troops into Gaza and Hamas fired rockets toward Tel Aviv and residential areas across the country. Her friends' Twitter feeds are full of references to a supposed genocide committed by Jews against the Palestinian inhabitants of Gaza (*W*, 201), and her date Toni is more explicit in his outrageous paralleling of the Holocaust and Israeli military interventions: "Aber was da in Gaza und hinter der Mauer der Westbank passiert, ist nicht besser als Auschwitz." (But what's happening over there in Gaza and behind the wall of the West Bank is no better than Auschwitz; *W*, 33). For Lola, it is evident that antisemitism lurks behind much of the self-righteous criticism of Israel she witnesses, not only in Germany but also throughout the whole of Western Europe (*W*, 203).

Lola's personal encounter with German antisemitism changes her, "grundlegend, auf stille Weise" (completely, in a subtle way; *W*, 22). She becomes withdrawn and mistrustful, and engages in casual sex of a kind that implies self-negation. (Rebekah Slodounik makes the intriguing argument that through casual sex Lola asserts the one component of her identity as a German Jewish woman that is not contested by others. This is persuasive but does not mean that Lola's self-assertion is necessarily emancipatory.)²³ Alienated by Toni's comparison of Gaza and Auschwitz,

---

22 See Brudholm, *Resentment's Virtue*.
23 See Slodounik, "German, Jewish, and Female."

and by the tone of the discussion of the current conflict in the Middle East in the bar where they are drinking, Lola calls Benjamin, a Jewish friend with whom she occasionally has a masochistic form of intercourse that recalls the so-called "Stalaghefte" (Stalag books; *W*, 39), a form of Nazi-exploitation pornography that circulated widely in Israel in the 1950s and 1960s. Once Benjamin arrives, Lola slides under the table, gives him oral sex, and, after he has ejaculated in her mouth, takes her coat and leaves (*W*, 38–40). With both Toni and Benjamin—and during a later encounter in Israel that similarly hints at humiliation (*W*, 237–39)—there is also a power imbalance in Lola's relationships with men, Jewish and non-Jewish. Funk's protagonist is subjugated as a half-Jew by Jews, as a Jew by Germans, and as a woman by both, and can only respond by "living out" her absolute marginality.

Winternähe thus touches on the often-acrimonious debate about who "counts" as a Jew. Most immediately, Lola implies that German efforts to categorize Jewishness are themselves a form of antisemitism—even as these efforts are also stimulated and even legitimized by the Jewish community's own bitter disagreements on the matter. The lawyer for the colleagues who added a Hitler moustache to her image on a Facebook post argues in court that Lola is not Jewish according to Jewish law and that they therefore cannot be guilty of antisemitism (*W*, 56). Her German date Toni later tells her the same to her face: "Dann bist du ja gar keine Jüdin. Soweit ich weiß, muss deine Mutter Jüdin sein." (Then you're not even a Jew at all. As far as I know, your mother has to be Jewish; *W*, 34.) Benjamin, on the other hand, accepts her as Jewish, but her Jewish lover's preference for redheads suggests a degree of self-negation (*W*, 66 and 73). (Lola's father has a similar proclivity, as discussed later.) In contrast, a young Orthodox Jew she sits next to on a flight to Thailand simply dismisses her claim to be Jewish out of hand (*W*, 254–56). For her own part, when she has sex with Shlomo—the Israeli she met on Tinder in Berlin and then takes up with again after she arrives in Tel Aviv—she craves his Hebrew words while responding, unavoidably, in her mother('s) tongue: German (*W*, 143–44).

More generally, Lola's status as a *Vaterjüdin* (Jew "only" on the father's side) complicates her endeavor to define a Jewish identity in relation to both Germany, the country of her nationality, and to Israel, where, supposedly, a more authentic Jewishness can be forged. She is the daughter of a parent from each of the victim and the perpetrator collectives: "Sie war Täter und Opfer in einem." (She was a perpetrator and victim in one; *W*, 313.) This oxymoronic identity provokes confusion and even incomprehension in Israel (*W*, 313–44). As will be discussed shortly, Lola also feels alienated by both Israeli ethno-nationalism and the empty posturing of the leftist peace protesters that she spends most of her time with there. Unlike Shlomo, who also lacks a Jewish mother (*W*, 70), she is unable to commit to either side in the national debate and thus to take a position as an Israeli Jew. In Germany, likewise, she is aware that her lack of a Jewish mother means that she does not "count" for many in the community (*W*, 313). Her thought that she might formally convert is quickly frustrated. Rabbi Goldberg informs her that her efforts will only count for Reform congregations, and she is repulsed by the inauthenticity of her fellow students. These include the German men who enthuse about their Jewish wives while uttering Yiddish and Hebrew phrases, and a young Ukrainian woman whose great-grandfather had run a concentration camp (*W*, 59–64).

If Lola cannot be accepted as a Jew "by birth" and she cannot convert, she might instead ground her Jewish identity in family trauma and in solidarity with others. In fact, Jewish memory—and Jewish universalism—is anticipated in the novel's epigraph, consisting of a quotation from the well-known essay "Über den Begriff der Geschichte" (On the concept of history) by the German Jewish philosopher Walter Benjamin: "Das wahre Gesicht der Vergangenheit huscht vorbei. Nur als Bild, das auf Nimmerwiedersehen im Augenblick seiner Erkennbarkeit eben aufblitzt, ist die Vergangenheit festzuhalten." (The true picture of the past flashes by. Only as a picture that flashes its final farewell in the moment of its recognizability is the past to be held fast.)[24] Funk has most probably not engaged extensively with the vast scholarship on Benjamin's idiosyncratic philosophy of history, of course—she most likely simply wishes to signal a "Jewish sensibility."[25] Indeed, Lola's rather wooden allusions to "Erinnern, diesem im Judentum tief verankerten Brauch" (remembering, this tradition deeply rooted in Judaism; *W*, 217) and to "Eingedenken"— the "Erinnerungsgebot zwischen Gott und den Menschen, das das Judentum und seine Tradition prägt" (commemoration, the obligation to remember between God and people, that shapes Judaism and its tradition; *W*, 217)—suggest a desire to position herself within the broad Jewish tradition rather than a detailed knowledge.

Notwithstanding the likely superficiality of Lola's understanding of Jewish thought, her anchoring of her identity in concepts of Jewish memory and Jewish universalism has consequences. First and foremost, her internalization of memory as trauma—including her grandmother's experiences of the camps, her grandfather's experience of flight (*W*, 29–30), and her father's inherited distress (*W*, 120–24)—predisposes her to generalize her empathy to include others who are plagued by the past. Above all, this means Shlomo, who is tortured by his responsibility for the killing of a Palestinian boy when he was in the army. Following

---

24 Benjamin wrote the text in 1940 while interned in France. His subsequent attempts to flee the Nazis ended in suicide.
25 See Steinberg, ed., *Walter Benjamin*.

his discharge, he became a peace activist, a fervent critic of Israel's reference to the Holocaust to justify its military interventions (*W*, 71–72), and a campaigner for an independent Palestinian state (*W*, 137–43). Lola helps him with his sexual dysfunction (*W*, 76), refrains from judging him (*W*, 153), and creates a photo exhibition, "Shlomos Vergangenheit" (Shlomo's past; *W*, 241). She installs this exhibition in his flat before she leaves for Thailand, as a kind of making-material of his guilt but also of the trauma he endures: "Es war die Geschichte von Shlomo und seinem Schmerz." (It was the story of Shlomo and his pain; *W*, 247). At the same time, Lola's empathy also extends to the Palestinians who suffer the excesses of the Israeli army in Gaza. Here, in fact, she refers more specifically to Jewish memory and Jewish universalism. In conversation with her grandfather Gershom, she wants to know why he cannot relate to those now being oppressed by the survivors and their descendants: "Wo ist deine jüdische Identität, wenn es um Palästinenser geht?" (Where is your Jewish identity, when it's about Palestinians?; *W*, 162). Being Jewish, Lola implies, means an inclination, even an obligation, to look beyond Jewish suffering to embrace solidarity with others.

Yet this abstract elaboration of diasporic Jewish identity is quickly revealed as potentially vacuous and even suspect. Three Yeshiva pupils are killed, followed by the revenge killing of a Palestinian boy. Lola initially has empathy with all four victims, whereas Shlomo—the Israeli soldier turned peace activist—sees only Palestinian suffering and Israeli guilt, in a simple reversal of a discourse of mutual antagonism that is structured along ethnic and nationalist lines (*W*, 164–69). Instead of holding her ground and insisting on compassion for both sides, however, Lola quickly agrees to accompany Shlomo to the Palestinian boy's funeral. Solidarity with all, it seems, is an ideal that dissolves as soon as political realities intrude, and always whenever intimacy predisposes an individual to choose one side or the other. For Shlomo's sake, Lola will march with Palestinian rather than Israeli mourners.

Even more undermining of Lola's Jewish universalism is the suggestion that empathy is in any case always ultimately solipsistic, that is, directed toward the self rather than others. Shlomo, it turns out, weeps not for the boy whose funeral he is attending but for the youth he killed while in the army, and actually for himself, on account of the guilt that burdens him (*W*, 192). Equally, the supposed generalizability of traumatic memory to the suffering of others that underpins Lola's solidarity may engender a surprising and even dubious moral relativism. Lola thinks of traumatic memory as an anthropological constant: "Aus jedem Menschen blutet die eigene Vergangenheit und manchmal sogar die Weltvergangenheit." (Every person bleeds their own past, and sometimes the whole world's past; *W*, 151). In the understanding of empathy and solidarity with others that emerges from this, there are only victims.

Everyone is weighed down by the past, even the perpetrators—like Shlomo—and it seems that no distinction is to be drawn between different kinds and degrees of harm suffered. Lola's formulation that everyone bleeds their past—and indeed the trauma of the whole world—is adapted, she says, from Art Spiegelman's graphic novel *Maus* (1980–91), based on the American author's conversations with his father: "My Father bleeds History" (*W*, 151). However, this account of Holocaust victimhood is directly paralleled with Shlomo's act of perpetration—"aus Shlomo blutete die Vergangenheit" (Shlomo bleeds the past; *W*, 151)—perhaps suggesting an equivalence between the trauma experienced by the survivor and that endured by the Israeli soldier who killed a boy throwing rocks. Inserted between her account of the murders of the three Yeshiva students and her attendance at the funeral of the Palestinian youth killed in revenge, moreover, Lola writes a letter to Simon bemoaning how he has erased his own past—including his Jewish past—and, tellingly, how she is not permitted to dwell on the hurt that she has had to live with through the years. Lola's experience of being abandoned by her father is juxtaposed with the burden of guilt endured by Shlomo and even with the lasting trauma inflicted on Holocaust survivors (*W*, 170–74).

Lola is at least dimly aware that her grounding of her Jewish identity in solidarity is not only dubiously vague and relativizing but also a consumer choice, as it were. The peace activism that she becomes involved in is as much an opportunity to eat, drink, and stimulate the senses as it is a commitment to a cause. On the way to the funeral, Shlomo and Lola visit a museum (*W*, 180). Later, on the way to a demonstration, they stop for a banana-and-orange juice (*W*, 213). Similarly, Lola's photographing of violence and the mark it leaves on individuals contributes to the flood of images that shape consumer tastes, from Facebook—where Manuela and Olaf added a Hitler moustache to her portrait (*W*, 15–16)—to Instagram, even Tinder (*W*, 67), and the magazines she freelances for. On Instagram, Lola posts pictures "auf denen ihr Vergangenheit, Gegenwart und irgendwie auch die Zukunft verwoben schienen" (on which past, present, and somehow also the future seemed to her to be woven together), and then sells them for 33,000 EURO (*W*, 83). For her magazine work, she composes even more stylized images:

> Paar Füße, Lolas, die sie mit ziemlich viel Blitz von oben fotografiert hat. Der Fokus lag auf den Zehennägeln und dem roten abgeplatzten Nagellack. Wieder das sich durch Lolas Bilder ziehende Motiv: die Verbindung von Vergangenheit, Gegenwart und Zukunft. Da war mal Lack, bald wird er ganz verschwunden sein. Und so weiter.
>
> [Feet, Lola's, which she photographed from above, with lots of flash. The focus was on the toenails and the red nail varnish,

flaked-off. The same motif that goes through all Lola's pictures: the link between past, present, and future. Once there was varnish there, soon it will have completely disappeared. And so on. (*W*, 175)]

The motif of nail polish peeling away, suggesting the connection between past, present, and future, is conventional, even hackneyed, as she admits with the laconic "Und so weiter."

Lola, in fact, objectifies Shlomo: "Sie würde ihn fotographieren [. . .] Wie schläft ein Mörder? [. . .] Wie sieht sein weicher Penis und sein harter Penis aus?" (She would take his picture . . . How does a murderer sleep? . . . what would his soft penis and his hard penis look like?; *W*, 152). Elsewhere, she intrudes on his privacy to create art: "Lola machte Fotos von Shlomo, von Shlomos Tränen, von Shlomos Fingern, die sich um den Maschendraht klammerten." (Lola took photos of Shlomo, of Shlomo's tears, of Shlomo's fingers, clasping the wire fence; *W*, 192). In this image, empathy equates to commodification. For Walter Benjamin, history could be grasped "nur als <u>Bild</u>, das auf Nimmerwiedersehen im Augenblick seiner Erkennbarkeit eben aufblitzt" (only as a picture that flashes its final farewell in the moment of its recognizability). As Lola sees it, however, the current obsession with the fragile ephemerality of the past is little more than a commercialization of trauma.

Almost three months after her arrival, Lola quits Israel for Thailand (*W*, 242). Her disillusionment with the nationalist turn taken in the Jewish homeland is perhaps summarized within her recollection, a few weeks later in Southeast Asia, of seeing TV images of the assassination of Prime Minister Isaac Rabin, nineteen years earlier, on November 4, 1995 (*W*, 316–18). Rabin was killed by an Israeli ultranationalist who was opposed to his rapprochement with the Palestinians and signing of the Oslo Accords. For Lola, modern-day Israel no longer embodies the openness to dialogue and embrace of others that she—with other progressive Jews in the diaspora—sees as quintessentially Jewish values. More prosaically, in traveling to Thailand Lola is also retracing her father's route to Australia and even hopes that he will come and meet her halfway. Simon is present throughout the narrative, as the focus for Lola's attachment to Jewish identity, the proximate cause for her feelings of abandonment, and the recipient of lengthy letters, included in the text, that mostly go unanswered. On the one hand, Lola's father embodies the internalization of Holocaust trauma in the second and third generations, including an instinctive abhorrence of Germany. (A contrast is apparent with Lola's non-Jewish mother, Petra, a redhead who is not interested in dwelling on the past but only in accumulating wealth and social standing; *W*, 66.) On the other hand, Simon is elusive, even absent, impatient, and sometimes unforgiving, as intimated by an episode Lola recalls from her early childhood when, during a brief visit several years after he had left his daughter to flee West, he plays hide and seek with her but cannot be found. Lola panics, but her father can only express irritation that she had not thought to look upwards (*W*, 41–44). Simon, it seems, also encapsulates the fragility of Lola's connection to her Jewishness.

Simon's incessant travel through the tourist spots of Southeast Asia presents the novel's second—more pragmatic but ultimately less inspiring—possibility for a Jewish worldliness that is not fixated on either Germany or Israel. Simon quit communist East Germany (the GDR) in 1986, abandoning his young daughter to the care of her grandparents, but decided against settling in Israel, or even taking out Israeli citizenship (*W*, 23; 273). Now he refuses to think at all about the past, including his parents' Holocaust trauma and his childhood in the GDR. (As communists, Simon's parents had opted after the war to return to the Soviet zone. More generally, the novel touches on but doesn't explore in depth the ambivalent situation of the Jewish community in East Germany.)[26] To this extent, Lola's father might seem to embody an unburdened Jewish existence, or an existence in which ethnic, religious, and cultural markers no longer weigh heavily. Simon ends up in Australia and makes a new start with an American woman he met while busking in Melbourne.

There is nothing transcendent about Simon's globetrotting, however. He pursues only his own happiness, and his own interests. Likewise, Lola's own brief sojourn on an island off the coast of Thailand undercuts any notion that this diasporic existence can substantiate her Jewish identity in any meaningful way. What she experiences instead is consumerism, the smug complacency of Western tourists, and her own orientalizing impulses. She arrives in Bangkok, delights in architecture that reminds her (of her stereotype) of Shanghai in the 1930s,[27] imagines herself as an opium-addled white prostitute for rich Chinese men, and changes her Tinder profile to her new location before opting for a handful of Europeans only. She meets a Frenchman, and they undertake a tour of the city by tuk tuk (*W*, 262–67). On her taxi-boat crossing to the island, Lola's gaze lingers on the naked torso of her Thai pilot as he fixes an entangled propeller, and she takes a colonizing pleasure in his "archaischen Männlichkeit" (archaic manliness; *W*, 278–79). Later, she removes her bikini top, just as was the norm in the former East Germany and just as she used to do in Tel Aviv, but now without regard for the cultural norms prevailing in the Muslim part of the island (*W*, 290–91).

---

26 *W*, 307. See Ó'Dochartaigh, *Germans and Jews*, especially 55–67 and 91–101. Funk is the great-granddaughter of the East German writer Stephan Hermlin.

27 In the 1930s, Shanghai was a major destination for Jews fleeing the Nazis. There is no indication that Lola is referencing this history.

Above all, it is the uncanny symmetry between two couples—one German, the other Israeli—also sojourning on the island that most obviously undermines the prospect that Lola might be able to define a diasporic Jewish identity through world travel. Toni turns up, quite unexpectedly, with his girlfriend Peggy. This is the non-Jewish German man who, on their date in Berlin, had told Lola that she could not be Jewish without a Jewish mother. Also present on the island are Maya and Hillel, Israelis who are resident in Berlin. Though one is from the perpetrator collective and the other from the victim collective, the two couples seem to mirror one another in a way that suggests a progressive generation of young people from around the world embracing cosmopolitanism, anti-racism, and diversity, underpinned by a critique of Israel's treatment of the Palestinians and an idealized notion of Jewish values. However, as was evident from the earlier episode when Lola and Toni met in Berlin, Toni's stance on Israel is tinged by antisemitism. Likewise, his presumption that he, a German, can define who is a Jew is both reminiscent of Nazi precedents and, in its reliance on Orthodox precepts, fundamentally conservative. His insistence that Jewishness is simply a matter of a maternal bloodline is quite the opposite, therefore, of the liberal Jewishness that Lola hopes for. In any case, she implies, this worldly Judaism does not even exist, or rather no longer exists. Maya and Hillel, accordingly, reject Israel on account of what they perceive as its turn toward ethnonationalism and desire to find a more authentic Jewishness in Berlin. After the Holocaust, Lola demurs, this is pure nostalgia (*W*, 305–6). The truth is that the two young Israelis, like so many others, have moved to the German capital because of the freedom it offers to experiment personally and artistically—and because chocolate pudding is cheaper. This is a reference to the uproar caused in 2014 by a Facebook page run by a young Israeli, calling for his fellow citizens to immigrate to Berlin, where they could enjoy a cheaper cost of living (*W*, 305). As well as an affront to Israel's campaign to encourage the diaspora to make *aliyah*—the Minister of Finance described the website as "anti-Zionist"[28]—such a motive to live in the land of perpetrators is hardly a statement of universalistic Jewish values.

Lola seems unable to articulate either a self-confident Jewish identity, whether in Germany or Israel, or a more abstract notion of Jewish worldliness. She rejects Germany for its persistent antisemitism; Israel for its treatment of the Palestinians; and her father's peripatetic, self-denying Jewishness as a consumerist pose. All Lola is left with is what she had before her travels even began, that is, Jewish memory not as a universalistic imperative but as perhaps the only source of her persistently fragile identity. Lacking a Jewish mother, and with her father having abandoned

---

28 See Salloum, "The Chocolate Pudding Exodus."

her, Lola's Jewishness appears to derive solely, or at least primarily, from her grandmother's Holocaust trauma—not unlike Izy in *Superposition*, in fact. Indeed, Hannah's story grounds Lola's narrative, as it were, as the only memory that does not seem to be ultimately self-indulgent—whether the endless stream of letters Lola addresses to her father, which together make an exhibition of her sorrow akin to the thirty-three images of Shlomo's pain that she installs in his apartment, or indeed Shlomo's shedding of tears for his own guilt. In a letter to her granddaughter, to be read after her death, Hannah relates how her family remained too long in Germany, how she was deported with her parents and older brother, and how she alone survived. She ended up in Dachau, where she was pulled from a pile of bodies by an American GI, Joshua Simon Katz—Simon's real father (*W*, 226–27). Indeed, Hannah's Jewish story seems to resonate with Lola more enduringly than the connections she makes in the present day to either Israelis or Palestinians. She wears her grandmother's jewellery (*W*, 242) and writes *Winternähe* on her typewriter (*W*, 247). This investment in the *materiality* of Jewish memory, of course, suggests Jewish particularism rather than Jewish universalism.

At the end of the novel, Lola returns to the place she knows best: Berlin (*W*, 310). This homecoming perhaps signals a rejection of *both* forms of Jewish worldliness that she has tried out, in Israel and Thailand, and even an acceptance of her presence in Germany as the descendent of Holocaust survivors—if only on her father's side, of course. As she writes to Shlomo, she can now live with the legacy of the Holocaust without being overwhelmed by the past: "Die Geschichte im Jetzt zu fühlen, ohne davon überfordert zu sein" (*W*, 315; To experience history in the present day, without being overwhelmed by it.) At the same time, Lola is back where she started. She is still unsure of her Jewish identity, still fixated on Germany, and still driven by resentment rather than a positive vision of Jewish solidarity. In the closing pages of the narrative, then, Lola reveals that she had commissioned placards featuring the Facebook post Olaf and Manuela had doctored to add a Hitler moustache to her upper lip, and she had paid for these to be placed around Berlin in a week's time. The date is November 10—the morning after the anniversary of the pogrom of November 9, 1938.

"A Common Memory": Katja Petrowskaja's *Vielleicht Esther*

Kaufmann's *Superposition* and Funk's *Winternähe* exemplify the pop aesthetic that characterizes many recent German Jewish novels, including references to music and fashion; strongly sexual themes; and often with female protagonists who struggle to articulate a feminist response to their subordination to men. Channah Trzebiner's *Die Enkelin* (The granddaughter; 2013), examined in chapter 3, also falls into this category, although it lacks the meta-reflection that is present in *Superposition* and *Winternähe*. In these and other similar texts, the juxtaposition of "Jewish content" and "global form" manifests the tension between particularism and universalism. As shown above and as will be argued in relation to *Die Enkelin*, however, their protagonists generally mistake the fake cosmopolitanism of Western consumer culture for an authentic Jewish worldliness rooted in solidarity with others.

Petrowskaja's *Vielleicht Esther*, in contrast, is typical of a second strand of contemporary German Jewish writing, resembling twentieth-century modernism and in fact often citing German, German Jewish, and European authors of the period before the Second World War. In this novel—and in the novels by Grjasnowa and Salzmann that are analyzed in the next chapter—formal complexity, a questioning of historical truth, and a striking interest in narrating the past as a "what if" suggest ways of articulating a Jewish identity that is at least potentially available for reframing as truly worldly, that is, pointing beyond the immediate Jewishness of the Jewish experience. At the same time, of course, this provisional Jewishness is also highly unstable, oscillating between particularism and universalism. More than anything else, therefore, *Vielleicht Esther* is marked by radical uncertainty, as its Russian-speaking Ukrainian-born narrator Katja endeavors to formulate a philosophy of history—and an approach to storytelling—that can reconcile the in any case unrecoverable specificity of the Jewish experience with the potentially limitless generality of global solidarity.

Katja confesses at the very start of her narrative that her Jewish origins are "eher zufällig" (rather accidental).[29] Indeed, *Russian* vocabulary and references to *Russian* literature feature throughout the text—including Tolstoy, Akhmatova, Mandelstam, Blok, Turgenev, and Bulgakov—while, as Andree Michaelis-König notes, "we find only a few Yiddish words in the text, and almost all of them are treated rather contemptuously."[30] To this extent, Katja resembles many Soviet-born Jews who moved to Germany beginning in the early 1990s, including, of course, the novel's author, with whom she shares a first name and many biographical details. (Petrowskaja immigrated after the "quota refugees," in 1999). What Katja recounts in *Vielleicht Esther*, correspondingly, is her travel from Germany to Warsaw and Kyiv, where many of her kin had once lived, and her efforts to recover a Jewish family history that had faded in Soviet times, including as a result of antisemitism. Piecing together the sparse information she can glean in archives and from anecdotes, photographs, and

---

29 Petrowskaja, *Vielleicht Esther*, 10. Hereafter *VE*.
30 Michaelis-König, "Multilingualism," 151.

even recipes, Katja suggests the intellectual, cultural, and linguistic richness of Jewish life from the eighteenth century, including the *Haskalah*, or Jewish Enlightenment, until the Holocaust.

Most obviously, *Vielleicht Esther* is a work of painstaking historical reconstruction that also reflects on the impossibility of recreating the past as it actually occurred.[31] Indeed, the inadequacy of archival, photographic, or anecdotal evidence is demonstrated in a series of episodes interspersed throughout the narrative, all with a similar outcome. It is only luck, for example, that a photograph that an archivist in Kalisz procures for Katja from Ebay—most likely taken by a German soldier in 1940 (*VE*, 109)—shows the house that her ancestors had occupied (*VE*, 113–14). When she tries to examine files relating to her great-uncle Stern (*VE*, 151), the paper crumbles, and archival records are in any case inaccurate, for example when her ancestor Simon Geller is listed as running a school for the blind rather than for deaf and dumb children (*VE*, 54), or are unreliable translations of lost originals, as with the Russian rendering of the Yiddish newspaper article on which her family history depends (*VE*, 52–53). Names change, or are forgotten, as is the case for her great-grandmother Esther—"vielleicht Esther" (*VE*, 208–9)—as well as other relatives, known only by nicknames. The Holocaust caused ruptures in family history, of course, but there are often more prosaic reasons too. It would be tempting to link the uncertainty around Esther's name to her murder in Kyiv in 1941. However, the truth is that Katja's father only ever knew her as Babuschka (*VE*, 209).

Scholars have variously referred to Katja's—or Petrowskaja's—technique for compensating for the inadequacy of the historical record as "subjunctive remembering,"[32] as the "subjunctive approach" or "subjunctivity,"[33] and as a method of "finding and fabricating" through "interweaving documentation and invention."[34] Here, it is important to emphasize that this subjunctive remembering does not invent something that never happened in one form or another but rather gives access to particular events that would otherwise remain obscure. This is a distinction that underpins the novel's ethics: the obligation to narrate the past responsibly, even if the details must be fabricated. In one of the novel's most horrific episodes, Katja imagines her great-grandmother Esther dutifully responding to the German instruction for Kyiv Jews to present themselves for deportation. She pictures the German and Ukrainian patrols and speculates that Esther might have believed that Yiddish-speaking

---

31 See Osborne, "Encountering the Archive."
32 See Caspari, "'There Are No 'Other' People'" and Caspari, "Subjunctive Remembering."
33 Roca Lizarazu, "Moments of Possibility," 406–26.
34 Rohr, "On Finding and Fabricating."

Jews were the "nächsten Verwandten" (closest relatives; *VE*, 213) of the German occupiers and thus safe. Finally, she describes how an officer shoots her great-grandmother, "mit nachlässiger Routine, ohne dass das Gespräch unterbrochen wurde, ohne sich ganz umzudrehen, ganz nebenbei." (In a casually routine fashion, without his conversation being interrupted, without turning around fully, just in passing; *VE*, 220.) Katja admits that she has fabulated this event, decades after, and even celebrates the author's privileged perspective—"Ich sitze oben, ich sehe alles!" (I'm sitting upstairs. I can see everything!)—before she notes the inadequacy of her imagination and of historical accounts: "Ich sehe die Gesichter nicht, verstehe nicht, und die Geschichtsbücher schweigen." (I can't see the faces, don't understand, and the history books remain silent; *VE*, 221). Even though Katja cannot be sure of exactly how this one woman was killed, however, her duty is to narrate a possible, *plausible* version of a historical reality that, in its sum, is well evidenced and incontestable.

The subjunctive mode is not an imagining of infinite alternatives—even including a world in which the Holocaust did not happen—but an appropriate response to the uneven distribution of what knowledge has been preserved about the genocide. Notwithstanding Katja's proclivity for supposition, speculation, and even fabulation, *Vielleicht Esther* is a surprisingly grounded work of historical fiction. This is demonstrated, for example, when Katja relates how her father owed his life to her grandfather's insistence that a neighbor's ficus tree be removed from the cart on which families were fleeing the Nazis, to make room for the boy (*VE*, 217–18). Katja's narration of a foundational family myth stretches plausibility and is almost farcical. Her father denies ever having told her this story but relents when he sees how invested she is in it and indeed believes her own existence to depend on it. He consoles her, therefore: "Manchmal ist es gerade die Prise Dichtung, welche die Erinnerung wahrheitsgetreu macht." (Sometimes it's the pinch of poetry that makes memory align with the truth; *VE*, 219.) What is important here, however, is not whether her father's escape happened exactly in this manner but the historical reality that an individual's survival was often entirely dependent on the actions of others, and on circumstances. Immediately following this episode, Katja relates how all the other Jewish boys still in Kyiv were shot in the ravine at Babi Yar (*VE*, 218).[35] In all, more than 34,000 Jews were disposed of over two days, September 29–30, 1941. Esther was executed on her way to the ravine, as previously noted, and it is significant that Katja's reflections on poetic invention and the ficus tree that most likely never existed are interjected into the middle of her detailed fictionalization of how that particular killing could have happened. Esther's murder,

---

35 See Snyder, *Bloodlands*.

like millions of others, is historical fact, not supposition or speculation, even if the details are unrecoverable.

Vielleicht Esther is not only—or simply—a Holocaust novel, however. Its innovation derives from its interweaving of three complementary narrative strands ranging from the eighteenth century to the postwar Soviet Union. The first is Katja's efforts to recover her Jewish heritage. This endeavor underpins the entire novel. The second is her grandparents' proximity to the Holocaust, including the narrator's more abstract reflection on how the genocide *should* be memorialized. And the third is her repeated return to Soviet crimes and Soviet antisemitism. Each of these three strands, it can be argued, is fundamentally concerned with the relationship between Jewish particularism and Jewish universalism. To what extent are the Jewish lives (and deaths) that Katja imagines in her parallel narration of these interlinked pasts *universalizable* within a discourse of global solidarity and human rights?

As noted, Katja's connection to her Jewish heritage is initially weak. She summons her ancestors to her, "aus der tiefen Vergangenheit" (from the deepest past), they speak languages that seem familiar to her, and she hopes to populate her family album, "den Mangel auffüllen, das Gefühl von Verlust heilen." (To fill the lack, to heal the feeling of loss.) Ultimately, however, they appear to her in a huddled mass, "ohne Gesichter und Geschichten" (without faces, without stories; *VE*, 25). Unlike Samuel, the American Jew whom she meets at Berlin central station at the start of the book, Katja has no Jewish languages and no Jewish geographies. Sam is originally from Iran and still speaks Aramaic; he is traveling with his wife to the village in Poland that her grandmother emigrated from, even though they know that nothing remains of the thriving community that existed before the Holocaust (*VE*, 10). Katja, on the other hand, is a "Weichensteller," a pointsman whose job it is to switch railway tracks. On the one hand, this can be read as an affirmation of her role as narrator, managing the convergences of the different pasts she recounts. (Literary scholar Eneken Laanes argues that the pointsman is a "central metaphor for code-switching and linguistic and cultural translation in the text." In this persuasive reading, it refers also to Katja's switching between languages to create a transnational memory narrative.)[36] On the other hand, Katja seems to be without a history of her own, reduced to the function of an intersection rather than being an active participant in an ongoing story. Indeed, this applies to her Russian identity as much as her Jewish background. (Katja notes that in Russian the word pointsman, or стрелочник/strelotschnik, carries a negative connotation). She has married a German and is not teaching her children her mother tongue—she is a "dead end" (*VE*, 8–10) as far as her Russianness is concerned, she notes.

---

36 Laanes, "Katja Petrowskaja's Translational Poetics of Memory," 51.

Here, the English words in the German-language text reinforce the point about successive degrees of alienation from her first language.

Katja's efforts to recover her Jewish past appear, in part, to be in fulfillment of a debt that she feels she owes to older generations of her family. She recalls her mother's older sister, aunt Lida, who had been such a key figure in her childhood. Lida's death prompts her desire to research and write her family history and causes her to reflect on the transition from a living memory of the vitality of European Jewish culture before the war to her generation's dependence on photos, archives, and stories in the family to generate its own fragile and fragmented relationships with the past. To relate this past is an obligation as binding as the unpaid bills she discovers among Lida's effects: "als ob ich auch bei Lida Schulden hätte." (As if I too had a debt to pay to Lida; *VE*, 30–31.) More generally, Katja ponders how a recipe her aunt had left exemplifies the uncanny fusing of Jewish sensibility and European culture, which seemed to derive "aus einer Wurzel" (from one root; *VE*, 31). The recipe is at least partly Jewish but this element is now suppressed in favor of its description as Ukrainian, just as Lida prefers to suppress her youthful beauty and intellectual curiosity, the slaughter that followed, those who were murdered, or indeed anything at all relating to the traumatic past: "den Krieg und das Davor und das Danach." (The war and what came before and after; *VE*, 33–34.) As with the story of the ficus tree, Katja retells an eccentric family legend, honors its meaning for her and her relatives, but also intimates more general historical realities, for example the interdependence of Jewish and European culture and the hurt felt by Jews once the illusion of belonging had been destroyed in the mass shootings, ghettos, and camps.

Katja consults multivolume encyclopedias on the history of Judaism and of eastern European Jews (*VE*, 54), struggles to enunciate the Hebrew phrase *Sch'ma Israel* (Hear, O Israel; *VE*, 55), and tries to imagine her grandmother in Warsaw and what kind of Jewish life Rosa would have led if she had emigrated to America in 1915 (*VE*, 77). This follows an episode in which Rosa sings along to a Yiddish soundtrack after decades of forgetting her mother tongue. However, none of this brings Katja closer to her Jewish past—the thread is too tenuous. She wonders whether there is an echo of the Yiddish Wille in her uncle's name Wil (*VE*, 36) but knows that he was actually named for Wladimir Iljitsch Lenin. Her father had little connection to his Jewish background (*VE*, 36), and her own efforts to uncover family history depend on an unreliable Russian translation of a Yiddish newspaper article (*VE*, 52–53). Katja, in fact, is ignorant of her ancestors' languages: "kein Polnisch, kein Jiddisch, kein Hebräisch, keine Gebärdensprache, ich wusste nichts über die Shetl, ich kannte kein Gebet." (No Polish, no Yiddish, no sign language, I knew nothing about the stetl, I didn't know any prayers; *VE*, 101). Her brother is learning

Hebrew and studying the Torah, she reports, whereas she has married a German and writes in the language of the perpetrators (*VE*, 80).

Katja's account consists of six chapters, following a brief prologue in which she recounts how she met the American Jew Samuel at Berlin main railway station just as she was about to board a train to discover her family roots in Warsaw and Kalisz, the town inhabited by generations of her relatives. Each chapter focuses on an episode in her family history, except for chapter 1, which introduces the characters who will feature in the novel and inaugurates the meta-reflection on how the past is reconstructed that will be a major theme throughout the book. Chapter 1, then, introduces the reader to an almost unfathomable array of relatives. These include a Bolshevik revolutionary, whose decision to change the family name from the Jewish-sounding Stern to the "Russian" Petrowskaja resonates even in the present; a mention of several others who labored in a shoe factory in Odessa about whom nothing more is known; and a physicist who disappeared during Stalin's purges and whose brother-in-law, a secret policeman, was required to investigate. They also include a war hero nicknamed Gertrud, the husband of her aunt Lida; Katja's great-grandfather Ozjel, the grandson of Simon, who inaugurated the family vocation of schools for the deaf and dumb; and a reference to the many other ancestors who taught in such schools across Europe. And they include Katja's great-grandmother Esther, who was killed in Kyiv; her grandmother Rosa, and Rosa's mother Anna and sister Ljolja, murdered in Babi Yar; and Katja's great-uncle Judas Stern, who, in the interwar years, tried to assassinate the German envoy in Moscow and may have been manipulated by the forerunner to the KGB. Finally, there is Rosa's non-Jewish Ukrainian husband, Wassilij, who was a Soviet POW in Mauthausen and who, after his return to Kyiv, failed to make contact for forty-one years (*VE*, 18–20).

Most immediately, Katja's quest to reconnect with her ancestors seems to be focused on establishing the singularity of their lives. As discussed, this involves collecting—or speculating—details from family legends, archives, photographs, and even Google, and it appears designed to emphasize individuality, even exceptionality, over the ordinary. For example, there is her great-grandfather Ozjel, who moved from Warsaw to Kyiv in 1915. Katja's enquiries reveal that Ozjel's claim that his first wife Estera had died was untrue. He had in fact abandoned Estera and his sons, Zygmunt and the unfortunately named Adolf, following an accusation of spying for Austria and a period in prison (*VE*, 96). (Deaf and dumb people, Katja notes, are often presumed to be spies.) In addition, Ozjel was born a bastard, a disgrace the family strives to conceal even now (*VE*, 133). This account of Katja's Polish ancestors is narrated in chapter 3, titled "Mein schönes Polen" (my beautiful Poland), and her revelation of these secrets seems to suggest a personal reckoning with family history. Then there is her great-uncle Judas Stern. His story, Katja implies in a forty-page rendition of what she has found, is truly unique. Stern had tried to kill the German envoy in Moscow in 1932, was convicted by the Soviet authorities in a show trial, and executed. This bizarre episode is related in chapter 4, "In der Welt der unorganisierten Materie" (in the world of unorganized material), and seems to illustrate Stern's idiosyncratic nature, even madness. Later, Katja suggests that her paternal grandmother Rita might also have been insane (*VE*, 194–95)—with good cause, since she had witnessed how her baby brother's head was smashed against a wall during the 1905 pogrom in Odessa (*VE*, 195). As a final example, there is the story of the family's involvement in education for the deaf and the dumb, over seven generations, beginning with "Schimon der Hörende" (Simon, the listener) who founded a school in Vienna (*VE*, 49–50). (The name Simon is related to the verb "to hear" in Hebrew.) Indeed, the spread of Simon's descendants across Europe, founding schools for the deaf and the dumb everywhere they settled, is presented almost as the fulfillment of a biblical mission: "Abraham zeugte Isaak. Isaak zeugte Jakob. Jakob zeugte Juda und seine Brüder and so on and so forth." (Abraham begot Isaac. Isaac begot Jakob. Jakob begot Juda and his brothers and so on and so forth; *VE*, 50.) Katja admits here that she does not know whether she is alluding to the Old or the New Testament—more evidence of her lack of religious understanding—and the English addition further emphasizes her distance from this extraordinary history.

For all that Katja focuses on exceptional characters, however, her account of family history also presents, thus the title of chapter 1, "eine exemplarische Geschichte" (an exemplary story). Indeed, it can be argued that this representativeness motivates and propels her narrative. Her revelation of Ozjel's secret life thus prompts her search to discover the fates of his first wife Estera (deported, destination unknown; *VE*, 132), their son Zygmunt, who was shot to death in Lublin, and his spouse, Hela, who was murdered in Treblinka (*VE*, 108). This discovery, in turn, leads Katja to Zygmunt's niece, Mira, whose astonishing—but also entirely typical—story she learns when she speaks on the phone to the elderly survivor, now living in the United States: a ghetto; five camps; a death march; daring escapes; typhus; luck, cunning and deception; and occasional help from others (*VE*, 126–27). (Through Mira, Katja discovers living relatives on that side of her family, including distant cousins in London, who unwittingly are continuing the family vocation as teachers; *VE*, 125.) In the case of Stern, potential insanity initially appears to point, as noted above, to another family secret. Katja's lengthy description of his show trial, however, suggests that his assassination attempt might well have been orchestrated by the GPU—the precursor to the KGB and, nowadays, the FSB—in an effort to destabilize the relationship with Germany. And there is a related plot strand in which the secret police in Odessa visit her grandfather Semjon—Stern's brother—and intimidate the family, causing her father's premature birth (*VE*, 141–42). Semjon, the onetime Bolshevik revolutionary who changed the family name, doesn't tell his son about his uncle for many years and in any case keeps a low profile, for fear of attracting the attention of the authorities. At the same time, he too worked for the secret police, although he resigned when he was ordered to investigate his brother-in-law, a physicist accused of an unspecified crime (*VE*, 141–45). Both Stern's show trial and Semjon's harassment thus hint at something more general, namely the opaque, absurd machinations of the Soviet state—and quite likely Soviet antisemitism. Katja summarizes all this via an allusion to Kafka's *Der Prozess* (The trial; 1925), relating to the arrival of the GPU at Semjon's house to pursue a crime of which he is not even aware: "Dieses Gesetz kenne ich nicht, sagte K. Desto schlimmer für Sie, sagte der Wächter." (I don't know this law, said K. All the worse for you, said the guard; *VE*, 141.)

The most exemplary aspect of Katja's family history, however, may be contained within her account of her ancestors' commitment to educating deaf and dumb children. She comments: "Unser Judentum blieb für mich taubstumm und die Taubstummheit jüdisch. Das war meine Geschichte, meine Herkunft, doch das war nicht ich." (Our Judaism remained deaf and dumb for me and the condition of being deaf and dumb remained Jewish. That was my history, my origins, but it was not me; *VE*, 51.) At first glance, this confirms the gulf of incomprehension that separates her from her Jewish heritage. Yet her addendum that the state of being deaf and dumb is itself intrinsically Jewish is still more suggestive. Most obviously, this may be an allusion to family members who prefer not to speak about the past. Lida prefers not to speak about murdered relatives. Semjon remains silent about Stern. And her grandmother Rosa scribbles furiously in a notepad, slowly going blind, writing on the same sheet over and over, and never intending that her memories should be read (*VE*, 61–63). Yet there is also another possibility, even probability. For Katja, Jewishness cannot communicate itself to others and, as such, it remains esoteric at best and at worst "set apart." To what extent can—or should—Jews emerge out of their ethnic, religious, and cultural particularity and participate as hearing and speaking citizens in non-Jewish majority discourses?[37]

A response to this question is implied in her family's dedication to the education of deaf and dumb children, mostly Jewish, in schools founded across central and eastern Europe. Drawing on the Russian translation of the lost Yiddish newspaper article that is the starting point of her reconstruction of family history, Katja describes how her ancestor Simon Geller (or Heller) developed a technique for teaching the children to speak using a pencil to transmit the vibrations of the instructor's voice to

---

37 See Endelman, "Assimiliation and Assimilationism."

their mouths. In this way, she reports, the children learned to speak, in Hebrew and German, and with such great fluency that their speech was *hardly* different from that of people born hearing (*VE*, 53). This implies assimilation, even integration—Hebrew *and* German—even as it also alludes to how Jews are understood as not quite native. In addition, however, there are several other dimensions to the story—these are almost certainly unfamiliar to the reader, but we can suppose that the author Petrowskaja uncovered them in her research. First, Jews were overrepresented in the education of deaf and dumb children from the eighteenth century. Second, in the nineteenth-century debate between proponents of teaching sign language only and those who championed the acquisition of spoken language, Jewish instructors were pioneers of the new method, to better "integrate" their pupils into mainstream society. Third, both of these historical facts can be linked to certain features of Judaism, and especially to the *Haskalah*, or Jewish Enlightenment.

Teaching deaf and dumb children to speak made it possible for them to become fully accepted as active participants in Jewish ritual. Within a religious tradition with a strong emphasis on orality, Marjoke Rietveld-Van Wingerden and Wim Westerman argue, being able to speak was a precondition for being seen as legally and morally competent.[38] Katja's ancestors had been enablers of this "becoming Jewish" for deaf and dumb children. Like many European Jews, though, they had later fallen silent themselves—in giving them back their voices, Katja revives their Jewish identity, and her own. More generally, Katja's family is representative of the *Haskalah* that, from the late eighteenth century across central and eastern Europe, sought to introduce Judaism to Western modernity by emphasizing secular languages, abandoning traditional garb, and reforming Jewish ritual, and participating as active citizens in the majority society.[39] The long-lost Yiddish newspaper article about Simon Geller's pioneering work with deaf and dumb children was written by Faiwell Goldschmidt, a "Schriftsteller und Aufklärer" (writer and Enlightenment figure; *VE*, 52), and, as she researches this aspect of family history, Katja thinks of the "zahlreiche selbstlosen Männer der jüdischen Aufklärung" (numerous selfless men of the Jewish Enlightenment). These men (inevitably), she notes, were "beseelt von der Idee, Wissen zu verbreiten, es von Mund zu Mund weitertrugen. Für dieses vom Hören bessenene Volk war die gesprochene Sprache alles." (Inspired by the idea of spreading knowledge, transmitted it from mouth to mouth. For this people, obsessed by listening, the spoken word was everything; *VE*, 55.)

Katja's reconstruction of her family's past frames her ancestors as representative, therefore, and specifically of the emergence of European Jews

---

38 See Rietveld-Van Wingerden and Westerman, "'Hear, Israel.'"
39 See Feiner, *The Jewish Enlightenment.*

out of the ghetto over the course of the eighteenth and nineteenth centuries.[40] This was a journey toward emancipation, assimilation, and integration that, after the Holocaust, many would renounce as a fateful error on the part of a community that had fooled itself that it could truly belong. Indeed, Katja's account of the murder of her relatives in Babi Yar and elsewhere might appear to endorse this viewpoint, though there is no hint in the narrative that a different historical development would have been possible or even desirable, for example an embrace of the Zionist project of creating a Jewish state in Palestine.[41] (Unlike in many other recent novels, Israel does not feature at all.) More generally, however, Katja's family is representative of the relationship between Jewish particularism and a Jewish commitment to universalism that key proponents of the *Haskalah* movement emphasized time and again. Moses Mendelssohn's *Jerusalem* (1783), for example, attempted to reconcile a defense of the particularity of Jewish rituals and practices, including rabbinic traditions, with his embrace of "natural religion," that is, an Enlightenment view that all monotheist faiths are in essence expressions of a universalistic commitment to love, tolerance, and equality, and that these eternal truths can be arrived at through reason.[42] More concretely, Katja's family embodies this same tension—sometimes productive, other times less so—between their dedication to their Jewishness, including Yiddish and Hebrew, and their aspiration to be worldly, that is, to engage beyond their Jewish context on behalf of humankind as a whole, as teachers, scientists, or revolutionaries.

The Holocaust largely destroyed the dense networks of Jewish social and political activism that reached across Europe, or displaced them to the United States, Britain, and Palestine/Israel. Genealogies were interrupted or eliminated. This is the novel's second strand, and, here too, Katja's subjunctive narration suggests the representative nature of what her relatives suffered. A succession of passages relating how different relatives were connected to the massacre at Babi Yar typifies the different ways in which Kyiv's Jews more generally were exterminated in late 1941: the decision to flee or to remain, the march to the assembly point, casual executions, mass shootings and internment under mounds, betrayal, and—in very few cases—escape and survival. Katja reveals that she had requested books on the massacre from the library, and her account is no doubt shaped by the exemplary fates that works of history tend to offer up, therefore (*VE*, 183). A first section describes the ravine's location (previously at the edge of the city but now enveloped by postwar developments), Katja's visit to the site with her parents, the logistics of the killings, the memorialization of the event during the Soviet era, and a new memory culture after

40 See Sorkin, *Jewish Emancipation*.
41 See Wistrich, "Zionism."
42 See Breuer, "Rabbinic Law." See also Fogel, *Jewish Universalisms*.

Ukrainian independence in 1991 (*VE*, 183–93). A few pages later, Katja picks up again, with an account of how her maternal great-grandmother, Anna, was killed in Babi Yar, having decided to stay in the city, along with her daughter Ljolja (*VE*, 197–203). (She notes the coincidence of Ljolja's birthday with her nephew's. His Bar Mitzvah affirms the family's return to its faith seventy years after Ljolja, a non-practicing Jew, was killed; *VE*, 203.) Ljolja's husband, a non-Jew and much older, saves himself and flourishes after the war. The following chapter concerns her great-uncle Abram, who hid when the order was given for Jews to assemble but whose Christian wife was betrayed and shot (*VE*, 205–8). (After the war, Abram changed his name to Arnold to evade Soviet antisemitism. Thousands of deaf and dumb Kyiv residents attended his funeral.) Finally, there is Esther's story, including the invented account of how Katja's father was saved by the removal of a ficus tree during his family's escape (*VE*, 208–33).

Katja's reconstruction of her family's Jewish past and her reconstruction of her relatives' murder *as Jews* in Kyiv in September 1941 both oscillate between singularity and representativeness. In the first strand, key figures in family legend appear as extraordinary, even exceptional, while the clan as a whole is seen to embody the assimilation and integration of broad swathes of the Jewish population from the eighteenth century. In the second strand, integration is followed by extermination, and the fates of individual family members are imagined, even invented, and exemplify the Holocaust by bullets (*VE*, 185–86). The question now arises, then, of whether this representative function extends beyond Jews to encompass the world, as it were. Certainly, Sabine Egger suggests that Katja frames Babi Yar and other sites of atrocity as "multidirectional memory spaces,"[43] while Godela Weiss-Sussex argues that the novel's juxtaposition of pasts indicates an "extended and inclusive understanding of remembrance and belonging for the conceptualization of future communities."[44] Likewise, Maria Roca Lizarazu speaks of the novel's "futurity,"[45] and Susanne Rohr points to its "globalised transnational and trans-generational locus of consciousness."[46] For these scholars, in essence, Katja's narrative points toward a universalization of the Jewish experience of the Holocaust and implies—potentially, at least—a basis for global solidarity.

There is plenty of evidence for readings of this kind. In her introductory summary to what happened at Babi Yar, correspondingly, Katja notes that the ravine continued to be used for mass killings for two more years

---

43 Sabine Egger, "The Poetics of Movement."
44 Weiss-Sussex, "'Dass die tauben Geschichten aufflattern,'" 14.
45 See Roca Lizarazu, "Moments of Possibility."
46 Rohr, "On Finding and Fabricating," 538.

after September 1941, until the Red Army took the city, and the victims included not only Jews but also Soviet POWs, sailors from the Kyiv fleet, young women, passer-by's gathered up from the streets, Roma and Sinti, priests, and Ukrainian nationalists who had previously collaborated with the Germans (*VE*, 186). Later, Katja visits the former concentration camp at Mauthausen, in Austria. Her great-grandfather Wassilij had been interned as a Soviet prisoner-of-war, and she seems to parallel his fate not only with the Hungarian Jews who started a forced march from there in April 1945 (*VE*, 242) but also—with some ambivalence—the suffering of German POWs (*VE*, 253), when she cites the comments left by visitors to the website of the Austrian war graves commission.

Above all, it is during Katja's observations on her visit to Babi Yar that she comes closest to universalizing the (largely) Jewish suffering that occurred there as a template for expressions of solidarity with all victims of persecution and genocide. In a passage also cited by some of the literary scholars mentioned above, she comments:

> Babij Jar ist Teil meiner Geschichte, und anderes ist mir nicht gegeben, jedoch bin ich nicht deswegen hier, oder nicht nur. Irgendetwas führt mich hierher, denn ich glaube, dass es keine Fremden gibt, wenn es um Opfer geht. Jeder Mensch hat jemanden hier.
>
> [Babi Yar is a part of my history, and it's the only one I have, however I am not here for that reason, or not for that reason alone. Something else brings me to this place, for I believe that there are no strangers when it's about victims. Everybody has someone here. *VE*, 184]

This message here seems clear. There can be no distinctions between victims; Babi Yar epitomizes the suffering inflicted on all persecuted minorities, everywhere; and solidarity is the only appropriate response. Later, Katja is repelled by the erection of memorials for different victim groups. This recalls the "Selektion" in the death camps, she claims. (Jessica Ortner notes Katja's frequent use of the word "Selektion" through her narrative to suggest the exclusionary effect of the competition between Jewish, Russian, Polish, Ukrainian, and other "national" memories of the Second World War, the Holocaust, and other atrocities.)[47] Here, her desire for a "gemeinsame Erinnerung" (common memory, *VE*, 191) dramatically expands the scope of her refusal, earlier in the book, to discriminate between Jewish victims, namely between members of her family and countless others with the same surnames (*VE*, 26–27).

---

47 Ortner, *Transcultural Memory*, 115–19.

Katja's meta-reflections on her response to Babi Yar once again raise the particularism/universalism issue, this time more explicitly. If her reconstruction of family history alludes to the enduring debate on how Jews can negotiate between ethnic, religious, and cultural particularity, on the one hand, and assimilation and integration, on the other—perhaps including a commitment to universalistic values and the betterment of the world—then her account of her relatives' representative Holocaust experiences invokes a related discussion about what "meaning" is to be assigned to the genocide. Is the near-eradication of European Jews to be thought of as a singularly Jewish experience, or does it have universal significance as a crime against humanity? In some versions, this debate builds on a long tradition in Jewish and Christian religious thought of framing Jewish suffering as redemptive for all humankind[48] and is set against Orthodox responses to the Holocaust (God's absence, indifference, or anger, or the birth pangs of the coming of the Messiah) and restorative or Zionist interpretations (Jews must survive; they must be safe in their own state).[49] In recent years, specifically, the globalization of Holocaust memory has underpinned a broader political imperative to defend and even enforce universal human rights. This is what Daniel Levy and Natan Sznaider describe as "cosmopolitan memory."[50] The violence inflicted on Jews, it is suggested, embodies the violence inflicted on other minorities, in the past and still today, and forms an injunction to intervene, morally, politically, and even militarily.[51]

Katja's endorsement of a common—or cosmopolitan—memory is less emphatic than it at first appears, however, and it is not unconditional. When she asks her friend David whether any of his relatives were murdered at Babi Yar, for example, there is a hint of skepticism in her response to his pronouncement that it doesn't matter whether he has this personal connection or not: "oder wünschte er sich, dass es unwichtig war?" (Or did he wish that it was not important; *VE*, 184). Katja's interjection may suggest that, ultimately, we can only relate to suffering in which we are directly implicated. Immediately following this, Katja summarizes her own wishful thinking, that is, that she could walk through the site at Babi Yar and remain silent about the fact that her own relatives were murdered there:

---

48   See Moyaert, "Redemptive Suffering."
49   See Katz, "Shoah."
50   Levy and Sznaider, *The Holocaust*.
51   A. Dirk Moses argues that the construction of Jews as "exemplary victims" risks a depoliticization of the specific mechanisms of state violence. See Moses, *The Problems of Genocide*, especially 477–511.

als ob es möglich wäre, als abstrakter Mensch, als Mensch an sich und nicht nur als Nachfahrin des jüdischen Volkes, mit dem mich nur noch die Suche nach fehlenden Grabsteinen verbindet, als ob es möglich wäre, als ein solcher Mensch an diesem merkwürdigen Ort namens Babij Jar spazieren zu gehen.

[as if it were possible, as a person in the abstract, as a person *an sich*, and not as the descendant of the Jewish people, with whom I am still connected only by the search for missing gravestones, as if it were possible, to walk in this remarkable place called Babi Yar, as this person. *VE*, 184]

Katja is not, and cannot be, the universalistic abstraction—"Mensch an sich"—that is the implied subject of cosmopolitan memory. She is partial, and indeed partisan, the descendant of Jews, and her investment in their fate overwhelms the truth that her own Jewishness is attenuated at best. Eclipsing the universalizing framing of Jewish suffering cited by approving scholars—"Jeder Mensch hat jemanden hier" (*VE*, 184)—and a mention of other victims, including POWs, partisans, Roma and Sinti, young women, priests, is Katja's more expansive account of how all remaining members of the Jewish population of Kyiv were forced to strip, marched naked, beaten, and made to lie on top of the dead and shot in the back of the neck. Children, she reports, were thrown into the ravine alive (*VE*, 185–86). Next, Katja specifies that her own great-grandparents were executed there, along with their daughter Ljolja, and that Esther too "belongs" here even if she was actually killed on the way (*VE*, 187).

Just as undermining of the universalizing potential of Katja's Holocaust narrative is her detailed account of her grandfather Wassilij's internment as a Soviet prisoner-of-war in Mauthausen, and of her visit to the former concentration camp. This report comes directly after her reconstruction of her relatives' murder in September 1941. It could be assumed that the two episodes—Jewish suffering and the maltreatment of Soviet POWs—might shape a common memory of Nazi barbarism and the potential for solidarity. Indeed, Katja asks herself whether what she learns about Wassilij's internment in Mauthausen implies "eine Mission" for her in the narrative present: "Ich werde nicht in die Vergangenheit katapultiert. Es passiert jetzt. Wann, wo und mit wem es passiert spielt keine Rolle." (I am not catapulted back into the past. It is happening now. When, where, and to whom it is happening is not important; *VE*, 248.) It is not clear whether she means that the past is vivid to her today, or that similar things are still taking place, or both. In any case, she seems to imply that there is a responsibility to speak out on behalf of victims of persecution, whether then or now.

Yet Katja is not able to connect to her great-grandfather's experience in any real way. Just as she did during an earlier visit to Auschwitz (*VE*, 58–60), she is at a loss to truly feel her way into what the victims endured and is incapable of generating anything more than a ritualistic, empty, and fleeting solidarity. In part, this has to do with the routinized and sanitized nature of contemporary memory culture, which can never reproduce the real horror: "Es müsste doch überall Dreck sein. Ich habe davon gelesen. Der Tod müsste stinken." (There should be filth everywhere. I've read about it. Death should stink; *VE*, 247.) But it is also linked to our inability to put ourselves in others' shoes and to imagine our way into their lives. In a dream sequence that transports her back to Mauthausen in 1945, she is not able to cross the threshold of Wassilij's barracks in order to approach her grandfather in his bunk (*VE*, 245–48). (She also imagines herself pulling a variety of ribbons out of her pockets, as if to add color to a scene that she can only imagine in black and white; *VE*, 246.) If a descendant—with a special right of access to the victims' authentic suffering, she speculates (*VE*, 258)—cannot mobilize empathy as a bridge between traumatic pasts, what chance do those not directly affected have, including perhaps the narrative's likely non-Jewish readers?

Wassilij is not only a victim. He might have played a part in Stalin's collectivization program, which resulted in the starvation of millions of Ukrainians in the 1930s (the Holodomor; *VE*, 238). And Katja speculates that her grandfather might have mistreated fellow Jewish inmates in Mauthausen (*VE*, 249; 274–75), notwithstanding his marriage to a Jewish woman, Rosa, and their Jewish children. These possibilities again disrupt the potential for a common memory. After the war, Wassilij fails to contact his Jewish wife for forty-one years while living in secret in the same city. On his reappearance, it transpires that he has a vegetable garden, a typically Ukrainian pastime (*VE*, 234). His Jewish granddaughter Katja, however, is unable to enter this garden when she dreams of it decades later (*VE*, 238–39).

On his return from captivity, Katja's grandfather was suspected of collaboration, interrogated, and subsequently marginalized, as many Soviet former POWs were (*VE*, 231). Wassilij's story, therefore, connects Katja's Holocaust account—Babi Yar, Mauthausen, and, told in interwoven passages, the forced march of Hungarian Jews through Austria (*VE*, 271–77)—with the novel's third narrative strand, namely Soviet crimes. In general terms, these include show trials, the secret police, and torture (*VE*, 237–38), and Stalin's collectivization program in the 1930s (*VE*, 178; 238). More specifically, however, the narrator's focus is on the emergence of state-sponsored anti-Jewish sentiment from the 1950s.[52] The context, of course, is Stalin's execution of members of the

---

52 See Korey, "Soviet Anti-Semitism."

Jewish anti-fascist committee, Jewish intellectuals, and Yiddish poets—"Hitler hatte die Leser getötet und Stalin die Schriftsteller" (Hitler killed the readers, Stalin the writers; *VE*, 188)—establishing, Katja implies, a degree of continuity between the Nazis' murderous designs and Soviet persecution: "Diejenigen, die den Krieg überlebt hatten, waren wieder in Gefahr. Juden, Halbjuden, Vierteljuden." (Those who survived the war were in danger again. Jews, half-Jews, quarter-Jews; *VE*, 188.) The likely antisemitic machinations behind Stern's show trial and his brother's Semjon's intimidation by the GPU have already been discussed above. Above all, however, it is the Soviet regime's denial of the Jewishness of the Holocaust that concerns the narrator, since this amounted to a second erasure of those in her own family who were killed. It was only thirty-five years after the massacre at Babi Yar that the first monument was unveiled—for Soviet victims of fascism, as they were described, and "am falschen Ort und am falschen Tag." (In the wrong place, and on the wrong day; *VE*, 187).[53] The fact that the 34,000 people killed on September 29–30, 1941, were not named as Jews reflects Soviet antisemitism, Katja insinuates.[54] She describes how the ravine, once 2.5 km long and 60 m deep, had been filled with factory waste after the war and how, in 1961, the dam broke, resulting in 1,500 deaths (*VE*, 189). The Russian writer Yevgeny Yevtushenko is lauded for his (now well-known) poem recalling the Jewish tragedy—and ruing the Soviet repression of its memory—but this was a rare attempt to break the silence (*VE*, 189–90). (Yevtushenko's poem "Babiyy Yar" appeared in 1961 and sparked a forceful response from the authorities and even other artists.)

The three juxtaposed strands of Katja's narrative—Jewish family history, Nazi crimes, and Soviet repression—together present a picture of the violent disruptions that occur when one epoch ends and another begins, of the clash of ideas and ideologies, and of how ordinary people are caught up in conflicts that they can barely grasp. Within the broad sweep of eighteenth to mid-twentieth century European history that she describes, therefore, the near-extermination of Jews is clearly unique in its scale, geographical extent, and fanaticism, but it may also be *representative* of the persecution of other national, religious, and ethnic groups, including gypsies, Russian and even German POWs, Ukrainians, and many others not named in the novel. (And some, of course, were both victims and perpetrators.) Set against this exemplarity, however, is the *specificity* of what Katja discovers—or speculates—about her Jewish family, and especially

---

53 For a detailed analysis of Katja's reflections on the Soviet repression of the Jewishness of the massacre, see Ortner, *Transcultural Memory*, 122–28.

54 For the Soviet memorialization of Babi Yar, see Baranova, "Conceptualizations." For an account of how the Holocaust more generally was—or was not—remembered in the Soviet Union, see Weinberg, "The Politics of Remembering."

about the murder of her relatives. This includes her great-grandfather's first wife, their son and his wife, Katja's maternal grandparents, and, of course, Maybe Esther and her daughter Ljolja, as well as some more distant relatives, recently learned about, such as Benno, the seventeen-year-old brother of the niece of the son of her great-grandfather's first marriage, who was killed on a death march in May 1945 (*VE*, 276). These are the particularly Jewish stories that Katja seeks to recover from oblivion—and even erasure—and in imagining, or inventing, the detail of what might have happened to them, she also hopes to memorialize the millions of other Jewish victims of the Holocaust (*VE*, 268–69).

Like her fellow Soviet-born protagonist Izy in *Superposition*, Katja remains fixated on the specificity of the Jewish past that she has only just recovered. Yet she at least speculates what solidarity *could* look like, in contrast to Lola in *Winternähe*, whose sentimental empathy devolves into globetrotting and then back to resentment.[55] In *Vielleicht Esther*, in summary, Jewish particularism and Jewish universalism seem to be finely balanced. A conceptual framework is created for a truly "universalistic, cosmopolitan" (Kilcher) Jewish worldliness but in the end history, and historical detail—whether fabulated or real—weigh too heavily.

Worldliness?

In one of her more esoteric passages, Katja describes two quite different ways of inhabiting the world as a Jew. Some of her ancestors, she emphasizes, had dedicated themselves to the education of deaf and dumb children, "in dem hellen aber nie ausgeprochenen Glauben, sie würden die Welt reparieren." (In the clear but never expressed belief that they were repairing the world; *VE*, 17.) A term associated with classical rabbinic literature, the Kabbalah, *and* the Jewish Enlightenment, *tikkun olam* (repairing the world), has come to signify for many Jews a responsibility not only for their own welfare but also for the world at large.[56] Others of Katja's forebears, in contrast, "waren wie von Himmel gefallen, sie schlugen keine Wurzeln, sie liefen hin und her, die Erde berührend, und blieben in der Luft wie eine Frage, wie ein Fallschirmspringer, der sich im Baum verfängt." (Appeared as if they had fallen from a tree, they didn't put down any roots, ran here and there, touching the earth, and remaining hanging in the air like a question, like a parachutist who has become entangled in the tree; *VE*, 17.) This more whimsical image suggests rootlessness, dispersion, and—in the question hanging in the air, the parachutist caught in a tree—an unfathomable singularity. On the one hand, therefore, there is a universalistic mission in being a Jew that

---

55 Kilcher, "Diasporakonzepte," 135–36.
56 See Shatz, Waxman, Diament, and Hirt, eds., *Tikkun Olam*.

engages beyond the group. On the other hand, there is contingency and an introspective, even esoteric particularism.

Chapter 3 examines three recent novels whose Soviet- and German-born protagonists make a less ambivalent commitment to worldliness—whether to *tikkun olam* or a more prosaic kind of self-understanding within the Western secular mainstream—and who attempt to articulate more definitively what Jews are *for*, again with different outcomes. In these narratives, a more assertive self-positioning as post-religious, post-solipsistic, and even post-Holocaust implies less emphasis on Jewish particularism and instead a more allusive referencing of Jewish suffering as a *trope* connoting a history that inhibits integration into the global present or even as a *metaphor* that can be deployed as a resource for cosmopolitan engagement. In Trzebiner's *Die Enkelin*, then, the Jewish experience is a trauma to be overcome rather than an ethical imperative, and popular culture is embraced as an escape from its oppressive legacy. In Salzmann's *Außer sich* and Grjasnowa's *Der verlorene Sohn*, in contrast, the Jewish past—and Jewishness itself—is *queered*, meaning that it is deliberately alienated from its conventional context, as a memory of the genocide or of what Jews have endured *as* Jews, and inserted into new forms of relationality with others.

Once Jewishness is largely cited rather than expressly articulated, it may be that it becomes so diffuse that it appears hardly legible. This ambivalence of "Jewish purpose"—to adapt British historian Adam Sutcliffe's term[57]—and Jewish invisibility is explored in *Der verlorene Sohn*, and in relation to Polish Jewish philosopher Isaac Deutscher's typology of the "non-Jewish Jew."[58] It is further scrutinized in the conclusion, which asks whether and to what extent German Jewish writing is becoming increasingly less Jewish and speculates what its future might be following the atrocities of October 7, 2023.

---

57 See Sutcliffe, *What Are Jews For?*, 1–24.
58 See Deutscher, "The Non-Jewish Jew."

3: Worldliness: Channah Trzebiner, Sasha Marianna Salzmann, and Olga Grjasnowa

In the decade after the end of the Cold War, when hopes were high that the world might finally coalesce around (Western) liberal values, some Jewish and non-Jewish thinkers alighted on the reemergence of Jewish life some fifty years after the Holocaust as evidence that Jews could model and even help to shape a more united Europe. Intellectual historian Diana Pinto, for example, introduced the concept of a "Jewish space," as old and new democracies across the continent began to integrate the Holocaust into their national histories and set about promoting the Jewish past as an arena in which Europeans could engage and develop a common self-understanding.[1] In relation to the Jewish community in Germany specifically, Julius Schoeps wondered whether the arrival of post-Soviet Jews might foster a "cross-fertilisation of worldviews."[2] Likewise, David Shneer saw the emergence of a new "German–Russian–European Jewish identity."[3] Historian Dan Diner and literary scholar Oliver Lubrich both wondered whether newly arrived Russian Jews might point toward a post-colonial future for Europe, beyond empire and embodying hybridity,[4] and Sander Gilman and Y. Michal Bodemann (with Gökce Yuedakel)[5] were among a number of scholars who asked whether Jewish integration could serve as a model for Muslim integration. In each case, there is a suggestion that Jewishness, as the essence of intercultural exchange, might serve a higher aspiration, namely a new Europe characterized by diversity, openness, and tolerance. Dmitrij Belkin hints at this as well in his

---

1   See Pinto, "A New Jewish Identity." In subsequent articles Pinto adapts the concept to the increasingly challenging global geopolitical context from the late 1990s. See, for example, "The New Jewish Europe" and "A New Role for Jews in Europe." There has been much debate on Pinto's optimistic thesis. See Ganter and Oppenheim, "Jewish Space Reloaded."
2   See Schoeps, "Saving the German-Jewish Legacy," 58.
3   See David Shneer, "The Third Way."
4   See Diner, "Residues of Empire." See Oliver Lubrich, "Are Russian Jews Post-colonial?"
5   See Gilman, "Diaspora Judaism." See Bodemann and Yuedakel, "Learning Diaspora."

prognosis of an emerging "Patchwork-Judentum" (patchwork Judaism) in Germany and indeed across Europe.[6]

Recent scholarship on German Jewish authors and texts tends to affirm and even expand the suggestion of the fundamentally cosmopolitan significance of Jewish existence in Germany and Europe. Luisa Banki and Casper Battegay, for example, offer seven theses on the newest Jewish writing, including aspects addressed in this book—a focus on families and generations and on historical trauma rather than on the Holocaust as an event; transgression; the ambivalence of Israel; and how depictions of casual sex are used to explore stereotypes of Jewishness. Banki and Battegay's thesis seven is more abstract, and even programmatic, however: "contemporary German-language Jewish writing, therefore, points to the future of Europe: it contributes to a transnational, 'European Europe' and also even requires it."[7] Recent German Jewish writing, in this analysis, anticipates the essence of a European unity that is (yet . . .) to come, and embodies the imperative of global interconnectedness.

Jews, it seems, suggest the potential for a more integrated and harmonious future simply by *being Jews*. Indeed, their apparently intrinsic worldliness might even imply what British historian Adam Sutcliffe calls "Jewish purpose." In his 2020 book *What are Jews for? History, Peoplehood, and Purpose*, then, Sutcliffe examines the proposition, long debated in the Jewish tradition and in Christian and post-Christian frameworks, that "Jews are endowed with a particular historical purpose." This, he summarizes, has been construed in different ways at different times: to transmit the scriptural evidence for the truth of Christianity; herald the second coming of Christ (through Jews' return to Zion or conversion, or both); exemplify universalism through their overcoming of their own particularity; embody modernity with its myriad social, political, intellectual, cultural, and economic transformations; be a "light unto the nations" through their ethical behaviour; or—through their suffering—point toward the imperative of universal human rights.[8] Throughout, of course, there is a presupposition of Jewish singularity—Jews as the chosen people, or, more negatively, as "the people apart."[9]

For many Jews in Germany today, a framing of Jewishness, and Jewish purpose, as inherently cosmopolitan and socially engaged may have practical advantages. For younger Soviet-born Jews especially it likely accords with the lived experience of existing between nations, languages, and cultures. For these Russian speakers, in addition, *and* for secular Jews, those not considered "properly" Jewish, and those whose

6   Belkin, "Wir könnten Avantgarde sein."
7   Banki and Battegay, "Sieben Thesen," 47.
8   Sutcliffe, *What Are Jews For?*, 1–24.
9   See Vital, *A People Apart*.

gender identity or sexual orientation is at odds with Orthodox Judaism, it may validate their Jewishness vis-à-vis skeptics and infuse it with meaning. In short, solidarity might be an essential Jewish value—incorporating ethical injunctions from religious texts[10] and Jews' striking participation in progressive causes—but, as argued in previous chapters, it is also a form of self-positioning.

Chapter 2 analyzed three novels in which solidarity seemed to be contingent on a reconciliation of Jewish universalism and Jewish particularism, or, to put it another way, on balancing an aspiration to engage on behalf of others with a desire to recover the specificity of the Jewish experience. In each text, the past is presumed to be original and *originating*, that is, it both grounds and founds Jewish identity in the present—Izy's Soviet Jewish past in *Superposition* (2015), the Holocaust trauma of Lola's grandparents in *Winternähe* (Near winter; 2015) and, in *Vielleicht Esther* (Maybe Esther; 2014), Katja's efforts to reconstruct the fates of her relatives, including the manner of their execution by the Germans and their Ukrainian accomplices. Precisely because the past is so fundamental to their articulation of Jewish identity, however, all three struggle to fully embrace a worldly perspective. The same might be argued in relation to the protagonists of Altaras's *titos brille* (2011), Himmelfarb's *Sterndeutung* (2015), and Stein's *Rabbi Löw* (2014), who are all are concerned to find ways of living as Jews in modern-day Germany *despite* the traumatic legacy of the Holocaust.

This chapter begins with an analysis of Trzebiner's *Die Enkelin* (The granddaughter; 2013) and specifically its protagonist's wish *not* to integrate the past into her Jewish identity but rather to overcome Holocaust memory, and her Orthodox background, almost entirely in order to achieve a quite different kind of worldliness, now unburdened by trauma and fully aligned with the present. Following this, we turn to two novels that situate the Jewish past as a *resource* rather than as a legacy to be faithfully (or speculatively) reconstructed. The past, even including the Holocaust, becomes a literary trope, as it were, that can be reframed and even rewritten to underpin global engagement in vastly different contexts. In Salzmann's *Außer sich* (Besides oneself; 2017) and Grjasnowa's *Der verlorene Sohn* (The lost son; 2020), it is argued, a diffuse worldliness is communicated through generalized motifs of exile, marginalization, and persecution. How *Jewish* this is may be an open question.

Unorthodox?: Channah Trzebiner's *Die Enkelin*

Channah Trzebiner was born in 1981 in Frankfurt. *Die Enkelin* is her first, and to date only, literary work. It was well received by reviewers in the major German newspapers as an insightful reflection by a young

---

10 See Roth, *The Jewish Idea of Ethics and Morality*.

Jewish woman of the third generation on her grandparents' Holocaust trauma and the "abnormality" of Jewish family life seventy years after the genocide. Typically, reviewers emphasize the grandfather's erratic moods, angry outbursts, and even cruelty, or they frame the book as an education for the German reader, with details of Jewish customs and rituals, extensive use of Yiddish (and a glossary of Yiddish terms), and insights into the transmission of trauma through the generations. (The text's "Jewish authenticity" is guaranteed by a full-page photo of the author in its front matter.) Less often mentioned are the narrator's own preoccupations, including her petty jealousies, musings on sex and gender, her unhappy Orthodox marriage, divorce, and her new non-Jewish boyfriend Marco. The first third of the narrative, then, focuses on family, including her grandfather Abraham, sister Zoé, and aunt Rachel, and the Sabbath, strained relationships with non-Jewish acquaintances, and holidays in Israel, where her grandparents repeatedly emigrated, only to return each time to Germany. The other two thirds, in contrast, describe how Channah gradually moves further from her family and her Jewish context. Successive episodes are dedicated to taking a job in a bank and acquiring non-Jewish female friends, beginning a PhD. under the supervision of the Jewish academic and activist Micha Brumlik,[11] visiting Auschwitz, confronting German memory culture at Bergen-Belsen, spending time with New York Jews, Channah's growing intimacy with Marco but also occasional insecurities, and her decision to move in with him. Indeed, *Die Enkelin* is not just about the transmission of Holocaust trauma through the generations. It might also be considered, alongside international bestsellers such as Naomi Alderman's *Disobedience* (2006) and Deborah Feldman's *Unorthodox: The Scandalous Rejection of My Hasidic Roots* (2012), as a work that describes, for a gentile audience, a young woman's break with Orthodox Judaism. Hence, Trzebiner's description of Channah's integration into the secular mainstream relates as much to the global debate on how to live as a Jew in the twenty-first century as it does to her German context.

---

11 In the early 1980s, Brumlik presented an alternative position to the conservatism of the mainstream Jewish community, founding the magazine *Babylon*. He was also roundly condemned for his criticism of Israel and its treatment of the Palestinians. In later years, he has been more supportive of Israel, critical of left-wing antisemitism in Germany, and coeditor of the journal *Jalta: Positionen zur jüdischen Gegenwart* (Yalta—Positions on the Jewish Present). In 2015, he published *Wann, wenn nicht jetzt? Versuch über die Gegenwart des Judentums* (When, if not now? Thoughts on Judaism today), a reflection on the indispensability of the diaspora to the survival of a cosmopolitan Jewish identity and on the increasing ethno-nationalism of the state of Israel. In 2022, he published *Judentum. Islam: Ein neues Dialogszenario* (Judaism, Islam: A new scenario for dialogue; with Elisa Klapheck und Susannah Heschel) on the need for dialogue between Jews and Muslims. See Anna Corsten, "Jewish Left-Wing Intellectuals."

The juxtaposition of her grandfather's (and, to a lesser extent, her grandmother's) traumatic past and its continuing reverberations and Channah's incomparably less momentous present-day preoccupations generates the thematic and stylistic dissonance that is typical of many recent German Jewish novels. Even more jarring in *Die Enkelin*, however, is the extensive inclusion of Yiddish. On the one hand, then, there is the thoroughly modern feel of Channah's frequent references to sex, weight, and fits of jealousy. On the other hand, for the likely non-Jewish and secular reader, Yiddish invokes a traditional Orthodox Judaism, characterized by religious faith and ritual but also by patriarchy and the subordination of women. For the non-Jewish *German* reader specifically, moreover, Yiddish is distinctly uncanny, being both familiar but also only obliquely accessible, even with a glossary, and reminding of the near-extermination of eastern European Jews. The novel's opening third, correspondingly, goes beyond the introduction to Jewish customs that is often a feature of German Jewish literature, although this is present too, for example when it is reported that placing stones on a grave "ist ein [jüdischer] Brauch" (a Jewish custom).[12] Moving back and forth between her German narrative frame and Yiddish direct speech, Channah suggests both the intimacy of German and Jew and the unforgivable crime that was committed.

Each member of Channah's immediate family suffers the burden of Holocaust history differently, and with different consequences in the present day. Her grandfather Abraham's first wife was murdered in the gas chambers, along with their son and unborn child (*E*, 12). Decades after his own experience of the camps, Abraham remains obsessed with food and compulsively steals from grocery shops in Germany (*E*, 24) and market stalls in Tel Aviv, often implicating Channah in his transgressions (*E*, 24). At the time of the Chernobyl disaster Abraham is overwhelmed with a disproportionate sense of doom (*E*, 22), and his alternating outbursts of anger and affection point to his persistent traumatization (*E*, 12–14). Soon after the war, he married a fellow survivor, as was common in Displaced Persons camps (*E*, 210). His second wife, Channah's grandmother Rywka, had barely survived a Nazi doctor's attempts to sterilize her (*E*, 111). Rywka lost her husband in the Łódź ghetto; her baby was torn from her and deported to a death camp; her parents and eight brothers and sisters were murdered in Bergen-Belsen—Channah is named for the youngest girl (*E*, 12)—and she was conscripted as a forced laborer in one of its sub-camps (*E*, 132–34). In the present day, Rywka suffers partial blindness, since her left eye was stabbed out by an SS man for his amusement (*E*, 110).

Channah's mother Pola is encumbered by her parents' trauma and appears prone to depression. Pola is burdened, Channah believes, by

---

12 Trzebiner, *Die Enkelin*, 153. Hereafter *E*.

the survivor's guilt felt by Abraham and Rywka, which manifests in their daughter as an inability to participate fully in life (*E*, 73). This becomes especially acute after Channah's father dies. Born to a gentile mother and a Jewish father who had been hidden by Jehovah's Witnesses, Rick was less burdened than his wife and, for as long as he was alive, his drive sustained the family (*E*, 73). Channah worries that her mother will kill herself and obsesses about maintaining the semblance of order that Pola seems to need in order to ward off the chaos that threatens to overwhelm her: "Mama mochte keine Unordnung." (Mama didn't like any disorder; *E*, 72.) Pola's sister Rachel is equally affected, Channah reports. She too feels their parents' pain "als hätte sie es selbst erlebt" (as if she had endured it herself; *E*, 80) and, like Pola, seems to exist in their shadow.

In the third generation, Channah and her sister Zoé feel excluded from the intensity that exists between their parents and grandparents and overwhelmed by being exposed to a history that the survivors are not able to assess as entirely unsuitable for young children (*E*, 75). Above all, however, Channah feels "unsichtbar" (invisible; *E*, 69) for her mother, and she knows she exists only to remind her grandparents of those who had been murdered: "Meine Person war nicht von Bedeutung. Ich war ein Beweis dafür, dass es andere gegeben hat. Kinder, Mütter, Väter, Brüder und Schwestern." (My person was not of significance. I was proof that others had existed. Children, fathers, brothers and sisters; *E*, 12.) Even her name belongs to another, her grandmother's youngest sister, who was murdered in Bergen-Belsen.

The originality of Trzebiner's novel, however, lies in the potential transgression insinuated by its third-generation narrator's perspective on her grandfather's character flaws. Indeed, Channah consistently undermines the conventions surrounding the representation of Holocaust victims and thereby signals a certain critical distance for a younger cohort caught between veneration for the survivors' experiences and awareness of how these experiences deform their present, and their ability to be "normal"—if normal means being unburdened and fully part of their German milieu. Added to this, though less perceptibly, Channah's narrative frames her grandfather's self-absorption and occasional sexual transgressions—a patriarchal sense of entitlement that cannot be fully explained away as Holocaust trauma—in relation to a distinctly contemporary concern with gender. This, in turn, reorients the novel away from the intergenerational transmission of trauma toward a more expansive concern with the contradiction, whether real or perceived, between Orthodox Jewish values and "modern life." In essence, integration into mainstream society—aligning with the non Jewish German majority—may be as much an escape from what Channah perceives as the constraints of her Jewish context as an overcoming of her grandparents' Holocaust trauma.

Abraham is not only a Holocaust victim. He is also a bully, serial adulterer, and even predator. His thieving of food might be understood as a consequence of his experience of starvation in the camps, and survival no doubt required him to demonstrate a certain cunning and physical strength, as Channah notes: "Opa, und da bin ich mir sicher, hatte nur überlebt, weil er so Schlau wie ein Fuchs war und ihm von Natur aus die körperliche Stärke für alle Hunger- und Ausrottungsstrapazen gegeben war." (Grandpa, I'm convinced, only survived because he was as sly as a fox and because he had the physical strength for all the hardships inflicted by hunger and extermination; *E*, 15.) It is less clear, however, that the Holocaust was the cause of an indifference to the needs of others that seems distinctly male. "Opa," his granddaughter reports, "war irgendwie der Pate, er nahm sich, was er brauchte. Er nahm es sich so selbstverständlich und ohne Diskussion, dass keiner sein Verhalten je anzweifelte." (Grandpa was the patriarch, he took what he needed. He took it as if it were his right and without discussion, so no one ever questioned his behavior; *E*, 30.) Abraham's sense of entitlement, therefore, seems to be a predisposition rather than a response to trauma. More generally, his behavior appears to be expected, even normalized, within the wider family. There seems to be an acceptance of his repeated affairs, beginning in Sweden just after the war, when he was already married to Pola (*E*, 156), and continuing right up to his death, and of his regular groping of his wife's female acquaintances and, in later life, his care assistants (*E*, 30). The elderly man even comments on his granddaughter's clearly underage friends, naming one as fat, another as skinny, and a third as ugly: "Ich glaube, mehr als ihren Körper hat er nicht gesehen." (I think he never really perceived more than their bodies; *E*, 30.)

Most immediately, Channah's portrayal of her grandfather impinges on the sanctity of Jewish victimhood. Indeed, to have been designated for extermination does not—and should not have to—equate to moral purity, and to expect "better behavior" may be a form of antisemitism. Rafael Seligmann, Maxim Biller, and other authors suggest a similar critique of the sacralization of Jewish victims and often feature elderly male survivors with overactive libidos. In *Die Enkelin*, however, the grandfather's privilege has an additional significance. The fact that his Holocaust trauma dominates Channah's narrative, at least initially, is not incidental. It is only some way through the text that the reader discovers the full extent of her *grandmother's* suffering, when Channah hears the story from her aunt Rachel (*E*, 85–87), and it is not until even later that she realizes that, years before, Pola had implied but not explicitly disclosed that she had been forced to prostitute herself in the camps (*E*, 189). In highlighting her grandmother's gendered experience during the Holocaust, the fact that Abraham's story occludes Rywka's even within the family, *and* her grandfather's contempt for women in the present day, Channah hints at a more general theme of power relations between the sexes.

The first third of Channah's narrative, in fact, is concerned not only with the intergenerational transmission of Holocaust memory, or even with the gendered aspect of this intergenerational transmission—although it seems that the grandfather's story must be told first. It is also about the patriarchal structure of the family more generally, and specifically the patriarchal structure of Orthodox Jewish families. The second two thirds of her narrative, therefore, tell the story not only of Channah's liberation from the burden of her grandparents' trauma but also of her self-emancipation as a woman, and as a Jewish woman. This entails an embrace of the secular mainstream of German society that recalls Altaras's *titos brille* (tito's glasses; 2011), examined in chapter 1, but which is potentially even more transgressive in its accommodation of Holocaust memory and Jewishness to her immediate concerns as a young woman, beginning a career and settling down with her (German) boyfriend. The "normality" Channah craves might be thought trivial, even trite, but it is her choice to make.

Channah's divorce from her (Jewish) husband involves both predictable financial insecurity (*E*, 88) and a repudiation of her previous socialization, therefore: "Ich wurde dazu erzogen, eine brave Ehefrau zu sein. Ohne Mann hat eine Frau keinen Wert." (I was raised to be a good wife. Without a man a woman has no value; *E*, 88.) In fact, as Channah sees it, being subordinate to a man is an intrinsic part of her Jewish identity. After her grandfather's death and the dissolution of her marriage, she reports, she no longer feels motivated to observe Shabbat, even though she longs to, every Friday (*E*, 81). What's most significant about Channah's self-emancipation, however, is that she rejects not only the most obvious manifestation of traditional roles—Orthodox Judaism—but also two options that might seem to offer the possibility of combining a visible Jewish identity with gender equality. When she is in New York, researching for her book, it is unsurprising that she would be repelled by the suggestion, in an Orthodox area of the city, that women should sit at the back of the bus and is alienated by the wigs and identical long skirts that they wear in public: "Ich fühle mich nicht wohl, das erste Mal unter eigenen Menschen fühle ich mich sehr fremd." (I didn't feel comfortable, for the first time among my own people I felt alienated from myself; *E*, 185.) (In the next pages, she also recalls women survivors in Tel Aviv, friends of her grandmother who scolded her in Yiddish for displaying her skin, and she associates this experience with feelings of shame about her own sexuality; *E*, 187–89.) At the same time, she also rejects the liberal Judaism embodied by Lily, a professor at a New York university. Lily is married to a non-Jew, surrounds herself with left-leaning academics and senior colleagues at the United Nations, invites a Jewish lesbian couple to dinner, and displays an openness and tolerance that Channah sorely misses in her "Ghetto" (*E*, 159–60). Yet Lily too has rules, including how cookies are to be arranged on a plate, not mixing up Harvard and Yale, and that Channah should, on demand, be able to recite the four questions for Passover in English (*E*, 162). (Traditionally, the youngest capable person present at Passover asks the four questions. These are referenced in the novel's full title.) Likewise, in Tel Aviv, she is also not able to align herself with the easy-going self-confidence she encounters on the city's famous beaches, filled with young Jews from across Europe. She flirts with a young Israeli but is upset by his questioning of why she would want to live in Germany, avoids his attempt to kiss her, and spends the following week visiting his grandmother, a Holocaust survivor (*E*, 37–39).

Channah's urge to assert herself against her conditioning pushes her not, as might be expected, to embrace a more liberal version of Judaism, therefore. Instead, she is compelled to explore the world beyond. Most immediately, this means negotiating a new relationship with her German context. Subsequently, however, it implies a fashioning of femininity, which—even if it might appear to the reader to be somewhat clichéd and even simply another version of conformity—for Channah at least represents a kind of worldly self-realization.

After her divorce, Channah secures a job in a Frankfurt bank, largely following a stereotypical display of *chutzpah* at her interview, when she grossly embellishes her previous experience and views the entire exercise as revenge on Germans for what they inflicted on her grandparents and mother (*E*, 92–95). Moving past her excruciating reflections on her efforts to beguile a senior manager (*E*, 97–110)—a throwback to her previous socialization, perhaps, as noted above—the key breakthrough she makes in her first proper employment is that it is possible to be friends with non-Jews, including "drei herzensgute, intelligente und zum Schreien witzige Damen" (three warmhearted, intelligent, and hilariously funny ladies; *E*, 101). She learns to trust strangers—Germans—and experiences this as "heilsam" (healing; *E*, 101). The next step on her journey toward reconciliation with her German homeland comes when she secures a place to study for a PhD. at the university. She meets Charlotte, an empathetic young German woman, who, Channah reports, has an uncanny ability to sense her Jewish friend's hesitation "in der neuen fremden Welt" (in the strange new world; *E*, 102). Channah begins to teach tutorials and is gratified by the positive feedback she receives, especially from a handsome young man, who, she imagines, resembles Brad Pitt (*E*, 105–6). Again, this episode signals her embrace of—and acceptance into—the non-Jewish German mainstream.

More difficult is the indifference, ignorance, and sporadic insensitivity she encounters whenever the Holocaust is mentioned. A series of short chapters coming in the middle of the narrative detail variations on a theme of the gulf that exists between her fixation, as the granddaughter of survivors, on the genocide and the inconsistent, even thoughtless responses of her non-Jewish compatriots. An acquaintance of Marco's family is anxious to tell Channah about a local memorial for deported Jews—Channah, internally, makes a list of the injuries inflicted on her family for which actual rather than symbolic compensation would be required (*E*, 107–12). Later, she plans a visit to Auschwitz but postpones rather than embarrassing Marco's family by traveling directly from their home, at Christmas, to the extermination camp (*E*, 116). Slowly, in fact, she comes to appreciate that Marco gives her what she has never had, that is, distance from the Holocaust and "einen zeitlichen oder räumlichen Abstand zu meinen Großeltern, meiner Tante oder meiner Mutter." (A temporal or physical distance from my grandparents, my aunt, or my mother; *E*, 125.) Still, Marco accompanies her on a trip to Bergen-Belsen—where her grandmother was liberated in 1945 (*E*, 132)—shares her outrage when the ticket office at Celle railway station is intentionally unhelpful (*E*, 137–38), and benefits both from her gratitude and her musings on the burden that third-generation Germans are forced to carry for their grandparents' crimes (*E*, 142). Despite her misgivings about his lack of romance (*E*, 146), "unjewish" independence from family members (*E*, 118; *E*, 148), and worries that he might fall for a pretty (non-Jewish) French girl (*E*, 195–97), Channah's decision to move in with Marco surely signals her willingness to now "trust" Germans.

For the reader primed to expect Jewish writing to be focused on the Holocaust, mentions of Brad Pitt, a stereotypically seductive French girl, and Marco's wandering eye might appear incongruous and even alienating. The same is true, for example, when Channah serves up clichés about the benefits of sharing an apartment with a gay man, more sensitive and attentive than a boyfriend could ever be (*E*, 167–69), or when she extemporizes about how women want to be treated as princesses and urges men—if they value their sex lives—to remember to compliment and indulge their wives. This latter thought is expressed during a lengthy and inescapably hackneyed depiction of a Russian Jewish mother in New York, who urges her to find a good Jewish man and settle down (*E*, 173–78). Yet Channah's references to movie stars, gender clichés, and self-conscious citations of Jewish stereotypes provide her with a point of entry "into the world." Popular culture, then, offers a way out of the perceived constraints of Orthodox Judaism and Holocaust trauma and into an unburdened "normality." Here, *Die Enkelin* can be compared to Deborah Feldman's bestseller *Unorthodox* (2012). Feldman was raised by her Yiddish-speaking grandparents in the Orthodox tradition, entered an arranged marriage at seventeen, and fell pregnant, but then left her husband, repudiated her New York Hasidic roots, and—most scandalous of all—revealed to the world the secrets of the inward-looking community that she had left behind.[13] Both *Die Enkelin* and *Unorthodox*, accordingly, narrate their female authors' emergence into a form of worldliness while also profiting from the fascination with sects fostered in the media and mass entertainment.

Trzebiner's *Die Enkelin* is less aesthetically challenging and thematically complex than other novels analyzed in this book, and its articulation of contemporary Jewish identity, beyond Orthodox Judaism and even beyond Holocaust memory, is less expansive and less inspirational. A skeptical reading of Channah's integration into the secular mainstream, in fact, might conclude that she has abandoned her heritage—with only a residual concern for the sanctity of her grandparents' suffering—and simply swapped subordination to her Jewish grandfather for subordination to the skewed gender norms of fashion magazines and movies. (She also overlooks the significant strands within modern Jewish practice aiming to include feminist, lesbian, and progressive voices, sometimes even within Orthodox congregations.)[14] Yet this mundanity is surely significant in itself. *Die Enkelin*, it can be argued, thus offers an important corrective to ethnographic and especially literary scholarship that may overstate the cosmopolitan and even utopian orientation of Jews today, particularly younger Jews. As we move on to examine Salzmann's *Außer sich* and Grjasnowa's *Der verlorene Sohn*, it is vital to bear in mind that the global solidarity they imply may be an elite discourse of authors, artists, and activists, and an aspiration rather than a reflection of the mindset of the Jewish community as a whole.

Queering the Jewish Family Novel: Sasha Marianna Salzmann's *Außer sich*

A key characteristic of contemporary writing in German by self-identified Jewish authors is the juxtaposition of multiple strands of reflection within the overarching frame of family history. In *Der gebrauchte Jude* (the used Jew; 2009), Biller's story of growing up in West Germany in the 1980s and negotiating inherited trauma and the prejudices of the majority culture sets the scene for his reflections on his journey to becoming known as a Jewish author. Similarly, Altaras's recounting in *titos brille* of her parents' persecution during the war, flight from Yugoslavia in the 1950s, and leading role in the reestablishment of the community initiates her deliberations on reconciliation with the land of the perpetrators and the

---

13 Feldman moved to Germany in 2014. *Überbitten* appeared in 2017 as a German-language version of her memoir, *Exodus*, from 2014. The Yiddish title—"reconcile"—and the echoes of Yiddish throughout the text have a special resonance in the German context, of course.

14 See Ferziger, "Feminism and Heresy."

mass arrival of post-Soviet Jews today. In Stein's *Rabbi Löw*, family history is fantastical. In Himmelfarb's *Sterndeutung*, it is historically contextualized, notwithstanding occasional literary artifices. In these novels, family history encompasses other narratives touching on German Jewish memory culture, what it means to be Jewish today, and Jewish migrants from the former Soviet Union. In Trzebiner's *Die Enkelin*, Petrowskaja's *Vielleicht Esther*, and Funk's *Winternähe*, a focus on Holocaust trauma in the second and third generations is the starting point for reflections on Orthodox Judaism, gender, Israel's treatment of Palestinians, and the limitations of the archive but also of literary efforts to recover the Jewish past.

In Salzmann's *Außer sich*, in contrast, an expansive retelling of the lives of the protagonist's great-grandparents, grandparents, and parents is juxtaposed with two other plot strands that, at first glance, appear to be quite unrelated to Jewish identity, Jewish memory, and Jewish solidarity. Certainly, the novel's central concern with its protagonist Ali's transition from woman to man, on the one hand, and, on the other, with protest and repression in Turkey challenges the reader to find connections and even coherence across the text.

Three narratives are presented in *Außer sich*, therefore. First, there is a relatively conventional focus on great-grandparents, grandparents, and parents in the Soviet Union and then in Germany, following the family's migration in the early 1990s. Unlike Petrowskaja's *Vielleicht Esther* and Himmelfarb's *Sterndeutung*, however, the novel is not concerned with integrating the Soviet Jewish experience of the Holocaust into German and German Jewish memory culture—although there are several brief mentions of the genocide—but largely with the protagonist's reconstruction of Soviet antisemitism, persecution, and repression before, during, and after the war; belief in socialism and disillusionment; and the prejudice the family encounters in Germany, including, for example, familiar scenes of bullying at school. In this strand, which is woven through the other two narratives, Ali is frequently positioned as a listener, reshaper, and narrator of stories passed down by now deceased ancestors or solicited from living relatives. Second, there is a subtle exploration of the patriarchal structure of the family, the imposition and internalization of gender identities, and Ali's emergence as trans, including their attempts to account to parents and grandparents for their changed voice and face. Third, Ali tells the story of their apparent transformation into Anton. This relates to Ali's twin brother, their intense and even incestuous relationship; Anton's flight to Istanbul and Ali's search for him in that city; their merging into a single person; and (both) their involvement with various trans, non-conformist, and dissident characters caught up in anti-government protests centered on Istanbul's Taksim Gezi Park. In 2013, this square was the focal point for environmental and political opposition to the authoritarian regime of President Recep Tayyip Erdoğan. At the close of the novel, moreover, the state's violent suppression of these protests appears to be conflated with the attempted coup of July 2016 by elements of the Turkish military.

Each of these narratives is analyzed in greater depth in what follows, including how they interconnect. In essence, the argument will be that Ali/Anton's narration of family history creates an affective connection to what their great-grandparents, grandparents, and parents endured in the Soviet Union and Germany while also creating a space for Ali/Anton's queering of this Jewish story—a rearticulation of diasporic Jewishness beyond the nation, gender conventions, and even ethnicity. This act of listening, retelling, and redefining Jewish family history then initiates Ali/Anton's attempts to relate their own trans story—a metaphor for a fluid permeability with others, or a boundless cosmopolitanism—and to insert it back into the "Jewish canon." Finally, in tracing Anton's concurrent, coinciding experience of Istanbul and the (con)fusion of the twins into a single persona, Ali hints at the limits of their efforts, through their queering of Jewish family history, to redefine solidarity with others. Notwithstanding the seeming disparateness and even disconnectedness of its three plot strands, therefore, what *Außer sich* actually presents is both the radically utopian potential of Jewish worldliness and the persistence of privilege that inhibits its full realization.

Chronologically, Ali's Russian Jewish narrative starts with their great-grandfather Schura, although his story is only actually told following an account of Schura and Etinka's daughter Emma (Ali's grandmother) and her husband Daniil. (Daniil's family history is also related, as will be discussed shortly.) Schura presents Ali with a ten-page folder just before his death, which motivates the composition of the family history that is dispersed throughout the novel. Ali doesn't know why they—using the gender-neutral pronoun—began to bring together texts and images from the past or "warum ich angefangen habe, mich als mich zu denken, zu sprechen, sogar zu schreiben"[15] (why I began to think me as me, speak, and even write), but they do know that their simultaneous emergence as family biographer and as an "I" began at the time they received this folder, or after their return from Istanbul. Schura's "Mappe" (folder; *AS*, 142), "Aufzeichnungen" (records; *AS*, 157), or diary (*AS*, 181) make it possible for Ali to sketch their great-grandparents courtship at medical school in the 1930s; Schura's service as a doctor in the war years (*AS*, 158); Soviet propaganda in the 1950s lionizing and possibly inventing his and Etinka's medical accomplishments during the fight against the Nazis (*AS*, 145; 164–66); his dismissal in Stalin's anti-Jewish purges (*AS*, 153, 156); and his stubborn faith in socialism (*AS*, 166). In Germany, until

---

15 Salzmann, *Außer sich*, 142. Hereafter *AS*.

his death, Schura's speech is curtailed by dementia, though this does not inhibit the clarity of his writing.

Two elements stand out as especially significant in Schura's story. First, he wanted to be an actor, playwright, and set designer rather than a doctor but his father insisted that he forgo a place at the arts academy, although he continued to write plays during his medical training, especially when pining for Etinka (*AS*, 151–55). For Schura's father, acting was a disreputable profession and even too "Jewish," as summed up in the Yiddish "balagula," an itinerant who travels between villages hawking his wares. (The peddler was a stereotypical Jewish profession in medieval Europe.)[16] Ironically, Schura was in any case already well on his way to becoming properly Russian, or at least to playing a properly Jewish role in Russian society—his Yiddish was too rudimentary to argue with his father and so he signed up for medical school (*AS*, 152–53). Performance, writing, and Jewishness are associated with one another as marginal and even shameful and must be given up in favor of integration. Second, and suggesting resistance to this suppression of Jewish identity, Ali relates how Schura had managed to engage Etinka by speaking a few words of Yiddish to her, as they both checked for their names on a list of exam candidates. (Etinka came top; he was second.) Knowing that this display of ethnic and especially Jewish belonging was frowned upon by the Soviet authorities, they begin their relationship in a mode of subversive excitement (*AS*, 148–50).

Performance—singing, acting, writing—is a key motif throughout Ali's narration of family history. Etinka, for instance, would have liked to have been a singer, according to her daughter Emma (*AS*, 182). Emma is described as a "zartes Geschöpf" (delicate creature), who reads poetry, plays piano, does theater, and looks at herself for hours in the mirror (*AS*, 175–76), and she and her husband Daniil conduct their courtship through passionate conversations on the films of Grigory Alexandrovich Alexandrov and the poetry of Nikolay Alexeyevich Nekrasov (*AS*, 184–85). (Alexandrov was a favorite of Stalin and Nekrasov was known for his empathetic depictions of Russian peasantry and political liberalism.) Similarly, Ali's father Kostja enrolled in the Music Academy and appears to have had some talent (*AS*, 84). In Istanbul, Ali sings Soviet war songs with Katho, also known as Katharina and Katüscha, in the club that will be the locus of their social life (*AS*, 44). In an underground theater in the same city Ali also imagines encountering their lost brother Anton and, for the first time, seems to merge with him to become Ali/Anton (*AS*, 34–36). And, of course, Ali is also a storyteller, and—thus the novel's literary conceit—the composer of the text itself (*AS*, 144).

---

16 See Deutsch, "Hawkers and Peddlers."

On the one hand, performance is associated with Jewishness, invoking stereotypes of Jewish inauthenticity, "passing," inconstancy, and the failure to integrate into respectable bourgeois society. On the other hand, as will be discussed shortly, performance also relates to the construction of gender, and to the construction of nation—and to the queering of these categories. Throughout the novel, allusions to the practice of placing singing birds into small cages, in which they are concealed by a cloth, and inviting men to pay to enjoy their melodies most immediately relates to the sexual abuse that Katho suffers at the hands of strangers (*AS*, 123–25; 364–65). However, the image of entrapment and exploitation also serves more generally as a metaphor for the fate of those whose performances stand out as different, even—or perhaps especially—when this difference exerts an exotic appeal for the majority.

Ali's father Kostja, who enrolled in the Music Academy but ends up working shifts in the VW factory following the family's migration to Germany (*AS*, 245), is a drunk, a wife-beater, and an all-round failure. This is a different kind of performance, therefore—a performance of angry, resentful, and vicious masculinity. On the one hand, Kostja's violence toward his wife reenacts the violence he suffered as a child—he was abused by an uncle (*AS*, 69)—and even the antisemitic violence meted out to his parents in their village (*AS*, 66). On the other hand, Kostja's disappointment with life and consequent aggressiveness are a result of his own shortcomings. At the time he was introduced to his future wife Valja, he was in love with a *Schickse*, a non-Jewish girl, but was incapable of going against the prejudices of both sets of parents (*AS*, 70–72). In Germany, he struggles to make a new life, is Jewish only when he discovers he can have time off from work on the Sabbath (*AS*, 244), and hankers for Russia but allows himself to be ripped off when he tries to sell the apartment in Moscow he has inherited (*AS*, 254–56). Kostja moves in with a Jewish woman, Vika, perhaps because her name reminds him of Valja, but he longs for the wife who left him and for the children he hardly sees (*AS*, 251–53). He remains a drunk, leaving frequent abusive messages on Ali's answering machine (*AS*, 237) and turning up inebriated for divorce proceedings. In court, he doesn't have an interpreter so Ali in effect falsifies what is being said to him in order to mitigate his rage (*AS*, 242–44). Later, it is suggested that Kostja killed himself and that Ali believes their transition was to blame (*AS*, 254). Anton confirms that their father threw himself off a balcony, which Anton believes is an embarrassing way to die (*AS*, 296–97).

What is striking about Ali's recounting of Kostja's story—part tragedy, part his own doing—is its lack of judgment, even though Ali is directly impacted. Instead of hurt or even anger, there is texture and complexity, as Ali relates Kostja's biography of family abuse and its reenactment through the generations, antisemitic prejudice, gender roles, and migration. Ali offers a nuanced account of how social and cultural norms shape individual predilections, without excusing Kostja but also without condemning him. Notwithstanding their difficult relationship, in fact, Ali returns to Kostja time and again, adding new layers of insight and allowing him to become knowable, as a person who existed before Ali and separately from Ali and whose life story intersects with moments of world-historical significance.

The same is true for Kostja's wife Valja, Ali's mother. Valja's parents had named her after the Soviet cosmonaut Valentina Tereshkova, the first woman to go into space, seeking to conceal her Jewish heritage—futilely, given that her surname is Pinkenzon—and to signal her parents' socialist convictions (AS, 58). Despite her "ordentliche sozialistische Frisur" (proper socialist hairstyle), "gerade Nase" (straight nose), and love of Tolstoy and Achmatowa (AS, 59), however, Valja cannot avoid the wrath of her heavy-drinking first husband Ivan, "ein echter russischer Mann" (a proper Russian man) and a violent antisemite (AS, 59–64). (Drinking and wife beating are not just gentile pastimes, though. Ali's great-grandmother, Valja's grandmother Etinka, was also abused by her husband; AS, 64.) Following her divorce, Valja is sent to Moscow to meet Kostja (AS, 65). Notwithstanding that they are cousins, they are encouraged to begin a relationship, to overcome the shame of Valja's failed marriage and to wrestle Kostja away from the *Schickse* he is in love with (AS, 70–71). They sleep together, Valja falls pregnant with Ali and Anton, nearly miscarries in hospital, is beaten by her future mother-in-law, and discovers too late that Kostja too is a drinker (AS, 73–83). A short while after her arrival in Germany, Valja divorces him and secures a well-paid job as a doctor (AS, 248).

In relating Valja's story, however, Ali complicates any simplistic notion that it can ever be possible to straightforwardly "know" other people, even within the family. Ali pictures Valja pregnant, in jeans and a turtleneck sweater, and hopes to recall the sensation, from inside the womb, of the mother-to-be's shallow breathing. "Aber das kann ich heute nicht wissen" (but I can't know that today; AS, 86), Ali concedes, and can only conclude, in relation to this episode and others from Valja's life: "ich kann mich an nichts festhalten, ich weiß, das wurde mir erzählt, aber anders." (I can't be sure of anything, I know, that was told to me, but differently; AS, 86.) Once again in a Jewish family novel, parents and children are unable to connect across their different historical experiences, and the past is a burden. Later, this distance is dramatically emphasized, as Ali seems to depict the actual conversation with Valja that underpins their understanding of the mother's past—this is Valja's original narration of her own life, "aber anders" (but differently). As Valja relates her childhood, unhappy marriage, and divorce, therefore, Ali appears to float in the air, as if in a dissociative state, and hovers above observing their own corporeal self and their mother in discussion (*AS*, 257–75). There is a gulf between them, it seems. Ali can narrate family history, or rather a version of what has been told to them, but this may not help them to move forward.

Just as Ali cannot comprehend Valja's experience of Soviet drudgery, domestic violence, and migration, so is Valja unable to grasp Ali's transition. Throughout the novel, Valja consistently fails, or refuses to acknowledge, Ali's physical transformation as a result of taking testosterone—neither the child's desire to dress as a boy and have short hair (*AS*, 90–91), nor the adult's preference for men's clothes (*AS*, 94–95), deepening voice (*AS*, 343), facial hair (*AS*, 261), and changes in physiognomy (*AS*, 90). During their conversation, however, Ali's "I" leaves their own body, becomes external to the self—*Außer sich*/besides oneself—and finds some comfort in this psychological detachment (*AS*, 263). This is an "andere Perspektive" (another perspective) that permits a novel view of the room they are sitting in but most likely also of their different histories, their relationship, and Ali's self-understanding (*AS*, 265). Ali begins to picture a different body and a different, longed-for self—that is, to become an "Er" (he). There is a great deal that still does not make sense, and Ali cannot yet imagine the self as a coherent "I," or, in Russian, an Я (*AS*, 274). But there is hope in reimagining the past and the people who inhabit it *differently*: "Ich erdenke mir neue Personen, wie ich mir alte zusammensetze." (I imagine new people, just like I piece together previous people; *AS*, 275.) And there is hope in waiting for things to be different, "Denn was ist warten sonst als eine Hoffnung." (For what is waiting other than hope; *AS*, 275.)

This "andere Perspektive" is implicit throughout Ali's narration, as they describe, deconstruct, and finally *queer* nation and gender. Russianness, then, is linked to normative expressions of heterosexual femininity and masculinity, for example in the Soviet films from which Valja learns how to be in love and even how to kiss (*AS*, 59) and in her first husband's drinking habits: "Wenn er nicht trinkt und heult, ist er entweder eine Schwuchtel oder ein Jid." (If he is not drinking or sobbing, he's either a gay or a Yid; *AS*, 61.) Valja is pushed and pulled by Kostja's mother, her mother-in-law, when trying on her wedding dress—her body is insufficiently appealing, it seems (*AS*, 75). Ali, in turn, is scolded as a "Lesbe" (lesbian) by aunts for failing to behave as a girl (*AS*, 36–37), and by Valja on account of her short hair (*AS*, 91; 116). When Ali presents their passport at the Turkish border, the official struggles to match the photo to the person standing in front of him, on account of the transformation in Ali's physical appearance (*AS*, 15). Gender identity and national belonging are intimately linked—and policed. And the same is true of ethnic identity, sexual orientation, and national belonging. Ali's paternal grandmother was taunted in her village—"Schau die Judensau, wie sie läuft, wie eine Schwuchtel" (look at the Jewish pig, how she walks, like a gay; *AS*, 66)—and Kostja, in Germany, hopes to show that he is properly Russian (and not a Jew) by mocking his friend Wowtschik's "Schwuchtelmusik" (gay music; *AS*, 239). Toward the end of the novel, as Ali narrates as Anton, Anton returns to Russia and is beaten up by childhood friends as, once again, a "Judensau und Schwuchtel" (Jewish pig and a gay; *AS*, 283). As the American scholar Sander Gilman argues, in nationalist discourses being Jewish has long been associated with being sexually deviant and therefore incapable of "belonging."[17]

Ali's great-grandparents', grandparents', and parents' repression of their proclivity to act, sing, or write poetry—their erasure of their Jewish otherness for the sake of becoming "properly" Russian—contrasts with the exuberantly gender-bending performances that Ali encounters in Istanbul, including the Russian trans man called Katho; the half Romanian, half-Hungarian Aglaja, who dresses as a male clown; and the drag artist Verka Serduchka (the invention of comedian, actor, and singer Andriy Mykhailovych Danylko, who represented Ukraine at the 2007 Eurovision finals). At the same time, these performances also prompt Ali to *imagine* the queerness that once was, in their Russian Jewish family too. Ali pictures how they might stand with Katho on the banks of the Bosporus and conjure up "Vorfahren, die so waren wie sie" (ancestors who were like them):

> Onkel mit rasierten Beinen, die nachts ihre Bäuche in Corsagen und Kleider zwängten, Tanten mit Wasserwelle und schwarzem Lippenstift, die in Anzügen durch die Straßen spazierten. Keine dieser Geschichten hatte je ihren Weg in die Erzählungen von Familie gefunden, aber es musste sie doch gegeben haben, also was war falsch daran, sie sich zu erdenken?
>
> [Uncles with shaved legs, who at night squeezed their stomachs into bodices and dresses, aunts with fingerwave haircuts and black lipstick, who walked the streets in suits. None of these stories had ever found their way into family legend, but they must have existed, so what was wrong with inventing them? *AS*, 135–36]

These queer Jewish stories have been repressed. Yet traces, hints, intimations of them may persist in the accounts that Ali does receive through the generations. Kostja, for example, continues to sing despite his father's injunction that performance is "too Jewish." Elsewhere, there may be a suggestion of homoerotic attraction in the boxing training that Ali's maternal grandfather Danıil undertakes with a friend at university. His

---

17 See Gilman, *The Jew's Body*.

boxing partner, a middleweight to his lightweight, beats him to a pulp but they continue to spar, go drinking, and confide in one another for three years: "Sie erzählten sich Dinge, die sie niemandem sonst erzählten." (They told each other things that they told no one else; *AS*, 198.) More obviously, Kostja more than once ends up in an intimate drunken embrace with his best friend Wowa, including after they have been listening to the cross-dressing artist Verka Serduchka (*AS*, 238–39).

As so often in recent German Jewish writing, it is a third-generation narrator's relationship with *grandparents* that initiates and even structures a rearticulation of identity. Indeed, for all that it innovates new themes and even ways of narrating, Salzmann's *Außer sich* is still recognizably part of a canon that also includes, say, Trzebiner's *Die Enkelin* and Funk's *Winternähe*. It is through their extensive renarration of the childhood wartime experiences of Emma and Daniil, and of how they migrated to Germany many decades later, that Ali is able to imagine a connection across the generations, therefore, and a familial intimacy within which queerness, long repressed for the sake of "integration," can once again be recognized, acknowledged, and even loved. (The norm-enforcing authority of parents is skipped over.) This re-queering of Jewish family history is rooted in the shared experience of trauma—albeit trauma of very different kinds—and, as we shall see, it is the basis for Ali's solidarity with national, sexual, ethnic, and political minorities in Istanbul. As discussed below, this involves another form of queering, that is, of the narrative's chronology.

Death is ever-present in the story that Ali narrates about her grandparents, drawing on what they tell her of their lives during and after the war. (At the start of their account of Emma and Daniil, Ali is still a "she.") Emma—the daughter of Schura and Etinka—almost died as a newborn (*AS*, 162–63); her maternal grandfather was wounded after he threw himself on her to protect her from a bullet fired by invading German troops; and she nearly died during a citywide food-poisoning scandal for which Schura, a senior doctor and public health official, would have been executed if he had not already been dismissed during the anti-Jewish purge that followed Stalin's death (*AS*, 170). Emma, it is suggested, was "von Anfang an dem Tod geweiht" (destined for death from the beginning; *AS*, 175). Of course, this predestination for death is true in a more general sense. Emma was a Jewish child, born during the German invasion and who grew up in the Soviet Union during the vicious antisemitism of the 1950s. In Daniil's story, references to the Holocaust—and to fortuitous survival—are more explicit. An aunt, Astra, married a German in 1932 and then emigrated to Kazakhstan, bringing her parents in 1940/41. In this way, she "verhinderte das Bekannte" (prevented what is known): "Und so lebte wohl dieser Zweig der Familie glücklich fern der Schrecken der Schoah." (And so this branch of the family probably lived happily far removed from the horrors of the Shoah; *AS*, 185–86.) On his mother's side of the family, all of Daniil's aunts and uncles—Orthodox Jews in Bucharest—made it to Palestine and were spared the war and the subsequent postwar communist dictatorship: "Alle wurden vom Krieg verschont und von der Partei. Clara nicht." (All were spared the war and the Party, except Clara; *AS*, 186.) Daniil's mother Clara, in fact, is rescued from the Germans by Communist Party colleagues sent by her husband Boris but later endures Soviet repression. Daniil too suffers discrimination at the hands of the Soviet authorities, who deny a school diploma to someone with the surname Pinkenzon and refuse to admit him to university in Lviv or Moscow (*AS*, 194–95). (He eventually resumes the Jewish faith that his father had abandoned for communism, and in old age he emigrates to Germany, of all places; *AS*, 184–85.) Finally, and making clear that the Holocaust killed Soviet Jews too, there is the story of Musja Pinkenzon, Daniil's second cousin, who was shot by an SS officer when Jews were being assembled for deportation. Apparently—so Daniil's father Boris claimed—the boy had played the *Internationale* on his violin whereupon the German emptied a magazine of ammunition into his body (*AS*, 194). It is likely that the heroic aspect of this account is apocryphal, of course, reflecting Boris's own unthinking commitment to the Party.

This narration and re-narration of trauma generates empathy across the generations, it seems, rooted in a common, though very different experience of precarious existence. Indeed, the grandparent's willingness to reach out and speak of themselves creates an opportunity and even an obligation for Ali to reveal who they are and to become knowable. Emma and Daniil have been so far ignorant of Ali's life—"und das war meine Schuld" (and that was my fault; *AS*, 209)—but now things have changed:

> Aber ab jetzt war es anders. Diese distanzierten, höflichen Menschen, mit den breiten, offenen Gesichtern [...] hatten etwas von sich preisgegeben, hatten mir Pfade gelegt und saßen nun nackt vor mir, während ich mich fühlte, als würde ich mich verstecken hinter dem, was sie glaubten von mir zu wissen.
>
> [From now, though, it was different. These distant, polite people, with their broad open faces [...] had shown something of themselves, had laid down a path for me and were now sitting naked before me, while I felt as if I were still hiding behind what they thought they knew about me. *AS*, 209]

In telling their story, the grandparents become vulnerable—"nackt"—but also show Ali the way toward self-actualization. Ali has returned from Istanbul with a changed appearance, however Emma and Daniil show care in welcoming their grandchild as "etwas Bekanntes" (something known; *AS*, 209). Still unused to speaking in the first person and knowing that they cannot demand that Emma and Daniil fully understand the transformation that they have begun, the novel's protagonist now sets out to tell the story of "Ali [. . .] und wie sie zu Anton wurde" (Ali [. . .] and how she became Anton; *AS*, 210). Ali hopes that Emma and Daniil might hug them, or just look at them: "das wäre schon viel." (That would be a lot; *AS*, 210.)

To the extent that Ali's queering—or re-queering—of Jewish identity comes *after* their return from Istanbul, it can be thought to depend on the solidarity they have experienced in the Turkish city. In this understanding of Ali's narrative, correspondingly, the affection, mutual support, and even love Ali develops with transsexuals, ethnic minorities, and political protesters instills the confidence to be open to narrating their transition for their grandparents and to belonging to their Jewish family once again. Yet the two narratives in fact interweave throughout the novel and often even mirror each other. Indeed, it is surely just as possible that the "relational subjectivity" that Bühler-Dietrich identifies in Ali's interactions in Istanbul—including the "ambiguous and emergent identities and belongings" (Roca Lizarazu)[18]; the "alternative we, an alliance of outsiders" (Balling),[19] and the "alternative ontologies beyond the binary" (Albé)[20]—is itself preceded by the openness to the world that, Ali's account suggests, characterized Jewishness before it was made to be "straight." In a nutshell, Ali's experience in Istanbul prompts them to re-queer Jewish family history, but this is only possible because traces of that queerness still remain—and these traces, it can be speculated, are what positioned Ali as able to respond to cosmopolitan encounter in the first place.

Newly arrived in Istanbul, Ali meets Katho in a club, and they strike up a conversation, connected by the Russian language, and perhaps even by nostalgia for shared cultural references and places (*AS*, 50). (Katho's nickname Katüscha recalls a Soviet-era song celebrating victory in the Great Patriotic War and a multiple launch rocket system; *AS*, 40.) This familiarity, rooted in national belonging, is challenged, however, by the sex they have together. Initially, gender conformity is confirmed by Ali's gaze upon Katho's body, which is clearly marked as female. (In this moment, Katho is referred to as Katharina.) Then Katho confesses that she is not a she but rather a he (*AS*, 45–46). Unsure how to respond, Ali goes into the bathroom, avoiding Katho's kiss, and tries to reflect on what this revelation means. Her skin itches—here, Ali has female pronouns—as

---

18 See Roca Lizarazu, "'Integration.'" See also Roca Lizarazu, "Ec-static Existences."
19 See Balling, "Intimate Associations."
20 See Albé, "Becoming Queer."

she tries to negotiate the tension between her desire for female bodies and what Katho has revealed about his actual identity. The next day, they walk to the park and Katho tells Ali about the hormones he is taking, and how the beard he is growing will soon disqualify him from his job as a female dancer (*AS*, 49). Later, Ali assists Katho with injecting testosterone while listening to—and re-narrating—the story he tells about his Ukrainian childhood, his father, prostituting himself, taking part in a political protest at which Aglaja is injured (more of this character shortly), and encountering Anton (though he is not named) (*AS*, 125–36). Katho also appears elsewhere in the text, as Aglaja's lover, the victim of an assault (*AS*, 231), and an increasing irritation to Ali as their relationship becomes ever more transactional (*AS*, 244–51). Ali imagines their wedding—with dead and living relatives present—and settling into bourgeois conformity (*AS*, 350), but this fantasy—or parody—is shattered when Katho steals Ali's passport (*AS*, 261).

Notwithstanding this betrayal, Ali learns to be open to Katho's experience. At the same time, Katho also impacts on Ali, by re-narrating Ali's life, as it were. After Katho relates his story, he then asks about Ali's life. Ali surmises how their great-grandparents might have met in Odessa, and then pictures Ali and Katho—in the present day—flicking through black and white photographs of this past. This is the moment when Ali first imagines a queer Russian Jewish genealogy, within this album of family photos, including uncles with shaved legs and aunts with fingerwave haircuts and black lipstick (*AS*, 136; already cited). Ali walks to the Bosporus, imagines Odessa across the Black Sea, thinks back to Schura's "Mappe" (folder) and begins to re-narrate—and then queer—Russian Jewish family history (*AS*, 140–42). Later, Ali starts to take testosterone and to undergo their own transition.

Ali's openness to queerness in Istanbul, queering of Russian Jewish family history, and transition, are facilitated by two further characters. The first is uncle Cemal, who is not an actual uncle but the relative of a friend from Berlin, Elyas. (There are a number of real uncles, including the uncle who sexually abuses Kostja and Valja's uncle Mischa, whom Ali seems to have been close to; *AS*, 92–93. Many characters also talk about their fathers, including Cemal; *AS*, 22.) In this way, the novel presents— and challenges—different models of masculinity. Cemal is a lawyer who defends dissidents against the Turkish state, including one of the founding members of the militant Kurdish Workers Party, Abdullah Öcalan, and Cemal had also spent eight months in prison (*AS*, 20–22). From that time onwards, his mother has refused to speak to him. Her piety—including now wearing a veil—reflects the growing divide in Turkish society between Islamization and secularism (*AS*, 21–22). Cemal looks after Ali when they faint on arrival at the airport (*AS*, 17), offers comfort following Valja's rejection (*AS*, 344), and supports Ali's transition into Anton

(*AS*, 265). These gestures of kindness toward a person who arrived as a stranger suggest a different model of family and, ultimately, solidarity, based on empathy and care for others rather than bloodlines.

The second character is Aglaja. Described as a mermaid in the dramatis personae that stands at the front of the novel, Aglaja is also an accordion-playing clown who features in both Ali's and Anton's narrative. She sleeps with Ali, Anton, and also with Katho, whom she helps with his transition (*AS*, 127). Above all, Aglaja connects the personal and the political, that is, the underground clubs that Ali frequents and the anti-regime demonstrations that are taking place across Istanbul. In an episode that is related by Ali (*AS*, 131–33) and then again by Ali-as-Anton, Aglaja is struck by a canister fired by security forces, containing tear gas, as they clear Taksim Gezi Park. She is injured, rescued—apparently by Anton (*AS*, 317–19)—and becomes the face of the resistance movement to President Erdoğan's government (*AS*, 317). Born in a circus, traveling the world without a home of her own, exploited as a child, abused and then abandoned by her father, an epileptic, and a foreigner (*AS*, 322–30), Aglaja embodies disadvantage, marginalization, and otherness itself, as well as political mobilization in solidarity with the oppressed. Her story, in fact, echoes elements of Ali's family narrative, including incidental details such as looking after relatives suffering from diabetes (*AS*, 66, 240; 326), and her quintessential displacement may even function as a cipher for Jewishness.

Thus far, the focus has been on Ali's retelling of the lives of great-grandparents, grandparents, and parents and on the protagonist's account of their experience of solidarity with transvestites, transexuals, and protesters in Istanbul. In essence, the argument is that Ali's re-queering of Russian Jewish genealogies as *worldly*—as unbounded by arbitrary categories of nation, sexual identity, and ethnicity—is motivated by, but perhaps also predicts, the emancipatory potential identified by Bühler-Dietrich, Roca Lizarazu, Balling, Albé, and others, and that Ali's re-narration of Jewish family history and of the start of their transition are therefore inextricably intertwined, for all that this initially appears unlikely.

The third strand of Ali's narrative, however, generally overlooked by scholars, introduces a more dissonant tone. Indeed, the story of Ali's brother Anton, and of how Ali *becomes* Anton, is a story of abuse, incest, and Ali-become-Anton's internalization of patterns of male violence and the denigration of those perceived as less "white." Even as *Außer sich* articulates a progressive vision of a re-queered Jewish worldliness, therefore, it also cautions against the presumption that long-established prejudices and assertions of relative privilege will simply fall away. As discussed below, this is an important nuance to Salzmann's own real-life engagement as an author-activist—along with the poet and polemicist Max Czollek—in advocating for solidarity across ethnic and sexual minorities.

Anton's story is designated as Part Two ("Zwei") of the novel and is ostensibly narrated by Ali's twin or by Ali-become-Anton. This narrative strand is framed at its start by Ali's confession of a propensity to fabulate: "Ich erdenke mir neue Personen, wie ich mir alte zusammensetze" (I imagine new people, just like I piece together previous people; *AS*, 275, as previously cited), and at its end by a more explicit admission that there is an element of invention in Ali's—or Ali/Anton's—depiction of Anton's activities after he lands in Istanbul: "so wie ich mir Antons Leben zusammengedacht hatte." (Just as I conjured up Anton's life; *AS*, 364.) At the same time, the story of Anton builds upon details about his childhood and migration to Germany as an adolescent already revealed earlier in the novel. The reader already knows, for example, that Anton once wore a dress of Ali's (*AS*, 36), that he taught her to read aged three (*AS*, 99), and that they were inseparable (*AS*, 99). Following the family's resettlement in Germany—described in an episode that echoes other Russian Jewish "arrival narratives" (Biendarra)[21]—Anton and Ali live for a time in an asylum-seekers' hostel. Anton takes up skateboarding, the twins suffer bullying at school, and, significantly, it is Anton who declares to their tormentors that he is not a Russian but a Jew: "Ich bin Jude." (I am a Jew; *AS*, 106.) After Ali and Anton are beaten up by their German classmates, there is a first hint of incest, as if their scandalous intimacy is motivated by discrimination and exclusion: "Ihre Münder standen offen. Erst als Anton Ali küsste, fing sie an zu weinen." (Their mouths gaped open. Once Anton kissed Ali she began to cry; *AS*, 107.) They examine each other's changing bodies in bed together and wear each other's clothes; Ali is jealous when Anton kisses his first girlfriend; and Anton strikes their father to defend his sister (*AS*, 122–24). The suggestion that the hostility of others provokes an incest-like codependency among immigrant Jews is also present in Kaufmann's *Superposition*, notably in Izy's relationship with Timur.

The consummation as adults of the twin's incestuous relationship is what drives Anton to flee to Istanbul, from where he sends the postcard—without any information about his precise whereabouts—that causes Ali to follow and try to find him (*AS*, 23; 87). (In a mirroring of narrative strands that is typical of the text, it is an allusive memory of their sex that prompts Ali, once in Istanbul, to return to Russia and Germany in order to queer Russian Jewish family history; *AS*, 139–42.) In Part Two, Anton describes how they kissed, how he discovered his sister's bandaged breasts—her transition was just beginning—how Ali penetrated his anus with her finger, how they fellated one another, and how she orgasmed (*AS*, 300–302). Following their sex as siblings, as twins, and even (in Ali's mind) as the same person, Anton craves genuine otherness, that is, to experience what it is like to be in the world. "'Ich habe

---

21 See Biendarra, "Cultural Dichotomies."

meine Sachen gepackt,'" he says: "'und wollte irgendwohin, ich glaube, ich wollte sehen, wie weit ich komme.'" (I packed my things and wanted to go somewhere, anywhere, I think I wanted to see how far I could get; *AS*, 303.) It is as if the twins' distinctly unworldly love pushes Anton to seek difference beyond the introversion—particularism—of his Russian Jewish family: "'Ich wollte irgendwo sein, wo ich nichts wusste und nichts verstand und die Sprache nicht konnte und die paar Freunde, die meine Sprache sprechen, würden still sein. Das Geld reichte bis Istanbul.'" (I wanted to be somewhere where I knew nothing and understood nothing and wasn't able to speak the language and the few friends who spoke my language would be quiet. The money got me as far as Istanbul; *AS*, 303.)

Following his arrival in Istanbul, Anton moves into a squat with Barış, whose father is a high-ranking officer in the Turkish army and who has run away from home (*AS*, 291–22), and he hangs out with the young men who congregate in front of the synagogue, and with sex workers (*AS*, 293–95). Later, he sleeps with Mervan, whose father canceled his German passport while he was attending a family wedding in Istanbul, leaving him as a reluctant Turk but "eigentlich Armenier" (actually an Armenian; *AS*, 334), and befriends Nour, a refugee from the civil war in Syria who resists arrest for theft because he fears a repeat of the torture he endured in his home country, and is deported (*AS*, 334–36). And he grows close to Aglaja, whom he rescued when she was struck by the gas canister at Taksim Gezi Park (*AS*, 317–19). Anton and Aglaja become lovers and he enters her world of queers, transvestites, and transsexuals, including Katho (*AS*, 330–31). Katho/Katharina/Katüscha, of course, is familiar to the reader from earlier in the novel, though as Ali's love interest. Anton's account of his time in Turkey, in fact, is the mirror of Ali's, or perhaps more accurately an alternative narration of Ali's experience as Anton. Just arrived in Istanbul, Ali is taken to a local theater by a friend of Cemal's, glimpses her (pre-transition) reflection in a chandelier, and then imagines Anton sitting next to her, smiling at her "in exakter Spiegelung zurück" (in an exact reflection; *AS*, 35). Later, in a club with Katho, she sees Anton's face in the mirror above the bar and believes it is hers: "Sah sie Antons Gesicht, das ihr Gesicht war." (She saw Anton's face, that was her face; *AS*, 226.) Anton too catches sight of his twin walking in the street (*AS*, 296), and—mirroring Ali's narration of the same episode—he imagines that he sees her at the protest at which Aglaja is injured. Anton, however, cannot confront their intimacy and so he flees (*AS*, 320–21). This fracturing of their oneness may have been predicted, in truth, in the earlier episode in the theater. A piece of crystal falls from the chandelier in which their faces appeared to be reflected side by side but also "verzerrt" (distorted; *AS*, 35).

Anton seems to embody the self-actualization that is denied to Ali, at least before his sister completes her transition into a "he": "Stelle mir das

Leben meines Bruders vor, stelle mir vor, er würde all das tun, wozu ich nicht in der Lage gewesen bin, sehe ich ihn als einen, der hinauszieht in die Welt, weil er den Mut besitzt, der mir immer gefehlt hat." (I imagine my brother's life, he would do everything that I am not in the position to do, I see him as someone who sets off out into the world, because he has the courage that I have always lacked; *AS*, 275.) Anton travels, has sex with men and women, and engages with otherness. Anton's Jewishness is not foregrounded in his Istanbul narrative, but the reader will likely remember his assertion as a newly arrived migrant in Germany: "Ich bin Jude" (I am a Jew; *AS*, 106) and surmise that this marginalized identity underpins his embrace of the ethnic and sexual minorities that he encounters in Turkey. Certainly, Anton's queerness—Jewish or not—predisposes him to live among the dispossessed, the marginalized, and the persecuted, and to engage in acts of solidarity with the young people protesting against the Turkish state. Wrapping a shawl around his face, he runs into a fog of tear gas fired by the massed ranks of police and is appalled that his current lover, İlay, fails to stand by his side (*AS*, 314–16).

Yet almost as soon as Ali begins to take testosterone, they wonder whether to *become* Anton inevitably means to adopt male privilege. It is not the change in voice and appearance or even the pain of the injections that is concerning for Ali, but the possibility "dass ich jetzt, wo ich ein Sohn war, werden würde wie mein Vater." (That, as a son, I would now become like my father; *AS*, 236.) Kostja was a wife beater, just like Valja's first husband, the Russian antisemite Ivan. Other instances of male violence include Kostja's own father, who regularly hit Kostja's mother (*AS*, 81); Valja's grandfather, who beat her grandmother Etinka (*AS*, 64); the schoolboys who assaulted Ali and Anton (*AS*, 106); Daniil's brutal, homoerotic sparring with his university friend (*AS*, 198); an attack on the trans man Katho (*AS*, 231); and the man who thrashed Anton when he intervened to stop him grabbing Aglaja's bottom (*AS*, 336). It is perhaps no surprise, therefore, that Ali-as-Anton also lashes out at Aglaja after they become lovers. Male violence mirrors state violence. Following his friend Nour's brutal deportation by the authorities, Anton finds that he can no longer tolerate Aglaja's sex with other men. He desires to marry her, to "regularize" their relationship, and is offended when she assumes his proposal is intended to facilitate her emigration to the West (*AS*, 337–40). As significant, his assault follows his retelling of his story (*AS*, 340). Anton, it seems, needs a woman to suffer in order to assuage his tale of failed masculinity, just like the men in his family before him.

Anton's privilege is not only male privilege, however. His desire to go out into the world—to become worldly—is realized not through making himself authentically known to others but through deception and even mimicry. He fakes interest in Barış's lamentations about his father in order to secure a place in the squat (AS, 291–92); he pretends to flirt with the men who come on to him in bars while stealing their wallets (*AS*, 303); and he plays the part of "exotic Turk" for an elderly German visitor whom he pleasures and then robs (*AS*, 306). Subsequently, he polishes tourists' shoes while narrating—fabricating—family life in his impoverished village in rural Turkey (*AS*, 307). He also allows himself to be picked up by İlay, a greying, middle-aged, bourgeois artist in denial about his sexuality, and mixes the roles of lover and male escort during a short vacation to the Aegean Sea (*AS*, 308–16). In effect, Anton abrogates to himself the experiences and stories of others, including the most marginalized groups. Moreover, even though he is a migrant, a queer, and a Jew, Anton can "pass as white." He cites a Russian proverb that his mother used to say to him when he was a child: "Ich wollte mir wie ein Weißer vorkommen" (I wanted to appear to myself as a white man), alluding to being in a position to enjoy luxury and social status but also, most likely, to concealing the family's Jewish origins. Now—in the world—Anton is finally able to actually "be white":[22] "Und hier war ich. Ich war raus, ich war weit weg [. . .] und trug ein weißes Hemd." (And here I was. I was out, I was far away and wearing a white shirt.) He frequents the hotel terrace in the evenings and gazes over the Bosporus, the famous Blue Mosque, and the city's slums, just like a rich Western tourist. This is where he picks up the elderly German man, although his earnings are taken off him by the barman, who tells him to beat it (*AS*, 305–6). For all that he lives among the dispossessed and the displaced, Anton is not the same as them. For this reason, his mimicry seems opportunistic, even exploitative.

Paradoxically, Ali's fabulation of how they became Anton may be the most concrete of the stories they tell in *Außer sich*. On the one hand, then, Ali's juxtaposition of Jewish family history with sexual and ethnic otherness in Istanbul presents a re-queered Jewish solidarity as a vision for the future, but this remains, for the time being, an abstraction. On the other hand, Ali-as-Anton's story suggests, albeit indirectly, the actually existing structural and ideological barriers to creating alliances between minorities, including in Germany. It might even be argued that a concern with Russian-speaking Jews' relative privilege today—quite different to the direct danger great-grandparents, grandparents, and parents endured during the Nazi and Soviet periods—is what constitutes the underlying coherence of Ali's narration. Like other recent novels by Soviet-born writers, therefore, *Außer sich* relates the experience of arrival, hostile German bureaucracy, prejudice, and first steps toward becoming established—in a reportage of more than ten pages, in fact (*AS*, 100–111). Yet Ali and Anton are (now) *German*, and they are *white*. Ali uses a German passport

---

22   There is a discussion, of course, of whether Jews are "white." See Gilman, "The Jewish Nose."

to enter Turkey (*AS*, 15) and is angry when Katho steals it (*AS*, 261), and Anton considers selling his (*AS*, 307).

Here, and by way of concluding our reading of Salzmann's extraordinarily complex and multivalent novel, it is worth mentioning one final character, whose interactions with Ali perhaps provide the most likely model for how solidarity between Soviet-born Jews and other minorities *can* work, in Germany, in the present day, and founded on a kind of queerness that is perhaps less performed and thereby more authentically radical than what Ali experiences in Istanbul. The son of Turkish migrants who arrived in West Germany as guest workers in the 1960s, Elyas exists at the margins of each of Ali's narratives (and of German society more broadly) and yet is also somehow foundational to all of them—Elyas introduces Ali to uncle Cemal in Istanbul, and thus ensures that Ali will be cared for; he accompanies Ali through their renarration of Jewish family history; and, crucially, he phones Ali in the final pages of the novel, as military helicopters swoop low during the coup of 2016, and directs his friend to safety. Ali thanks Elyas for his love over the years (*AS*, 357–58) and returns to Cemal's apartment. Cemal embraces his adopted niece-nephew and, in the closing lines, offers tea—çay, a traditional Turkish drink associated with hospitality toward strangers (*AS*, 365).[23]

At the beginning of the novel, Ali reports that Ali and Elyas grew up together, as it were—or rather *grew together*, that is, approached one another without necessarily becoming one: "So was wie aufgewachsen [. . .] oder eher zusammengewachsen" (grew up together, as it were, or rather grew together; *AS*, 17). Ali, in fact, is a "she" when they first meet at a party in Berlin. They are both appalled by the parody of queerness in the other guests' neon tops, pink muscle shorts, powdered hair, and glittery lips (*AS* 211), but are also unable to grasp the affinity they feel. It cannot be sexual desire, as their needs are so "unterschiedlich" (different; *AS*, 213)—he is a gay Turkish man, she is a Russian Jewish pre-transition transexual who sleeps with women. Shortly afterwards, however, they move in together, occasionally have sex, but are not a couple (*AS*, 214–16). A few months later, Ali departs for Istanbul.

What Ali and Elyas develop is an ethics of mutual care that acknowledges the differences that persist, even as they draw near to one another. Each remains authentically queer in their own particular way, unlike the *performances* they witness at the party in Berlin and, it might be inferred, that Ali observes in Istanbul. Nor does their intimacy, including their periodic sex, imply possession, or the subsuming of one into the other. Again, this is not the case for Ali's relationship with Katho in Istanbul and

---

23 Çay is listed by UNESCO as a part of Turkey's (and Azerbaijan's) intangible heritage. See: https://ich.unesco.org/en/RL/culture-of-ay-tea-a-symbol-of-identity-hospitality-and-social-interaction-01685. Last accessed July 25, 2024.

it is the absolute opposite of Ali's incestuous merging with Anton, which in any case ends up with Ali/Anton's reproduction of white male privilege. Elyas struggles to accept Ali's transition and seeks to return them from Turkey to Germany (*AS*, 222–25) but he nonetheless remains supportive throughout and, as already described, phones to lead Ali to safety at the moment when help is most needed.

Even before Ali travels to Istanbul, and even before they renarrate Jewish family history (or whichever comes first), therefore, it seems that Ali *already* lives an authentically queer, or re-queered, Jewish solidarity, in alliance with their gay, Muslim friend Elyas. This is Jewish worldliness as *praxis*—rather than as something to be theorized—involving the careful negotiation of difference and concrete interventions in social, political, and cultural discourses. This, of course, is precisely what the novel's author Sasha Marianna Salzmann exemplifies in their work at the Maxim Gorki Theater, as artistic director and then writer in residence, working primarily with playwrights with a migration background,[24] and their collaboration with Max Czollek on building coalitions across ethnic and sexual minorities to challenge concepts of integration and "majority culture."[25] The same emphasis on *action* with and in support of others typifies Salzmann's essays and interviews since the Russian full-scale invasion of Ukraine in early 2022 and, as will be discussed in the conclusion, following the Hamas attacks of October 7, 2023, and Israel's response. In summary, Ali perhaps never needed to renarrate family history and never needed to travel to Istanbul. At least some Jews in Germany, it can be argued, are already living a version of Jewish identity that insists on its fundamental—original—*queerness* as a metaphor for universalism and global solidarity.

A Non-Jewish Jewish Worldliness?: Olga Grjasnowa's *Der verlorene Sohn*

Of course, another possible implication of the suggestion that there was perhaps no need for Ali to re-queer Jewish genealogy—and no need to go to Istanbul to become open to their own and others' otherness—might be that the pragmatic solidarity they practice in Germany does not actually require Jewishness in the first place. Or, to frame it differently, if Jewishness is a metaphor for universalism, then might it eventually transcend itself, revealing its traces only through *citation*? In a note at the end of the novel, Salzmann claims that its title is taken from the literary magazine *freitext* and adds that this borrowing corresponds to the Jewish tradition of passing down names through the generations. (Salzmann

---

24 See Landry, "Rethinking Migration."
25 See Roca Lizarazu, "'Integration.'"

co-edited *freitext* for twelve years.) Here, Jewish motifs may function as prompts rather than as fundamental markers of identity.

In an interview with *Der Standard* in early 2022, Salzmann's fellow Soviet-born author Katja Petrowskaja is even more explicit about the relatively indirect influence in her work of Jewish faith, thought, and culture:

> "Meine Texte stellen vielleicht einen Versuch dar, mithilfe der Erinnerung etwas zu 'reparieren.' Es gibt diese jüdische Idee von 'Tikkun Olam,' von einer Reparatur der Welt. Ich weiß nicht viel über das Jüdische, aber das sagt mir etwas."[26]

> (My texts may represent an attempt to "repair" something with the help of memory. There is this Jewish idea of "Tikkun Olam," of a repair of the world. I don't know much about Jewish things, but that speaks to me.)

Jewishness, understood in this way, may be little more than an injunction to engage in solidarity with others and to do good in the world. In *Vielleicht Esther*, the narrator struggles to balance Jewish particularism with Jewish universalism. In Petrowskaja's recent public positions, it seems—including in this interview in response to the wave of refugees arriving from her native Ukraine after the Russian invasion—the author frames Jewishness more decisively as a moral imperative requiring little if any actual Jewish content.

We return, then, to historian and prominent Jewish voice Michael Wolffsohn's prognosis of "a community of Jews without Judaism."[27] In chapter 2, it was argued that a Jewish sensibility—even a Jewish *worldliness*—might exist despite the absence of religious faith, *halachic* credentials, or a deep connection to Jewish culture. For non-believing Jews or Jews with "only" a Jewish father or a single Jewish grandparent, seemingly, Holocaust memory can underwrite a principled and universalistic solidarity in the present day. In this chapter, the focus has been on Jewish self-positioning *beyond* Holocaust memory, and on contrasting articulations of Jewish worldliness emerging from a less emphatic fixation on that particularly Jewish historical trauma—Channah's embrace of popular culture and Ali's allusions to Jewish queerness as a generalized metaphor for marginalization, persecution, and solidarity with others. Finally, we turn to Olga Grjasnowa's 2020 novel *Der verlorene Sohn* to explore what happens when a text's Jewishness is so diffuse—beyond faith, *halachic* debates, *and* any direct thematization of Holocaust memory and family trauma—that it is not clear whether it is Jewish at all. Grjasnowa's account of the

---

26 Petrowskaja, "'Wie sonst möchten Sie Putin aufhalten?'"
27 Michael Wolffsohn, "Jews in Divided Germany," 28.

Russian conquest of the North Caucasus in the mid-nineteenth century and the taking-hostage of a Muslim prince may exemplify a "non-Jewish Jewish worldliness." As will be discussed, this term draws on Polish-born philosopher's Isaac Deutscher's typology of the "non-Jewish Jew."

From Grjasnowa's début novel *Der Russe ist einer, der Birken liebt* (All Russians love birch trees; 2012), to *Die juristische Unschärfe einer Ehe* (The legal haziness of a marriage; 2014) to *Gott ist nicht schüchtern* (God is not shy; 2017), her third, it is possible to discern an increasing sublimation of overtly Jewish themes—the Holocaust, Israel/Palestine, and Jewish identity—into a universalistic concern with human rights, specifically the rights of people fleeing conflict and persecution. Jewish characters, correspondingly, become ever less central and, in *Gott*, they disappear entirely, as the author turns to the civil war in Syria and the arrival of several million refugees to Europe in 2015. Instead, sporadic but strategically placed citations of the Jewish past and especially the Holocaust remind of where prejudice has led in the past and imply an imperative to intervene today.[28] All three novels, it can be argued, are motivated by a sense of Jewish purpose (Sutcliffe), to communicate the plight of others and to mobilize on their behalf. They also suggest a certain self-effacement, as Jewish identity—and Jewish suffering—frame but do not dominate the discussion.

Grjasnowa's fourth novel appears at first glance to be an unambiguously *Russian* novel, without any immediately obvious references to Jewish history or Jewish identity. In *Der verlorene Sohn*, then, Grjasnowa retells the story of the Muslim warrior and leader Imam Shamil, who in the mid-nineteenth century led resistance to the Russian Empire in the North Caucasus and slowed its conquest of Chechnya and Dagestan by twenty-five years. (The author follows Moshe Gammer's *Muslim Resistance to the Tsar: Shamil and the Conquest of Chechnia and Daghestan*, from 1994, which is acknowledged among the Russian, German, and English sources listed at the end of the novel.)[29] Through stylistic and thematic allusions to well-known works by Pushkin, Lermontov, and Tolstoy, *Der verlorene Sohn* invokes the significance of Shamil for what Rebecca Gould calls the "imaginative history of Russian colonialism,"[30] including Soviet vacillation between lionizing him as an anti-imperialist hero and fearing him as a radical Islamicist[31] and the fraught relationship today between Moscow and the autonomous republics. The novel knowingly replicates the Russian literary tradition's romanticization of the Caucasus and the

---

28 See Taberner, "Possibilities" and "Pragmatic Cosmopolitanism."
29 Gammer, *Muslim Resistance to The Tsar*.
30 Gould, "Imam Shamil," 118.
31 See Gammer, "Shamil in Soviet Historiography" and Creuzberger, "Freedom Fighter."

Muslim "other"—with descriptions of awe-inspiring nature and exotic local customs—while also drawing out the critique of Russian imperialism that is also often at least implicit in the texts it invokes.³² More generally, allusions to Gogol, Dostoevsky, Turgenev, the poet Tyutchev, and Lermontov suggest contemporary but also present-day debates on "Russianness," Russia's European orientation, and universal values.³³

Most immediately, therefore, *Der verlorene Sohn* tells a Russian story, replete with references to Russian history and Russian literature and with parallels between Tsar Nicholas I's expansionist ambitions and President Putin's imperial habitus today. The narrative is prefaced with an epigraph (first in Russian, then translated into German) quoting Viktor Stepanovich Chernomyrdin, Russian prime minister from 1992 to 1998 and one of the architects of the response to the Chechnya insurgency: "Wir wollten immer das Beste, doch es kam wie immer." (We always wanted the best, but it turned out like always.) At the same time, more global issues are also at stake that resonate beyond the Russian context. First, the narrative focus on Shamil's twelve-year-old son, Jamulludin, who is taken hostage by the Tsar's forces and then becomes part of elite society in St. Petersburg, invokes contemporary debates on the potential for Muslim immigrants to integrate. Second, the novel's discreet framing of prejudice against Muslims in terms of Enlightenment discourses on Jewish emancipation intimates the presence of a non-Jewish Jew as storyteller.

On the one hand, Jamulludin's Russian hosts bestow a gracious generosity on the stranger in their midst, assuring his safety, attending to his comfort, and facilitating his entry into society. (It might almost be forgotten that they had been responsible for his uprooting.) Jamulludin's education is provided by Tsar Nicholas, he attends balls, operas, and receptions at the Winter Palace with the progeny of the Russian aristocracy, and he is betrothed to Lisa, sister of his friend Alexej Olenin and the daughter of a former president of the Imperial Academy of Arts and of the Imperial Public Library, and a privy counsellor. On the other hand, however, acceptance is conditional. Jamalludin is admired for his mastery of languages but this means that he must suppress his native Avar.³⁴ Similarly, he is the object of great curiosity and even erotic fascination. The oldest sister of the family that he is placed with on his arrival barely speaks to him but, on his final night in her home, crawls into his bed to lie next to him (*S*, 119). At the academy, a fellow cadet, Dimitri, obsessively strokes his dark hair (*S*, 78–79). Jamalludin is "ein angesehener Gast" (respected

---

32 See Layton, *Russian Literature and Empire*.
33 I am grateful to Dr. Miriam Wray for drawing my attention to these references and their potential meaning as well as to possible links to German Romanticism.
34 Grjasnowa, *Sohn*, 119; 290. Hereafter *S*.

guest) but he knows that he can never truly belong: "Er würde eben niemals zu diesem Land dazugehören. Er war nicht gut genug, nicht russisch genug." (He would never belong in this land. He was not good enough, not Russian enough; S, 161.) At a ball, he dances with the empress, in a display of virtuosity intended to show that "sein Platz genau hier war." (That his place was exactly here; S, 132.) The stranger's need to impress merely confirms his lack of belonging, of course.

Essential for Jamalludin's integration is his gradual abandonment—or at least concealment—of his Islamic faith. When he first encounters Russian soldiers, he is shocked by their copious consumption of alcohol (S, 30). Likewise, he is irritated when he sees a woman with uncovered hair (S, 39), and he is puzzled when he sees a Russian officer gambling: "dass dieser so schamlos seinen Lästern frönte und fern von Gott war." (That he so shamelessly indulged his sins and was so distant from God; S, 45.) Once Jamalludin becomes an officer himself, however, he too devotes himself to "Frauen, Alkohol, dem Kartenspiel und lärmenden Spaziergängen durch die schlafende Hauptstadt." (Women, alcohol, cards, and noisy rampages through the sleeping city; S, 134.) He even visits a brothel with his comrades, although in the midst of his ecstasy he still knows that the prostitute's passion is "eingespielt" (performed; S, 137). Jamalludin is also playing a part, at least to a degree. He still prays, albeit only in his room and never five times a day (S, 94–95), but he will never be fully accepted. On occasion, the anti-Muslim prejudice he endures is obvious, for example when a tutor at the Academy seats him at the back of the class, despite his strong grades (S, 75), or when a young woman at court presses him to accept Jesus (S, 111–12). (He refers her to the Koran.) More often than not, though, the mechanisms of exclusion are more subtle. Jamalludin's betrothal to Lisa is welcomed by her family, well-known liberals who admit the famous anarchist Bakunin into their house (S, 190). Yet it is presumed, or rather expected, that he will allow himself to be baptized (S, 195–96, 205, 222), and Nicholas I imposes a lengthy engagement of two years and posts him to Warsaw (S, 215). Before the wedding can take place, Jamalludin is exchanged for the two Georgian princesses and returns to Dagestan. This is a homeland he barely knows and where, once again, he is destined to be an outsider.

Frequent references to the debates among the Russian ruling class on the abolition of serfdom (S, 152–53), the place of women in society (S, 186), and liberal, revolutionary, and anarchist alternatives to despotism—including Bakunin, Dostoevsky, and Pushkin—confirm the philosophical backdrop for the novel, notably the question of whether and how far Russia should open up to progressive ideas and to the West.[35] Indeed, the novel cites the scientific, philosophical, and literary innovations of the

---

35 See Gordon, "The Russian Enlightenment."

European Enlightenment more generally, for example Humboldt's expeditions in the New World (*S*, 101). Pervading the entire narrative is a distinctly Kantian interest in the nature of reason, political authority, and public discourse.

A significant dimension to the discourse about Enlightenment in Russia—as elsewhere in Europe, including Germany—concerned the emancipation of the Jews. Following the first partition of Poland in 1772 and then the second and third partitions of 1793 and 1795, when far greater numbers of Jews came under the control of the Russian Empire, Jews were permitted to reside only in the Pale of Settlement, that is, modern-day Belarus and Moldova, much of Lithuania, Ukraine and east-central Poland, and parts of Latvia, and western areas of what is now the Russian Federation. Their rights were severely restricted, and even more so by Nicholas I after he came to the throne in 1825.[36] Nicholas, in fact, was widely despised for his forced conscription of young Jewish boys—an episode that features in *Sohn*, as discussed shortly—and for his efforts to bring Jewish education under secular control, that is, to subject it to the interests of the Russian state.[37] At the same time, however, the Tsar's determination to carry out the administrative reform of his empire and disagreements among his advisors may have sowed the seeds for an eventual improvement in conditions for Jews in Russia and across its empire later in the nineteenth century.[38]

Adam Sutcliffe argues that from the seventeenth century "the question of the status of Judaism and of Jews was a key site of intellectual contestation, confusion and debate" within discussions of Enlightenment across Europe, including in Russia. Turgenev's antisemitic short story "The Jew" is directly referenced in the novel (*S*, 172), as discussed below, but Gogol, Pushkin, Dostoevsky, and other Russian writers generally thought of as progressive were also profoundly ambivalent about Jews and Jewish emancipation.[39] In fact, Sutcliffe continues, "the complexities clustered around Judaism are of central importance for a general understanding of the Enlightenment itself."[40] Jews, then, presented a "troublesome limit case."[41] To what extent could Jewish particularism be allowed, and to what extent could centuries of anti-Jewish prejudice be set aside in favor of tolerance and universal values?[42]

---

36 See Polonsky, "Nicholas I and the Jews of Russia" and Sorkin, *Jewish Emancipation*, especially "Russia and the Kingdom of Poland, I," 189–201.
37 See Edwards, "Nicholas I and Jewish Education."
38 See Stanislawski, *Tsar Nicholas I and the Jews*.
39 See Katz, *Neither With Them, Nor Without Them*.
40 Sutcliffe, *Judaism and Enlightenment*, 5; 6.
41 See Sutcliffe, "Judaism and the Politics of Enlightenment."
42 See Robertson, *The "Jewish Question"* and Mendes-Flohr, "The Emancipation of European Jewry."

Mentions of Jews in *Der Sohn* are infrequent, reflecting the general trend in Grjasnowa's work toward a focus on universal themes: state persecution, migration and forced displacement, and solidarity and privilege. Yet as a "troublesome limit case," Jews frame the novel's broader presentation of prejudice, including even among those who profess a commitment to Enlightenment values and to the liberalization of Russian society. Most obviously, incidences of direct persecution of Jews, or of discrimination or disdain, make explicit the pervasive bias—and even hostility—that infuses Russian attitudes toward all those who are perceived as inferior. Further to this, however, Jamalludin's witnessing of overt antisemitism, including the horrific treatment of Jewish boys recruited into the Tsar's army, sensitizes him to the limits of Russian tolerance more generally, in relation to his own treatment as a Muslim, but also to the treatment of serfs and women. Finally—and only to be inferred—the mobilization of these "Jewish moments" within the narrative may suggest a Jewish ethics. The unobtrusive, discreet manner in which this Jewish purpose is articulated within the text points to the presence of a non-Jewish Jew as narrator.

Dislike of Jews is normalized among the Russian elites. Members of the imperial court, including the empress, display their "Abscheu" (disgust; *S*, 111), a cadet at the military academy known for selling treats at inflated prices is nicknamed Itzig (*S*, 140), a derogatory name for Jews, and the Tsar barely attempts to conceal his contempt for the British Jewish financier and philanthropist Moses Montefiore, when he visits to plead for an improvement in the treatment of Russian Jews (*S*, 141–45). (The wider significance of these five pages will be discussed shortly.) These explicitly voiced examples of antisemitism reveal the truth of polite discourse, namely the prejudice toward those considered not to belong that is never far from the surface.

Jamulladin gradually becomes aware that, as a Muslim, he too is subject to prejudice and that discrimination is more generally a defining characteristic of Russian society. This realization seems to begin when he witnesses a column of Jewish boys being force-marched toward St. Petersburg. Jamalludin is shocked both by the adolescents' pitiful appearance and the callous indifference of their guards. The Jewish boys have been taken from their parents, are afflicted by hunger and hypothermia, and are destined to be conscripted (*S*, 167). Prior to this episode, which takes place during a military excursion, Jamalludin had appeared not to notice the ways he is excluded, even though they were obvious to the reader, of course. Most immediately, this episode of Jewish suffering prompts introspection, as Jamalludin reflects on what would happen to the children of his homeland if the Russian Empire were to defeat his father (*S*, 168) and thinks back to his own forced removal: "Mitleid mit sich selbst. Bilder der jüdischen Jungen ließen ihn nicht mehr los und die seiner Abreise aus Akhulgo kamen wieder hoch." (Sympathy with himself. The images of the Jewish boys would not leave him be and images of his own departure from Akhulgo came flooding back; *S*, 172.) More generally, however, he is repulsed by the abject cynicism of his fellow officers. When Alexej, the scion of his future wife's supposedly liberal family, and Kasparow, another officer, conduct an innuendo-laden conversation with some local hunters, Jamalludin demands answers:

"Gibt es denn viele Juden in der Gegend?," fragte Kasparow.

"Nicht mehr." Die Jäger lachten.

"Und woran liegt das?," fragte Jamalludin und nun war es Alexej, der ihm einen besorgten Blick zuwarf.

Pjotr räusperte sich: "Zum einen, wie Sie sicher wissen dürfen sich Juden in dieser Gegend nicht niederlassen . . ."

"Zum anderen?," fragte Jamalludin.

"Zum andern," sagte Nikolai und seine Augen leuchteten, als er sprach: "Zum anderen gab es heute ein kleines Volksfest."

["Are there lots of Jews in the area, then," Kasparow asked.

"Not any more." The hunters laughed.

"Why not?," Jamalludin asked and now it was Alexej who threw him a worried look.

Pjotr cleared his throat. "For one, as you will know Jews are not allowed to settle in this area . . ."

"And what else?," Jamalludin asked.

"Well," Nikolai said and his eyes lit up, as he spoke: "Today there was a little folk festival." *S, 171*]

The intimation of a pogrom is all too obvious, as is the repellant mix of conspiratorial half-acknowledgments and malice. Jamalludin loses his temper when Alexej, with great relish, recounts Turgenev's antisemitic short story "The Jew" (1847), throwing his plate against the wall and walking away, ashamed of his friend and of everything around him (S, 172).

Antisemitism is positioned as the foundational prejudice, as it were, a format for oppression in Imperial Russia more generally: "Der Zar entschied über jede Kleinigkeit der öffentlichen Ordnung, selbst das Rauchen auf der Straße hatte er verboten und graue Hüte, die ihn aus irgendwelchen Gründen an Juden erinnerten." (The Tsar decided every little thing in public life, even smoking on the street and grey hats, which for some reason reminded him of Jews; S, 242.) Two days after his meeting with Montefiore, and following an invitation from his loyal Jewish subjects, Nicholas I arrives late at the temporary synagogue in St. Petersburg (Jews were still not officially permitted to live outside the Pale of Settlement) and storms out on account of what he views as the depravity of Jewish rituals (S, 145–46). Linking calls to emancipate the Jews with his duty as Tsar to resist dangerously liberal ideas arriving from France, Nicholas I instructs Jamalludin: "Mach dir nichts aus den Juden." (Have nothing to do with Jews; S, 146.) If the Jews were tolerated, it is implied, then all the other forms of exclusion underpinning Russian society would also be thrown into question.

Subsequently, Jamalludin becomes conscious that, even among the liberal elites, freedom only ever exists in the abstract. Even as they celebrate the "Freiheit des Geistes" (freedom of the intellect) and criticize the authoritarianism of the Tsar (S, 188), Lisa's mother and father continue to beat their servants—their children protest, but weakly, "damit sich an der Ordnung der Dinge bloß nichts änderte." (So that nothing actually changed in the order of things; S, 222.) Lisa's parents, moreover, invite the anarchist thinker Bakunin into their home—where he no doubt repeats his thoughts on women's emancipation—and appear to tolerate their daughter's attachment to the novels of the proto-feminist George Sand (S, 185). Yet they will not allow her to travel to Göttingen to study. With Lisa, Jamalludin suddenly grasps that women might hope for the same things he desires—rights (S, 186–87). He also has sympathy with the prisoners that fill the Tsar's jails—activists circulating emancipatory ideas from France—because he too knows what it means to be confined, unable to speak freely, and forbidden to return home (S, 242). In time, he begins to develop an understanding of universal rights: liberty and freedom of expression: "Dieses Land war ein gläsernes Gefängnis—die Polizeispitzel waren überall, Briefe wurden aufgebrochen, gelesen." (This country was a glass prison—police informers were everywhere, letters were opened, read; S, 242.) If Kant defines Enlightenment as man's [*sic*] emergence out of self-incurred immaturity then this is the journey that Jamalludin has embarked on, as he deploys his innate reason to grasp the general principles that ought to apply equally to all human beings.

The encounter with anti-Jewish prejudice, therefore, seems to prompt Jamalludin's growing awareness of intolerance as an indispensable pillar of Russian society. At the same time, it can be argued that the novel as a whole is infused by the Jewish experience, albeit in a highly allusive fashion. A reference early in the text to the use of forced labor in the construction of St. Petersburg—including those who died "an der Erschöpfung, der Kälte, dem Hunger, Skorbut oder Ruhr" (of exhaustion, cold, hunger, scurvy, dysentery; *S*, 50)—reminds of the Nazi camps in which Jews (and others) were worked to death, just as the later scene featuring the Jewish boys anticipates the death marches at the end of the war. More generally, of course, the narrator's focus on trauma, memory, and solidarity may suggest a Jewish ethics of care, as was the case in Grjasnowa's previous novels. In *Der Russe*, for example, Mascha's retelling of her grandmother's flight from the Nazis frames her own, formerly repressed memory of the bloody clashes between ethnic Armenians and Azeris that she witnessed as a child in 1992 and, ultimately, her empathy with Palestinians.[43]

Jews are the central focus for the five pages of *Der verlorene Sohn* that recount the (real-life) visit of Moses Montefiore to Russia in March 1846. In St. Petersburg, Montefiore met with Nicholas I, the Tsar's Minister of National Enlightenment, and Jewish delegations from across the Pale of Settlement. In Russia, as elsewhere on his international travels, he asked that Jews be granted rights while also urging his coreligionists to learn the vernacular language and engage with the majority culture.[44] A religiously observant Jew, Montefiore embodies the only overtly Jewish positionality in the novel, defining Jewish emancipation as just as urgent as the end of hostility toward Muslims or the introduction of equal rights for women and serfs.[45] At the same time—as Jamalludin discovers—integration, or even assimilation, offers no guarantee that prejudice will abate and discrimination cease.

Yet the key character in this brief episode is actually Montefiore's private secretary, Louis Loewe. The real Loewe was an accomplished linguist from Silesia who learned Arabic dialects and local languages during extensive travels throughout the Middle East, a translator of interfaith dialogues, and a writer of treatises on cultural artifacts as well as of a dictionary of the Circassian language (widely spoken in Jamalludin's region). Inserted between the Tsar's abrupt dismissal of Montefiore's

43 See Skolnik, "Jewish Writing."
44 See Green, *Moses Montefiore*.
45 After his death, Montefiore was revered by diaspora Jews for his intercessions with local rulers. After the Holocaust, however, his "emancipation politics" was seen by many as suspect—a naïve belief that Jews could ever be accepted and that persecution would end.

entreaties and his disparaging of the St. Petersburg Jewish community at the Synagogue, accordingly, comes a conversation between Jamalludin and Loewe, a demonstration of Loewe's intercultural expertise. He addresses Jamalludin first in Circassian, then in the Damascus and Palestinian dialects of Arabic before trying the classical version, and finally English, a language that is now more familiar to the young Muslim than the idiom of the Koran. Through his switching between languages and his eagerness to learn about Dagestan, including its architecture and Avar grammar (*S*, 142–44), Loewe clearly reprises the traditional Jewish role as a "middleman minority,"[46] that is, as intermediaries who facilitate trade, finance, and cultural and intellectual exchange, often operating between dominant elites and subordinate groups.[47] Here, however, a more specific articulation of Jewish purpose is also implied—as a bridge between the particular and the universal.

Loewe's presence articulates a more discreet Jewish perspective, consequently, as translator, mediator, and even curator of other people's worlds. This is a universalistic perspective that ultimately elides its own original Jewishness—contrasting with the partiality of Montefiore, who intercedes as a Jew on behalf of Jews. It might even be argued, in fact, that it is the perspective adopted by the novel's unnamed third-person narrator. Just as Loewe translates between idioms and cultures, so does the narrator transmit exchanges originally in Russian, French, German, English, and languages from across the Caucasus, along with anthropological insights. (The bibliography at the end of the text lists the sources for the author's and thus the narrator's learning.) Likewise, just as Loewe appears in the novel as an agent of Jewish purpose, advancing the cause of cosmopolitanism, so can the narrator be understood to be the instrument through which Jewish experience is curated as a stimulus for Jamalludin—and the reader—to grasp the universal significance of his story for debates on prejudice, empathy, and rights. Certainly, the novel's episodic structure lends credence to this notion of narratorial curation. A succession of encounters prompts the young protagonist to develop greater moral understanding, including horrific vistas of Jewish suffering that appear especially, or even expressly, intended to accelerate his emotional and intellectual growth.

The narrator is not identified as a Jew. Indeed, the reader might assume that he or she is an insider—a Russian and a Christian—since this is the convention of the socially-engaged nineteenth-century Russian novel on which *Sohn* is modeled, with its unadorned prose, attention to detail, occasional throwbacks to Romanticism, and focus on the hypocrisy

---

46   See Blalock, *Toward a Theory of Minority-Group Relations*.
47   See Schama, *Belonging*.

of the Russian nobility.⁴⁸ Yet the fact that the novel also includes a subtle critique of the blind spots of the tradition it draws on—the mention of Turgenev's antisemitic "The Jew" and the anti-Jewish slurs used by the liberal elites who consume Gogol, Pushkin, and Dostoevsky—suggests a certain detachment. This does not mean that the narrator must be Jewish. Non-Jews too have sometimes broken ranks to expose antisemitism among enlightened elites. But it is suggestive at least, and what is at stake here is not the narrator as a real (or even imagined) person but whether the narration can be argued to embody a Jewish ethics.

In an essay of 1958, published ten years later in 1968, the Polish-born philosopher Isaac Deutscher coined the phrase "non-Jewish Jew" to describe Baruch Spinoza, Heinrich Heine, Karl Marx, Rosa Luxemburg, Sigmund Freud, and Leon Trotsky, intellectuals and activists for progressive and revolutionary causes who left behind their particularistic origins and engaged in the world on behalf of humanity as a whole. For Deutscher, this transgression against the core tenets of Judaism is itself quintessentially Jewish: "The Jewish heretic who transcends Jewry belongs to a Jewish tradition."⁴⁹ Deutscher too was a heretic who rejected orthodoxy of any kind and spoke out in solidarity with the marginalized and the persecuted: as an adolescent he rejected his Orthodox upbringing; in his twenties he joined the Polish Communist Party but was expelled in 1932; after he moved to Britain in 1939, he was briefly interned as a potential subversive; in 1965, he took part in the first "teach-in" at Berkeley; and he was also fiercely critical of Israel's occupation of Palestinian land after the Six-Day War in 1967.⁵⁰ Notwithstanding his transcendence of his origins, however, Deutscher located his activism firmly in the Jewish experience—dwelling on the "borderlines of various civilizations, religions, and national cultures" and "in society and yet not of it" (*NJJ*, 27)—and in his understanding of Jewish values as universalistic. Deutscher's is a vision of Jewish worldliness, correspondingly, that is diasporic, self-transcendent, and displays solidarity with others: "I hope, therefore, that, together with other nations, the Jews will ultimately become aware—or, regain the awareness—of the inadequacy of the nation-state and that they will find their way back to the moral and political heritage that the genius of the Jews who have gone beyond Jewry has left us—the message of universal human emancipation" (*NJJ*, 41).

Deutscher is directly cited in Grjasnowa's *Gott ist nicht schüchtern*, when the unnamed narrator inserts an epigraph into her account of the two protagonists' flight from the civil war in Syria: "Someone in a Cambridge common room asked the self-designated 'non-Jewish Jew'

---

48 See Freeborn, "The Nineteenth Century: The Age of Realism."
49 Deutscher, "The Non-Jewish Jew," 26. Hereafter *NJJ*.
50 See Horowitz, ed., *Isaac Deutscher*.

and Marxist historian Isaac Deutscher about his roots: 'Trees have roots,' he shot back scornfully, 'Jews have legs.'"[51] In *Sohn*, a brief mention of the Italian writer Natalia Ginzburg (author of *The Little Virtues*, originally *Le piccole virtù*, 1962) provides further evidence for a Jewish universalism that is rooted not in religious observance but in a general sense of a Jewish ethics. Ginzburg is quoted in a second epigraph at the start of the novel, praising parents' care for their children, most likely to sensitize the reader to the story of human suffering—a Muslim child torn from its parents—that lies behind the military and political machinations that will be described in the novel. Ginzburg was born into a Jewish family in 1916 (her mother was Catholic). During the war, she was harassed by the fascists, and her Jewish husband was tortured and killed.[52] *The Little Virtues* is a collection of essays, a number of which reflect on the author's wartime experiences and all of which circle around the question of belonging. In the 1980s, Ginzburg became politically active in the Italian communist movement and later, having quit the Party, as an independent leftist deputy. Her conversion to Catholicism surprised many, however her engagement on behalf of oppressed minorities, including the Palestinians, was always underpinned by her own experience of persecution and frequently referenced the Holocaust and Jewish suffering more generally. Literary biographer Nadia Castronuova describes this as "Jewishness as moral identity."[53]

In Grjasnowa's *Sohn*, it can be surmised, a non-Jewish Jewish narrator articulates a non-Jewish Jewish worldliness that largely bypasses faith, alludes to Jewish thought and culture tangentially, and cites the Holocaust only indirectly, as a basis for its commitment to universal human rights. For those Jews for whom religious conformity, the Holocaust, and Israel are indispensable to Jewish identity, this may seem challenging, even heretical, although many will also follow the injunction of *tikkun olam*. For those for whom Jewishness is just one aspect of an instinctively progressive, globally-engaged self-positioning, it may be a more appealing version of the future of Judaism, in Germany and perhaps everywhere.

The Limits of Solidarity, Jewish Writing, and October 7, 2023

At the start of this chapter, reference was made to the hope expressed by some Jewish and non-Jewish intellectuals in the 1990s that newly vibrant Jewish communities might herald a new era of pan-European solidarity.

---

51   Grjasnowa, *Gott*, 137.

52   Grjasnowa also references Ginzburg, including her experience of flight, in a discussion about the theatrical version of *Gott ist nicht schüchtern* (online transcript no longer accessible).

53   See Castronuova, *Natalia Ginzburg*.

The collapse of communism and the spread of liberal democracy, philosophers, historians, and sociologists speculated, had created the conditions for a reemergence of Jewish life across the continent, which would in its turn both embody and inspire a more cosmopolitan future. Literary scholars too believed that this renaissance of Jewish thought and culture might anticipate more hybrid and fluid identities, in Europe and indeed globally. More recently, they have focused less on the specific context of the end of the Cold War and revived a more general association of Jews with diaspora, even nomadism, cosmopolitan exchange, and the emancipatory potential of mediating between cultures.

The three texts examined above respond to this expectation that there should be a *purpose* to Jewish existence beyond simple self-perpetuation, that is, to point the way toward a more enlightened future for all humankind. Each novel positions its Jewish protagonist or (likely) Jewish narrator differently in this regard, confirming that Jews are of course not all alike while perhaps also exemplifying the complexity, choices, and compromises of actually living "in the world" as a Jew. In Trzebiner's *Die Enkelin* (2013), accordingly, worldliness means exiting Orthodox Judaism, keeping Holocaust memory alive but not being defined by it, and integration into the mainstream: becoming "normal" by *not* deriving a specific mission from Jewish suffering or from Jewish particularity. For Ali in Salzmann's *Außer sich*, Jewish solidarity—which may not be all that Jewish—must be *lived* rather than only theorized, via pragmatic engagement that builds alliances across minorities while acknowledging persisting differences. Finally, Grjasnowa's nameless narrator in *Der verlorene Sohn* may embody a Jewish imperative to mobilize on behalf of others that tends toward the transcendence of Jewishness itself. More negatively, however, this may appear as a kind of self-erasure.

In Salzmann and Grjasnowa in particular, the reference to the concrete situation of Jews in contemporary Germany—their self-positioning vis-à-vis other Jews and in relation to the non-Jewish majority and to other minorities—may be less obvious than in the texts by Altaras, Himmelfarb, Stein, Funk, Kaufmann, and Petrowskaja analyzed in chapters 1 and 2, but it can still be inferred. Indeed, it might even be argued that relative privilege and the *limits* of solidarity with other minorities are just as central to the debate on Jewish identity today as Holocaust memory, disagreement about who "counts" as a Jew, and divisions on Israel. For the younger generation especially, it might even be *more* important. Following a brief summary of the close readings in chapters 1–3 and how they relate to the theoretical framework set out at the beginning of this study, accordingly, the conclusion returns to this overarching concern. The argument is that the trend in recent writing for Jewish protagonists to position themselves no longer primarily in relation to the non-Jewish German majority but now in relation to other "others" reflects the broader development of what scholars including Erol Yıldız and Naika

Foroutan term a "postmigrant society." This new self-positioning, however, does not mean that the question of what it means to be a Jew in Germany has been resolved—it has simply been reframed. The final section of the conclusion reflects on self-identified Jewish authors' responses to the atrocity perpetrated by Hamas on October 7, 2023 and speculates about how the most lethal attack on Jews since the Holocaust—and Israel's ferocious offensive in Gaza—might shape the next evolution in German Jewish writing.

Conclusion: The Postmigrant Society and the Limits of Solidarity—After October 7, 2023

This book started out from the dramatic demographic transformation of the Jewish presence in Germany since the early 1990s. The Holocaust survivors from eastern Europe who largely reestablished the community after 1945 have now almost all passed away. Their second- and third-generation descendants are in the minority compared to the more than 220,000 people who arrived as *jüdische Kontingentflüchtlinge* from the successor states of the former Soviet Union and their children; and immigrants from America and Israel in particular have also made a contribution, albeit far smaller. Along with demographic renewal, there has also been a pluralization of Jewish life, including Orthodox, Conservative, and Reform congregations, a strongly secular understanding of Jewish heritage and culture, and the emergence—or importation from overseas—of feminist and LGBTQ challenges to traditional Judaism.

The next section presents a summary of the outcomes of the close readings in chapters 1–3 of recent novels by Adriana Altaras, Jan Himmelfarb, Benjamin Stein, Mirna Funk, Kat Kaufmann, and Katja Petrowskaja, Channah Trzebiner, Marianna Sasha Salzmann, and Olga Grjasnowa. Cross-cutting themes and key stylistic features are identified as well as a unifying concern across the diversity of the New German Jewish literature with the rearticulation of Jewish identity. This is followed by a discussion of the emerging trend in German Jewish writing to position Jews in Germany in relation to what sociologists Erol Yıldız and Naika Foroutan describe as the "postmigrant society," that is, explicitly in relation to a public discourse in Germany that now accepts the reality of migration and its profound reshaping of politics, culture, and identity. Here, the focus is on protagonists' engagement with other minorities but also on the *limits* of their solidarity. A final section examines interviews and essays by some of the authors examined in this book that appeared in the months after the horrific attack by Hamas on Israel of October 7, 2023, and Israel's ferocious response. As this study was being finalized, the war was still ongoing, provoking polarized responses around the world—including among Jews in Germany and across the diaspora.

Holocaust Memory, Solidarity, Worldliness

The main argument of this study has been that reading recent German Jewish literary fiction within the context of the demographic transformation and pluralization of the community makes it possible to understand key texts as interventions in the ongoing debate about what it means to be a Jew in Germany today, recognizing too that there is a *global* dimension to this debate centered on the diaspora's relationship with Israel, its treatment of the Palestinians, different interpretations of who "counts" as a Jew, and integration/assimilation, etc. At the same time, formal and stylistic characteristics have been emphasized throughout. In some novels, then, a pop aesthetic indicates integration into the majority culture or the potential for a version of Jewish worldliness unburdened by trauma or the expectation that Jews should be somehow exemplary. This is the case in Trzebiner's *Die Enkelin* (The granddaughter; 2013) as well as in Funk's *Winternähe* (Near winter; 2015). In others, a revival of early twentieth-century literary modernism might imply a self fragmented into different component identities. Salzmann's *Außer sich* (Beside oneself; 2017) is the most obvious example of this, but an intense focus on the instability of the "I" and the unreliability of the narrator telling his or her own story also characterizes Stein's *Rabbi Löw* (2014), Himmelfarb's *Sterndeutung* (Star reading; 2015), and, of course, Petrowskaja's *Vielleicht Esther* (Maybe Esther; 2014).

In many recent novels, casual sex is an especially significant marker of the protagonists' desire to participate in the secular non-Jewish mainstream, although it often also signals female and/or Jewish (self-)debasement, as in Funk's *Winternähe*. In other texts, gender and sexuality more generally—and especially *queerness*—are linked more explicitly to the exploration of Jewishness. Salzmann's *Außer sich* is the most striking example, of course, but gay and bisexual characters also abound throughout Grjasnowa's work. It is surely also significant that women writers—or, in Salzmann's case, a trans author—dominate in recent German Jewish literature and that their themes very often include gender and sex norms, discrimination, and the body as well as Jewish identity. A detailed study of gender, sexuality, and Jewishness in contemporary German Jewish novels is yet to be written.

Intertextual references to the German, German Jewish, and Russian literary traditions are a further stylistic feature of contemporary German Jewish writing. In Grjasnowa's *Der verlorene Sohn* (The lost son; 2020), for example, there are obvious allusions to, and even quotations of, the nineteenth-century Russian novel and the debate on parochialism and Europeanness. Other novels by Grjasnowa similarly cite Russian classics—most obviously *Der Russe ist einer der Birken liebt* (All Russians love birch trees; 2012)[1]—while in *Gott ist nicht schüchtern* the author again invokes early twentieth-century modernism and especially German Jewish and non-Jewish exiles from National Socialism, namely Erich Maria Remarque, Anna Seghers, and Bertolt Brecht, to establish a parallel with refugees in the present day. In an article on *Gott*, Jonathan Skolnik also speculates that Grjasnowa might have modeled the novel on Frank Werfel's *Die vierzig Tage von Musa Dagh* (The forty days of Musa Dach; 1933), which narrates the Armenian genocide, and its foregrounding of a "Jewish authorial voice" speaking out on behalf of other minorities.[2] Elsewhere, Skolnik notes how, in *Der Russe*, the collected works of Lion Feuchtwanger are prized possessions in the Russian Jewish protagonist's childhood apartment in Baku, next to family photographs. Andree Michaelis-König also identifies Feuchtwanger's influence as well as that of the nineteenth-century satirist Heinrich Heine and the early twentieth-century lyricist Alfred Wolfenstein, both Jewish exiles from Germany just as Feuchtwanger was.[3] (Feuchtwanger fled to France after Hitler came to power in 1933, spent a few months in the Soviet Union in 1936–37, and then emigrated to the United States in 1941.) In September 2022, Grjasnowa curated a workshop on exile at the Berliner Ensemble to accompany its dramatization of Feuchtwanger's 1939 novel *Exil*. As Skolnik points out, such references suggest Grjasnowa's resumption of the German Jewish literary tradition,[4] and Michaelis-König makes the same argument for Petrowskaja's *Vielleicht Esther* and another Soviet-born writer, Dmitrij Kapitelman, whose 2016 début novel *Das Lächeln meines unsichtbaren Vaters* (The smile of my invisible father) has clear echoes of Kafka.[5] For these Soviet-born authors, allusions to German literature indicate prior familiarity with German culture—in *Sterndeutung*, Arthur quotes Goethe, Kafka, Rilke, and Grass—and references to early twentieth-century German *Jewish* writing hint that they might be the heirs to its "decidedly diasporic model," to paraphrase the literary scholar Andreas Kilcher, as "essentially universalistic, cosmopolitan, exterritorial or transnational."[6]

Kafka especially is a key intertext for both Soviet-born and German-born writers: Stein, Himmelfarb, Petrowskaja, Salzmann (in their second novel *Im Menschen muss alles herrlich sein* / Glorious people; 2021), and Grjasnowa, including a direct mention of Kafka's parable "Vor dem

1 See Braese, "Auf dem Rothschild-Boulevard." See also Jeffreys, *The White Birch*.
2 See Skolnik, "'Jewish Writing.'"
3 Michaelis-König, "Exterritoriale Visionen," 75.
4 Skolnik, "Memory," 131.
5 Michaelis-König, "Exterritoriale Visionen," 75.
6 Kilcher, "Diasporakonzepte," 136.

Gesetz" (Before the law; 1915) in *Die juristische Unschärfe einer Ehe* (The legal haziness of a marriage; 2014).[7] Most obviously, the early twentieth-century Prague writer provides a prototype for authors' engagement with the question of what it means to be a Jew—Kafka was riven with ambivalence, of course—and many have argued that that his work even predicts Nazi and Soviet totalitarianism. More generally, however, Kafka is also a model for the autobiographically inspired writing that is perhaps the most salient characteristic of contemporary German Jewish literature. The burden of family expectations, including the responsibility to honor parents' or grandparents' traumatic experiences, shape almost all of the narratives examined in this study, as protagonists struggle to tell their *own* stories, which, more often than not, are versions of their authors' experiences. In Altaras's *titos brille* and Petrowskaja's *Vielleicht Esther*, the lead characters even share their author's first name; in other novels, the correspondence is less overt but still obvious. This does not mean, of course, that literary texts are simply a reworking of "real life." As in Kafka's work, the actual life lived is only the starting point. In recent German Jewish novels, moreover, the autobiographical self is almost always positioned in relation to broader currents of history, primarily twentieth-century fascism and totalitarianism but also—in Petrowskaja's *Vielleicht Esther,* Salzmann's *Außer sich,* and Grjasnowa's *Der verlorene Sohn*—Jewish life in Europe from the period of the Enlightenment. As important, of course, is the *self-positioning* of autobiographically inspired protagonists as they navigate the continuing debate on Jewish identity today.

Self-positioning is a key term throughout the close readings that are presented in chapters 1–3. Specifically, how Jewish protagonists position themselves vis-à-vis *other* Jews is as significant as how they position themselves with regard to the non-Jewish majority. In some novels this "inner-Jewish" dialogue is prominently staged in the narrative, for example *Sterndeutung*, in which Arthur is determined to show the Holocaust survivor Roth that he has fully assimilated into German Jewish memory culture, and indeed has expanded it to include the Soviet Jewish experience. In others, it remains in the background even as it clearly drives the plot. In Funk's *Winternähe*, Lola references the Orthodox establishment only briefly, but her urge to prove that she is "properly" Jewish is clearly a response to its doctrinal inflexibility.

Self-positioning, moreover, is a *dynamic* process. In Altaras's *titos brille* (titos glasses; 2015), when Adriana asserts her claim to embody the established Jewish community against the Russian speakers recently arrived from the former Soviet Union, she also signals a shift in her attitude toward the German majority, and most likely a more general shift in how second- and third-generation Jews relate to the land of the

7   Grjasnowa, *Ehe*, 102.

perpetrators. Accommodation, if not reconciliation, is a marker of difference from the "not quite Jewish" newcomers. In Stein's *Rabbi Löw*, this *plasticity* of identity in response to changed circumstances and competing claims is even more apparent. Rottenstein's unorthodox Orthodox Judaism thus draws on Jewish heretics such as Sabbatai Zevi in order to *reinvent* German Jewish identity. On the one hand, he defies the religious establishment with its insistence on an unbroken Jewish lineage. On the other, he berates the laxity that characterizes how many, if not most, Jews in Germany actually practice the faith. Both Adriana and Rottenstein, moreover, implicitly call into question the centrality of Holocaust memory for Jewish identity today. Adriana, then, emphasizes her Sephardic Jewish family's experience of antisemitism at the hands of Yugoslav communists *after* 1945 as well as at the hands of Germany's Croatian fascist allies during the war. Rottenstein's observant though scandalously transgressive Judaism alludes, of course, to the genocide but puts belief and ritual at the core of Jewish identity.

Rearticulating Holocaust memory, in fact, may be the most momentous way in which protagonists reposition themselves and define Jewish identity anew. In Funk's *Winternähe*, Lola first plays the conventional second- and third-generation role of decrying German hypocrisy—even possibly channeling *provocateurs* such as Maxim Biller—before rethinking the legacy of the genocide, in Israel, as a basis for empathy with all oppressed minorities, even Palestinians. (Of course, she subsequently deconstructs this universalistic empathy.) In Trzebiner's *Die Enkelin*, Holocaust trauma must be (largely) consigned to the past if Channah is to emerge into the "normality" of the non-Jewish mainstream. The protagonists of Petrowskaja's *Vielleicht Esther* and Himmelfarb's *Sterndeutung*, in contrast, reconstruct or even fabulate the details of Holocaust family trauma in order to reassert the Jewishness of Russian Jewish identity against the skepticism of the established community. As noted above, Adriana does much the same in *titos brille* with regard to her Sephardic Jewish heritage.

Above all, Trzebiner's *Die Enkelin*, Stein's *Rabbi Löw*, Altaras's *titos brille*, Himmelfarb's *Sterndeutung*, Funk's *Winternähe*, and Petrowskaja's *Vielleicht Esther* all challenge, more or less explicitly, the dominant role of Orthodox Jews in the community and as the custodians of Holocaust memory. In *Die Enkelin*, Channah overcomes the Holocaust fixation of the largely eastern European survivors so that she might "integrate." *Rabbi Löw* puts the emphasis on faith rather than the genocide. The novels by Altaras, Himmelfarb, and Petrowskaja focus on other Jewish geographies as well as the "use" liberal and secular Jews make of Holocaust memory. And all of these texts by writers born between the 1960s and early 1980s assert the right of the children and grandchildren to define the meaning of the Holocaust for themselves, including from a defiantly non-religious perspective that might also even criticize Israel, as in Funk's

Winternähe and Altaras's *titos brille*. *Winternähe* and *Rabbi Löw* also confront Orthodox strictures, of course, with protagonists who insist that a lack of a Jewish mother does *not* mean not Jewish at all. The challenge posed by the queerly Jewish—or Jewishly queer—Ali/Anton in Salzmann's *Außer sich* is obvious here too. Though not explicitly mentioned, the context for this novel may be the increasingly visibility in recent decades of gay and lesbian Jews in Berlin synagogues and even as rabbis.[8]

German-born Jews, therefore, position themselves in relation to Soviet-born newcomers. Observant Jews position themselves vis-à-vis their secular counterparts. Jews without a Jewish mother set themselves against those who insist on *halachic* conformity, just as gay, lesbian, and trans Jews similarly reinterpret Jewish identity. And all of these second- and third-generation Jews position themselves against the establishment, largely dominated for so long by the survivors, and largely Orthodox. Holocaust memory is the focal point of these maneuvers, but rethinking the legacy of the genocide is not an end in itself.

The close readings in chapters 1–3 further demonstrate that a key aspect of a protagonist's self-positioning in relation to other Jews—and to the non-Jewish majority in Germany and ultimately globally—is whether and how he, she, or (in *Außer sich*) they is/are able to resolve the tension between Jewish particularism and Jewish universalism. To the extent that they position themselves as "worldly" in contrast to the conventional fixation of the postwar Jewish community on Jewish victimhood and the uncanniness of Jewish life in the land of the perpetrators, both younger German-born and Soviet-born Jews find that they need to express just what this Jewish worldliness means, for them. This can imply different degrees of willingness to accept the subsuming of the specificity of the Jewish experience into a universalistic framework that emphasizes its significance for humankind as a whole.

Stein's *Rabbi Löw* is perhaps the most *un*worldly of the texts considered in chapters 1–3, with its allusions to the esotericism of Jewish ritual and Kabbalah, even as its *non-halachic* protagonist seeks to lift German Jews out of their introspective, arguably parochial focus on the Holocaust and to reconnect them to the wider Jewish tradition. There is no hint in *Rabbi Löw* that Jews should be *for* anything else other than their own survival. Likewise, in Trzebiner's *Die Enkelin* and Funk's *Winternähe*, Channah and Lola conclude that Jews have as much right as anybody else to be focused on their own history, although they are also determined to participate in the non-Jewish mainstream, unlike Stein's Rottenstein—but the price to be paid for "integration" may be their relinquishment of overt markers of their Jewish identity. Adriana, in contrast, sees no

---

8   See Becker, "A Revived Congregation's New Vision" and Igelhaut, "Young, Jewish and Queer."

contradiction between her insistence, in *titos brille*, on the specificity of her Jewish family story and her participation in secular society. However, she is also aware that, as a well-known author and actress, she is called upon by the majority to "represent" the Jewish presence in Germany. For the Soviet-born heroes of Kaufmann's *Superposition*, Himmelfarb's *Sterndeutung*, and Petrowskaja's *Veilleicht Esther*, matters are complicated by the urge to assert a Russian identity in addition to a Jewish identity, and by the fact that this Jewish identity must in any case be first reconstructed. In all three novels, the worry that becoming more engaged "in the world" might dilute the particularity of a Jewish past that has only just been recovered from its historical erasure is limiting.

Expressing solidarity with others is both an articulation of Jewish worldliness and a form of self-positioning, of course. In general terms, the solidarity with refugees, trafficked women, and Muslim victims of neo-Nazi violence demonstrated in the work of writers such as Rabinowich, Lux, Vertlib, Dischereit, Martynova, Grjasnowa, and others—discussed at the start of chapter 2—asserts a vision of what Jews are *for*, of "Jewish purpose" therefore (Sutcliffe), that contrasts with the established community's focus on Jewish concerns and its interactions with the non-Jewish German majority. The close readings presented in chapters 1–3, however, nuance any suggestion that Jewish solidarity is either easy or without limits. To the extent that Jewish protagonists position themselves not only in relation to other Jews and the non-Jewish *white* majority but *also* in relation to other minorities—whether Turkish Germans or recent refugees from predominantly Muslim countries—they become enmeshed in discussions of relative privilege, "Western" values, and liberal preconceptions.

The Postmigrant Society and the Limits of Solidarity?

Mascha, the Russian-Jewish protagonist of Grjasnowa's first novel *Der Russe*, associates almost exclusively with other migrants. The sole significant exception is her German boyfriend Elias, whose "hohe Wangenknochen, blaugraue Augen und dunkle Wimpern"[9] (high cheek bones, blue-gray eyes and dark eyelashes) mark *him* out as the exotic other. Elias's family, in fact, is originally from the former German Democratic Republic, a place "to the east" that appears as backward, provincial, and racist. For Mascha and the other minority characters who inhabit the narrative, in fact, Germany is hardly relevant. Mascha and her friends define themselves not in relation to the German majority but through reciprocal empathy and solidarity. She is, she says, "postmigrantisch" (postmigrant; *DR*, 12).

9   Grjasnowa, *Der Russe*, 10. Hereafter, *DR*.

With the term "postmigrantisch," Grjasnowa's protagonist is most likely citing the "postmigrant theater" introduced by Shermin Langhoff at the Ballhaus Naunynstraße theater in 2008 and then at the Maxim Gorki Theater, following her appointment as manager and artistic director in 2013. Langhoff's concept placed migrants and migrant themes at the heart of the production and thus at the center of cultural discourse.[10] Alternatively, although perhaps less likely, Mascha may be alluding to the work of sociologists including Naika Foroutan and Erol Yıldız, who—also drawing on Langhoff's theater work—reference the term as a conceptual tool in their rethinking of German (and Austrian) society today. While they have different emphases and objects of study, Foroutan and Yıldız broadly understand postmigrant society to mean: first, a theoretical lens in academic research that focuses on migrants and the migrant experience as fundamental to the study of contemporary Germany; second, a social reality that has been comprehensively shaped by migration, with this fact now acknowledged in social, political, and cultural discourses; and, third, the preponderance of cultural artifacts by migrants, about migrants, or with migrants central to the performance or text.[11]

The close readings presented in this book have focused on Jewish protagonists' self-positioning vis-à-vis other Jews and, to a lesser extent, in relation to the non-Jewish majority. Applying the lens of the postmigrant society, however, opens up a new perspective on the *other* characters that inhabit recent German Jewish novels, sometimes at the margins—such as the migrants and gypsies in Kaufmann's *Superposition*—and sometimes at the heart of the narrative, as in Grjasnowa's *Der Russe*. How Jewish protagonists position themselves with regard to other minorities may be just as significant as the dynamics that exist between Jews and between Jews and non-Jewish Germans. Reading—or rereading—German Jewish writing as a reflection of and an engagement *with* the social reality of the postmigrant society, then, can deepen our understanding of both the texts themselves and how Jews in Germany might respond in quite different ways to the challenges and opportunities it presents. As we shall see, for some protagonists the postmigrant society is largely ignored as they align themselves, even implicitly, with the white German majority. For others, engagement and empathy is tempered by caution and even detachment. And for a third set of Jewish lead characters, there is a potential for situating Jews not as a "people apart"[12] but as fundamentally connected through alliances and activism, albeit with concerns regarding their own relative privilege and power.

---

10   See Sharifi, "Postmigrant Theatre."
11   See, for example, Foroutan, *Die postmigrantische Gesellschaft* and Yıldız and Hill, eds., *Postmigrantische Visionen*.
12   See Vital, *A People Apart*.

In Altaras's *titos brille*, accordingly, there is *no* mention of any other minorities—excepting, of course, the Russian-speaking immigrants who arrive after 1991. This is striking, given the fact that the period that Adriana describes from the mid-1960s—when her family fled Yugoslavia and settled in Germany—largely corresponds to the period in which several million Turkish, Italian, Portuguese, Greek, Spanish, and even Yugoslav "guest workers" arrived. (In fact, the recruitment of foreign workers began in 1955.) For Adriana, it could be argued, Soviet-born Jews after 1991 may represent yet another wave of newcomers from whom the established Jewish community might wish to distinguish itself. Unlike, say, Maxim Biller's *Esra* (2003), which at least imagines a Jewish-Muslim intimacy,[13] Adriana is entirely focused on her situation—and status—within the Jewish community and in relation to the non-Jewish German majority. Her narrative is certainly not a "touching tale" of engagement between minorities, to use the term American scholar Leslie Adelson introduced to describe a subset of novels by Jewish and Turkish authors in the 1990s.[14] Channah, in Trzebiner's *Die Enkelin*, similarly makes no reference to other minorities—with the exception of her parody of a Russian Jewish mother—and defines herself only in relation to her non-Jewish German friends and her non-Jewish German boyfriend. Of course, there is no *requirement* for German Jewish writers to allude to other minorities—any more than authors from the non-Jewish majority are obliged to cite Jews—but in these two novels the omission seems significant.

In most of the other texts examined in this study, other minorities are more visible, and Jewish protagonists more consciously define themselves in relation to these "other" others. In Kaufmann's *Superposition*, as noted above, homeless people, migrants, and gypsies exist at the margins of the narrative, which is otherwise largely focused on Izy's interactions with her German-majority friends, her fellow Soviet-born Jewish on-off lover Timur, and Sascha, a Russian woman who was admitted because (like 1.8 million others) she could prove German ancestry.[15] In fact, Izy's engagement with *non-white* minorities is limited and betrays her own prejudice and privilege. She assumes that Muslims automatically dismiss women while she also objectifies a young Iranian woman in a way that is both misogynist and orientalizing. In Himmelfarb's *Sterndeutung*, Arthur is less condescending toward the asylum seekers whose hostels are being

---

13 Even in *Esra*, however, it turns out that the jilted Jewish protagonist's Turkish German ex-lover hails from a family of *Dönme*—"hidden Jews" who were once followers of the heretic Sabbatai Zevi. (See the discussion in chapter 1 of Benjamin Stein's *Rabbi Löw*.) See Taberner, "*Esra*."
14 See Adelson, "Touching Tales."
15 Kaufmann, *Superposition*, 98. See Panagiotidis, *Postsowjetische Migration*.

burned down (and to the victims of genocide in Rwanda, taking place in the narrative present) but he too is unable—or unwilling—to overcome the difference he perceives between his experience and that of other migrants to Germany. His journey from Russia, he notes, was comfortable, by train, and without bureaucratic delays or hostile border guards. He could be confident that his belongings would not be stolen by local police in Ukraine, and he only left behind his books because it wasn't possible to pack them all in his suitcases.[16] (The relative comfort of Soviet-born Jews' transit to Germany is a theme in other recent novels. The narrator of Kapitelman's *Das Lächeln*, for example, compares his family's arrival, facilitated by bureaucrats and border guards, with the hostility faced by Syrian refugees in 2015.)[17]

In her widely read study of how Jewish immigrants in the United States marked their difference from other minorities, assimilated, and eventually achieved success in their new country, anthropologist Karen Brodkin Sacks argues that they effectively "became white."[18] In a similar vein, literary scholar Karolina Krasuska has recently argued that for Gary Shteyngart, David Bezmozgis, and other Soviet-born Jewish writers who arrived in America beginning in the late 1980s or as part of the large migration wave after 1991—in parallel with those who went to Germany—a concern with whiteness, and white privilege, is central.[19] There are hints of this same concern in Kaufmann and Himmelfarb, as indicated above. In Funk, Petrowskaja, and Salzmann, it is addressed more directly. In Funk's *Winternähe*, Lola flees the Israeli-Palestinian conflict—and the complexities of solidarity—to a remote Thai island, where she meets a German couple and an Israeli couple and indulges, with these *white* Western tourists, in a neo-colonial exploitation of the local Muslim population. In Petrowskaja's *Vielleicht Esther*, Katja travels to Kalisz in Poland and is shown around the city by a Muslim immigrant, including the Hebrew letters on paving stones made out of recycled gravestones. This passage is the only one in the narrative that names another minority group in the present day and appears somewhat incongruous until the reader grasps that a parallel is being drawn. Katja comments that her Muslim tour guide was "die perfekte Andere" (the perfect other)[20] and that this is a term that is also applied to her by non-Jewish Germans. On the one hand, there is a suggestion here of solidarity between Jewish and Muslim minorities, a kind of "vernacular cosmopolitanism," to use Homi

---

16 Himmelfarb, *Sterndeutung*, 247–48.
17 Kapitelman, *Das Lächeln*, 23–24.
18 See Brodkin Sacks, *How Jews Became White Folks*.
19 See Krasuska, *Soviet-born*.
20 Petrowskaja, *Vielleicht Esther*, 134.

Bhabha's term.[21] On the other hand, it might be that Katja repeats—and even endorses—the prejudice behind the ostensible compliment aimed at the good-natured foreigner who integrates and asks for nothing in return.

As discussed in chapter 3, in Salzmann's *Außer sich* Ali/Anton appropriates the exotic otherness of Turkey's marginalized minorities in order to rip off German sex tourists while also playing at being white on the terrace of one of Istanbul's finest hotels. In fact, *Außer sich* can be read as a counterpart—but also potential corrective—to the author's collaboration with Max Czollek on the "Desintegrationskongress" (de-integration congress) in 2016 and the 2017 "Radikale Jüdische Kulturtage" (radical Jewish cultural days). (Czollek was mentioned in the introduction as the target of Maxim Biller's ire. Biller accused Czollek of exploiting his grandfather's wartime exile in Shanghai to "fake" Jewish credentials.) The "Desintegrationskongress" and the "Radikale Jüdische Kulturtage" brought together minority artists, activists, and intellectuals to debate their resistance to "integration" into the white German mainstream.[22] Both events took place at Berlin's Gorki Theater—where Shermin Langhoff is the director—and sought to build coalitions across ethnic and sexual minorities to challenge concepts of "majority culture" and "belonging."[23] What *Außer sich* offers, therefore, is a literary reflection on what is required to actually *achieve* this solidarity, insofar as Jews in Germany today enjoy a degree of privilege—or at least "passing"—that is not available to people with darker skin. Holocaust memory plays a relatively minor role in both the novel and Salzmann's wider program, with Czollek, of forming Jewish-Muslim-queer alliances. The impetus for solidarity comes instead from a shared experience of marginality, it seems, but effort is still needed to acknowledge significant differences and impacts.

Grjasnowa's first novel *Der Russe*, as discussed above, presents the postmigrant society as a given. Mascha and her friends from other minorities support one another and Mascha eventually connects her grandmother's tale of flight from the Nazis to the ethnic clashes in Azerbaijan in 1992 and to Palestinians in the narrative present. In *Die juristische Unschärfe einer Ehe*, released two years later in 2014, the focus is on *differences* between minorities and on how citizenship and legal residence confer rights on some while excluding others. Jonoun, Leyla, and Altay express their Jewish-Christian-Muslim solidarity through their queerly three-way relationship and travel freely on their Western passports, in contrast to the refugees, asylum seekers, and sex workers who ghost through the background of the narrative but are never directly named. Indeed, this contrast may be summarized in a passing reference to a reproduction

---

21   See Bhabha, "Unsatisfied."
22   See Landry, "Rethinking Migration."
23   See Roca Lizarazu, "'Integration.'"

of (one of) Maurycy Gottlieb's self-portraits, in which he appears as Ahasuerus, the wandering Jew, with regal hints of the Persian king also of that name who—in the Old Testament—spared the Jews of his realm following the pleading of his Jewish wife Esther.[24] Maurycy Gottlieb was one of the most significant Polish Jewish artists of the nineteenth century, at the time of the *Haskalah*, or Jewish Enlightenment. In his work—and in his life—Gottlieb confronted the dilemma of remaining loyal to his Jewish roots versus complete assimilation, and his self-portrait of 1876 hints at this with its obvious suggestions of stereotypically Jewish traits combined with an aspiration to Polish nobility. At the same time, the figure of the wandering Jew[25] also suggests a contrast between the novel's privileged protagonists and the "'irregular' migrants" at its margins. Like the mention of the reproduction of Gottlieb's self-portrait on the wall of Altay's well-connected Azeri lover, they simply add detail to the setting in which the main action takes place. In the New Testament, Ahasuerus taunted Christ en route to crucifixion and was thereafter condemned to wander the globe for all eternity. Today, people attempting to flee war, persecution, and poverty are similarly doomed to live without rights and always at risk of violence. More generally, Grjasnowa has acknowledged the work of Judith Butler and Jasbir K. Puar[26] on how the West now embraces gay rights—and philosemitism—as a means of asserting its moral superiority over "Islamic intolerance." *Ehe*, accordingly, is clearly inspired by the author's reading of Puar's *Terrorist Assemblages: Homonationalism in Queer Times* (2007). The "juridical haziness of their marriage" (*juristische Unschärfe einer Ehe*) can be tolerated as long as Jonoun, Leyla, and Altay conform to Western liberal norms and distinguish themselves from the fundamentalist, women-hating, and antisemitic Islamicists supposedly threatening to terrorize Europe. Salzmann too cites Puar's book as a key influence.[27]

As described in chapter 3, Grjasnowa's 2017 *Gott is nicht schüchtern* is about the civil war in Syria and the sudden arrival of between one and two million refugees in Europe in the summer of 2015.[28] In part, the novel responds to the representation in sections of the media and political discourse of the predominantly Muslim refugees as a faceless mass, a threat to "Western civilization," and especially a danger to women. Some public figures—including members of the Jewish community—also claimed

24 Grjasnowa, *Ehe*, 203. Mendelsohn, *Painting a People*, 110–11.
25 See Cohen, "The 'Wandering Jew.'"
26 Sheaffer, "Olga Grjasnowa."
27 See Salzmann's essay "Unsichtbar," especially 19.
28 FRONTEX recorded 1,802,267 border crossings for 2015, but that may include a number of multiple attempts by the same people. See https://frontex.europa.eu/along-eu-borders/migratory-map/. Last accessed July 25, 2024.

that they represented an existential threat to Jews in Germany.[29] In relating why and how each of the three Syrian protagonists flee, accordingly, the third-person narrator emphasizes their humanity. Beyond this, infrequent but unmistakable references to the Holocaust provide a framework for the German reader to grasp the brutality of the Syrian regime and the suffering of its victims. At the same time, however, the Holocaust is *provincialized*—or decolonized—as a peculiarly European (and North American) obsession. The narrator—Jewish, it can be inferred—and the most likely non-Jewish German reader thus assimilate the conflict in Syria into their shared discourse of Holocaust memory, including via allusions to Jewish and non-Jewish writers who fled Nazism (Anna Seghers, Erich Maria Remarque, and Bertolt Brecht). The refugees themselves, however—insofar as their words are directly reported at key moments in the narrative—make no mention whatsoever of this most horrific episode in European history. Indeed, the narrator's abstract invocations of Jewish suffering—resonating with European publics[30]—are relativized by more visceral episodes in which Syrians, North Africans, and other migrants speak with one another and shape their own "refugee solidarity" by exchanging stories of state repression, forced conscription, torture, and indiscriminate bombing.[31] The suggestion may be that while in Europe Jews and the non-Jewish white majority are (broadly) aligned, those with roots in other parts of the world have different experiences, and memories.

In her essay "Aus sicherer Entfernung" (From a safe distance; 2015) on the civil war in Syria and the "refugee crisis," Grjasnowa directly invokes—and even instrumentalizes—Holocaust memory as a call for intervention on behalf of others: "Wozu brauchen wir überhaupt noch das Gedenken an den Holocaust, wenn sich daraus keine Maxime für unser Handeln ergibt?"[32] (What do we need commemoration of the Holocaust for at all, if nothing results for the way we act?). The author's 2021 book-length essay *Die Macht der Mehrsprachigkeit* (The power of multilingualism) likewise frames (her) Jewish family history as underpinning a philosophical position that emphasizes multiculturalism, antiracism and pro-migrant activism, and global solidarity.[33] Her novel *Gott*, though, suggests that while Holocaust memory may be useful—and even necessary—to mobilize a European public, it also implies a position of privilege. In an interview with Katja Garloff and Agnes Mueller, then, Grjasnowa confirms that she considers her novel to be "Jewish writing"

29 See Arnold and König, "'One Million Antisemites?'"
30 See Diner, "Restitution and Memory."
31 Grjasnowa, *Gott*, e.g., 243.
32 Grjasnowa, "Aus sicherer Entfernung," 62.
33 See Grjasnowa, *Die Macht*.

because "migration is a very Jewish topic,"[34] yet this does not—cannot—mean that the experiences of Jewish refugees in the past are the same as those of Muslim refugees now, or that Soviet-born Jewish writers can necessarily relate. Likewise, in her essay "Privilegien" (Privileges), published in the collection by migrant writers *Eure Heimat ist unser Alptraum* (Your home is our nightmare; 2020), Grjasnowa notes that the arrival of dark-skinned, dark-haired refugees from the Middle East means that she is no longer regarded as foreign. On vacation with her daughter in Istanbul, her German passport distinguishes her from the Syrians begging for their help. She further reflects on the term "migrant literature" as a racist category and how Muslims in Europe are denied the security that she—white, and with German papers—easily enjoys.[35]

Finally, rereading Grjasnowa's work through the lens of the postmigrant society adds an important dimension to the close reading of her most recent novel, *Der verlorene Sohn* (2020), presented in chapter 3.[36] There, the emphasis was on the—likely—Jewish narrator as a mediator of sorts between the experience of the nineteenth-century Muslim protagonist and the present-day non-Jewish German reader. It was argued that the narrator's allusive framing of Jamalludin's abduction and subsequent marginalization in Tsarist Russia illuminates the broader failure of the Enlightenment to realize its promise of tolerance and equality for all—including for Muslims today. What was left unexplored, however, was the relationship between Jewish narrator and Muslim protagonist, *both* minorities in relation to the (probable) German-majority reader. If the novel as a whole functions as an allegory for the treatment of Muslims in contemporary Germany, and Europe, then it is surely *also* an allegory for the possibilities—and limitations—of Jewish-Muslim solidarity. This novel about nineteenth-century Russia, it seems, might actually be about today's postmigrant society.

Now, the complexity of privilege is more fully articulated. In Grjasnowa's *Der verlorene Sohn*, it can be argued, a (likely) Jew explains the dynamics of anti-Muslim discrimination for the majority while "passing" for the conventional narrator of a European novel in the nineteenth-century tradition, that is, as white and a Christian. (Imagining *Gott*'s narrator as a Jewish *woman* further undermines this tradition, of course.) On the one hand, this suggests privilege, or at least proximity to privilege.

---

34   Garloff and Mueller, "Interview with Olga Grjasnowa," 227.
35   Grjasnowa, "Privilegien," 130-9.
36   Grjasnowa's *Juli, August, September* was due to be released in September 2024, several months after the completion of this manuscript. The pre-publicity describes a plot centered on a Berlin-based post-Soviet Jewish family, who travel to Gran Canaria to meet their Russian-speaking relatives from Israel and to explore their Russian Jewish identity.

On the other hand, it suggests self-effacement, as the unnamed narrator benefits from the presumption of authority only for as long as she conceals her true identity. The non-Jewish Jew must not *appear* Jewish. Equally, it is an open question whether mobilizing on behalf of others supersedes Jewish interests.

After October 7, 2023

The question of solidarity and Jewish self-interest became still more fraught following the atrocity perpetrated by Hamas on October 7, 2023, when the Palestinian terror group murdered more than 1,200 people during a rampage through southern Israel, including sexual assaults and other heinous crimes. The ferocity of Israel's response, killing tens of thousands in Gaza and leveling much of its infrastructure, shocked people around the world, including many of Israel's staunchest supporters and many Jews in the diaspora. At the time of the completion of this book in mid-2024, the war was still raging, angry protests against Israel and its Western allies were taking place in cities and on university campuses across Europe and North America, and Israel and its leaders were being arraigned in the International Court of Justice and elsewhere, including on charges of genocide. At the same time, a huge surge in antisemitic rhetoric and even violence was apparent almost everywhere around the world.

In Germany too, news emerged of spontaneous celebrations of the Hamas attack, especially in sections of the Muslim community.[37] Jews reported that they felt unsafe, as antisemitic slogans, harassment, and even physical attacks increased dramatically.[38] The German authorities clamped down hard—citing Holocaust memory and Germany's historical responsibility to defend Israel[39]—arresting protesters, banning Muslim groups considered to be extremist, and withdrawing invitations to prominent artists and intellectuals deemed to be skeptical about Israel's actions in Gaza. At the same time, Muslim organizations reported a steep rise in Islamophobia, just like following the Al Qaeda terror attacks on the United States of September 11, 2001—or 9/11—and during the Western "war on terror" that ensued.[40]

How October 7 and its aftermath will impact on the Jewish community in Germany cannot yet be known, of course. Equally, the novels that might reflect on actual and potential rearticulations of Jewish identity

---

37 See Angelos, "Israel-Hamas."
38 See Nöstlinger, "Antisemitic Incidents."
39 In a widely watched video posted to the social media platform X on November 2, 2023, vice-chancellor and Green Party Leader Robert Habeck spoke of the historical imperative for Germany to stand with Israel.
40 See Strack, "Muslims in Germany."

after 10/7 are still to be written. So, what can be speculated about how Jews might position themselves in future, vis-à-vis each other, the non-Jewish majority, and, in the postmigrant society, Germany's large Muslim minority? Can solidarity be sustained? Will Jews in Germany retreat inward or continue to engage in a *worldly* way?

Authors' essays and interviews in the months after 10/7 offer some insight here, albeit limited. First, and perhaps contrary to expectations, Jewish writers remained largely silent about events in the Middle East, suggesting shock, uncertainty about what stance to adopt, a reluctance to be co-opted as a voice for all Jews, or for Israel, or possibly a feeling that their identity is not in any case closely tied to the Jewish state. (Soviet-born authors Katja Petrowskaja and Sasha Marianna Salzmann had been vocal about the Russian invasion of Ukraine in early 2022.) Second, as will be evident from the examples that follow, authors generally reiterate their previous preoccupations but with different emphases and a greater or lesser evolution of their emotional and intellectual positions. Third, the potential for Jewish writers to shape public discourse on matters touching on their identity seems—once again—to have become restricted, as louder voices dominate in perhaps predictable ways.

For Mirna Funk, then, October 7 and the surge in antisemitic incidents in Germany definitively resolves the question of where she stands in relation to her Jewish identity and to Israel. These were the issues that animated her protagonist Lola in *Winternähe*, as discussed in chapter 2. In essays and interviews published since late 2023, the author berates German antisemitism, recounts Hamas's depravity, asserts Israel's right to defend itself, rails against the "Islamisierung auf der ganzen Welt" (Islamicization of the whole world), and commits to making *aliyah*.[41] (It should be noted that Funk has moved to Israel several times, only to return, just like Lola in *Winternähe*.) This authorial self-positioning is less nuanced—and more strident, even polemical—than Lola's probing of what it means to be a Jew without a Jewish mother and a diaspora Jew caught between loyalty to Israel and discomfort with its treatment of the Palestinians. It might be speculated, therefore, that—for at least some Jews in Germany—the Hamas attack and Israel's invasion of Gaza have in some way *resolved* the doubts, whether their own or imposed by others, about where they belong. At the same time, there may arguably be a performative dimension to Funk's uncompromising defense of Israel and her pledge to move there. Certainly, her sharply expressed criticism of the prominence of Deborah Feldman in the media after 10/7 may suggest an urge to prove her own credentials. Funk decries the American Jewish author of *Unorthodox*

---

41   See Funk, "'Wir brauchen Israel.'"

(2012), now resident in Germany, as anti-Zionist (anti-Israel) and ignorant of the postwar history of the Jewish community.[42]

In a public reading in February 2024, Altaras was reminded by the moderator that her novel *titos brille*, published in 2011, opens with the words: "Meistens bin ich unbekümmert" (mostly, I'm unworried).[43] Does she still feel that way, after 10/7, she was asked? Her reply that she is now more cautious than before and disappointed by her fellow Germans' seeming lack of immediate empathy then leads to a reframing of her position in relation to the non-Jewish majority. Whereas previously, she had focused on the Nazi past and reconciliation, she says, now she is more concerned to engage in the *present*. This means asking about the surging electoral support in recent years for the far-right Alternative für Deutschland.[44] In another article, however, the author emphasizes that life goes on and humor is still permitted, as are holidays.[45] On a roundtable discussion with other Jewish writers and intellectuals, she also forcefully rejected—like Funk—Deborah Feldman's self-positioning as a representative voice for Jews in Germany. Her objection was that Feldman's assertion that the German police was not prepared to defend Jews demanding an end to the war was completely untrue. Here, she joined fellow panelist, the historian Michael Wolffsohn, in insisting that Jews could be safe in Germany, and that the country was fundamentally committed to a just peace.[46] For all her reservations, it seems, Altaras remains confident about the future of Jews in Germany.

Finally, there is Sasha Marianna Salzmann's exchange of letters with the Israeli musician, journalist, and author Ofer Waldman, which was published in mid-2024 with the title *Gleichzeit* (Real Time; 2024). (Waldman moved to Berlin in 1999 as one of the first members of the West-East Divan orchestra, founded by Argentinian-Israeli composer Daniel Barenboim and Palestinian-American academic Edward Said to promote artistic collaboration among musicians from across the Middle East. Waldman reports on Israel for German radio and writes radio plays and short stories.) In their correspondence between mid-October 2023 and late January 2024—roughly a letter a week from each, sent by email, and also a transcript of an online conversation conducted in real time—the two writers discuss their emotional responses to the Hamas attack, protests and counter-protests in Germany, and the situation in Israel, where friends and relatives are being mourned, hostages remain unaccounted for, and anger at Prime Minister Netanyahu's government is rising. They

---

42 See Funk, "Beänstigend."
43 Altaras, *titos brille*, 5.
44 Altaras, "Das Lachen, das im Hals stecken bleibt," 21.
45 See Altaras, "Zwischen den Welten."
46 See Luz, "Bei Lanz bringt Deborah Feldman alle gegen sich auf."

also comment, briefly, on the suffering endured by Palestinians as a result of Israeli military action. In sum, *Gleichzeit* expresses Salzmann's (and Waldman's) immediate but also relatively expansive reflections on 10/7, including the challenge the massacre and the global response to Israel's subsequent devastation of Gaza present for a progressive and universalistic Jewish identity.

In Salzmann's first few letters to Waldman, what is striking is the extent to which the author emphasizes Jewish family history, Holocaust memory, and anxiety about the surge in antisemitism in Europe, including violent incidents. Sasha recounts for Ofer the story of a grandfather who managed to escape the Germans by hiding in the forests of Ukraine; a visit just after 10/7 to the Shoes memorial in Budapest (commemorating the murder of 20,000 Jews by Hungarian fascists from December 1944 to January 1945); and how a friend, in a café in Vienna, refused to retract his assertion that all Jews deserved to be killed because of what Israel was doing to Palestinians in Gaza.[47] Indeed, the refrain throughout is the author's wish to sit *shiva* for the Jewish victims of 10/7 and their upset that it is too early, because it is not yet over. With rockets raining down on Israel and friends and relatives engaged in military action, there will be more deaths to mourn (*G*, 20).

Salzmann's letter to Waldman of December 15, written just over two months after 10/7, relates how, as a child, the author heard her great-grandparents speaking Yiddish. Also included are accounts of how Salzmann's family fled the Nazis, antisemitic persecution under Stalin, hate speech following the collapse of the Soviet Union, and how immigrants to Germany became "the Russians" for the existing Jewish community (*G*, 74–78). In this letter, then, the author seems to align with Soviet-born writers such Himmelfarb, Kaufmann, and Petrowskaja in articulating the *specificity* of Russian Jewish identity. In addition, Salzmann may even regret their rejection of Israel in younger years, recalling arguments with their great-grandfather Shura (who appears in *Außer sich*, of course)[48] on the subject of the Jewish state (*G*, 77). After 10/7, might it be that Salzmann has retreated from worldliness—and from solidarity with others, including Muslims—into a more particularistic Jewish identity?

Yet mentions throughout Salzmann's letters of the indispensability of *friendship*—substantiated by a reference on January 15 to German Jewish philosopher Hannah Arendt and her thinking on friendship, sociability, and dialogue (*G*, 115)—hint that engagement with others remains a

---

47 Salzmann, *Gleichzeit*, 36; 12–14; 45–48. Hereafter *G*.
48 Elsewhere, Salzmann mentions a Turkish friend, E., who took part in demonstrations against the Erdoğan regime, became the "face" of the queer movement, and wrote plays, pamphlets, and flyers (*G*, 117–18). The character Aglaja in *Außer sich* is most likely based on E.

key value for the author, notwithstanding the particular(istic) hurt felt in the immediate aftermath of 10/7. In every letter, Salzmann reports that a friend has called to enquire about the author's well-being; Salzmann responds to Waldman's allusions to caring for others in mental or physical distress; or they imagine comforting others: "Eine hinter der anderen. Wir sind eine unendliche Kette." (One behind the other. We are an endless chain; *G*, 12.) Indeed, friends—especially including Muslims such as Salzmann's friend Mehmet—are the promised land. "Wir alle haben einen Morgen," the author writes to Waldman, "und meine Zukunft, mein Eretz Israel, seid ihr." (We all have a tomorrow [. . .] and you are my future, my Land of Israel; *G*, 21.) Friendship, it is suggested, is more important than nation, and more important even than ethnic belonging. It is what Ali experiences with their Muslim friend Elyas in *Außer sich*— a pragmatic acceptance of difference, a commitment to dialogue, and a demonstration of solidarity.

Initially, Salzmann feels pressure from outside, from the non-Jewish German majority, to justify their focus on Jewish suffering. "Warum habe ich das Gefühl," the author asks, "dass die Veranschaulichung jüdischer Realität immer auch unter einer Art Rechtfertigungsdruck steht: Ja, ich weiß, wir sind nicht die Einzigen, die leiden." (Why do I have the feeling that making vivid Jewish reality always needs to be justified: Yes, I know, we are not the only ones that are suffering; *G*, 65.) Soon enough, though, empathy with Palestinians (re-)emerges spontaneously, and from within. On December 20, seven weeks after the Hamas atrocities and as the ferocity of Israel's military response was beginning to become apparent, Salzmann reports a dream in which they found themselves in Gaza, confronted by a young girl. The author continues: "Ofer, es gibt keinen Tag, an dem ich nicht über Gaza nachdenke, die Menschen dort in den Trümmern, ohne Lebensmittel, ohne Versorgung." (Ofer, not a single day passes that I don't think about Gaza, the people in the ruins, without food, without care; *G*, 86.) Significantly, Salzmann immediately associates the plight of Palestinians in Gaza with two Syrian refugees they shared an apartment with in 2015 and with Ukrainian women who had fled the Russian invasion in early 2022 (*G*, 86–87). The fortitude of these *strangers* inspires Salzmann to overcome hopelessness and to reengage on behalf of others. This letter of December 20, moreover, is the very next missive the author sends following their account of family history. Identifying as a Jew predicts Salzmann's empathy with Israelis killed and kidnapped on 10/7. It also underpins their empathy *globally*, for those in Gaza, Syria, and Ukraine, and wherever injustice and suffering reign.

The atrocities perpetrated by Hamas on October 7, 2023, Israel's overwhelming and violent response, and protests around the world—some tainted by antisemitism—do not yet seem to have prompted dramatic shifts in Jewish writers' self-positioning vis-à-vis other Jews, the non-Jewish majority, or other minorities, even Muslims. Rather, what is noticeable is a restatement, and perhaps even solidifying, of core beliefs. Funk reaffirms her attachment to Israel, setting aside previous doubts, at least for now. Altaras expresses greater caution about the surge in antisemitism but remains fundamentally committed to Germany, though with a greater emphasis on fighting the far right. Salzmann defines Jewishness as a basis for worldly engagement while asserting a right to care about Jews *as* Jews. These positions may not be representative of the wider community, of course. But they are at least suggestive.

The response of the German government, regional authorities, and cultural institutions to the atrocities of 10/7, on the other hand, frequently appears less nuanced. Senior politicians quickly reaffirmed their solidarity with Jewish victims and reiterated that Germany's *Staatsräson*—very purpose as a state—includes ensuring the security of Israel. On the one hand, official support most likely reassured Jews unnerved by reports of celebrations by some Muslims and of antisemitic slogans and even harassment in some of the protests taking place against Israel's military actions. On the other hand, German enthusiasm for protecting Jews may also have had the perverse effect of establishing non-Jews as the arbiters of what Jews themselves could and could not say. In mid-February 2024, the Israeli filmmaker Yuval Abraham was denounced as anti-Israel and even anti-Jewish by German politicians following an acceptance speech he had given on receipt of a prize at the Berlinale for his documentary *No Other Land* (2024). In his remarks, Abraham—whose grandmother was born in a concentration camp and whose father lost most of his family—had condemned the "situation of apartheid" existing in his country and called for a ceasefire in Gaza.[49] Abraham's comments were provocative, to be sure, but he was not alone among progressive Israeli and diaspora Jews in expressing such opinions. The desire of the German state to propagate its overcoming of the Nazi past may enforce a stifling homogeneity—even on Jews—with regard to Holocaust memory, the fight against antisemitism, and discussion of Israel.

Chapters 1–3 of this book demonstrated that the New German Jewish Literature illuminates debates on Jewish identity in Germany, and indeed globally, and explores a range of possible—and potential—articulations of what it means, *today*, to live as a Jew in the country responsible for the Holocaust but also, in a large proportion of recent novels, "in the world." Following the caesura of October 7, 2023, Jews in Germany and across the diaspora more generally will no doubt evolve new understandings of Jewishness and new ways of engaging with others, though most likely still drawing on the past. The future is always open. What is just as certain, regrettably, is that other people—the German state, well-meaning

---

49 See Oltermann, "Israeli Director."

sympathizers as much as overt antisemites, non-Jews everywhere—will believe that they have a right, even an *obligation*, to define the meaning of what happened on that horrific day and in the aftermath, for Jews, for Israelis, and for Palestinians and an entire region where war and suffering constitute everyday reality.

Bibliography

Abramson, Henry. "A Double Occlusion: Sephardim and The Holocaust." In *Sephardic and Mizrahi Jewry: From the Golden Age of Spain to Modern Times*, edited by Zion Zohar, 285–99. New York: New York University Press, 2005.

Adelson, Leslie. "Touching Tales of Turks, Germans, and Jews: Cultural Alterity, Historical Narrative, and Literary Riddles for the 1990s." *New German Critique* 80 (2000): 93–124.

Albé, Francesco. "Becoming Queer In/Human in Sasha Marianna Salzmann's *Außer sich* (2017)." *Seminar* 58, no. 3 (2022): 231–50.

Almog, Yael. "Politics and Literary Capital in Tomer Gardi's *Broken German*." *German Studies Review* 45, no. 3 (2022): 557–76.

Alt, Arthur Tilo. "Yiddish and Berlin's 'Scheunenviertel.'" *Shofar* 9, no. 2 (1991): 29–43.

Altaras, Adriana. "Das Lachen, das im Hals stecken bleibt." *Mittelbayerische Zeitung*, Kultur, February 24, 2024: 21.

———. *titos brille*. Frankfurt am Main: Fischer Taschenbuch, 2015 [2011].

———. "Zwischen den Welten." *Jüdische Allgemeine*, June 10, 2024. Online at: https://www.juedische-allgemeine.de/kultur/zwischen-den-welten-5/. Last accessed July 25, 2024.

Amit, Hila. *A Queer Way Out: The Politics of Queer Migration from Israel*. New York: SUNY Press, 2018.

Angelos, James, "Israel-Hamas War Cuts Deep into Germany's Soul." *Politico*, October 21, 2023. Online at: https://www.politico.eu/article/israel-hamas-war-germany-germany-berlin/. Last accessed July 25, 2024.

Arendt, Hannah. *Eichmann in Jerusalem: A Report on The Banality of Evil*. New York: Viking, 1963.

Arfa, Orit. "Modern Orthodox Jewish Life blossoms in Berlin." *Jewish Journal*, September 26, 2016. Online at: https://jewishjournal.com/news/worldwide/190349/modern-orthodox-jewish-life-blossoms-in-berlin/. Last accessed July 25, 2024.

Arnds, Peter. *Representation, Subversion, and Eugenics in Günter Grass's "The Tin Drum."* Rochester, NY: Camden House, 2004.

Arnold, Sina, and Jana König. "'One Million Antisemites?' Attitudes Toward Jews, The Holocaust, and Israel: An Anthropological Study of Refugees in Contemporary Germany." *Anti-semitism Studies* 3, no. 1 (2019): 4–44.

Atshan, Sa'ed, and Katharina Galor. *The Moral Triangle: Germans, Israelis, Palestinians*. Durham, NC: Duke University Press, 2020.

Axelrod, Toby. "Chabad Opens Germany's Largest Jewish Center Since Before WWII." *The Times of Israel*, June 30, 2023. Online at: https://www.timesofisrael.com/chabad-opens-germanys-largest-jewish-center-since-before-wwii/. Last accessed July 25, 2024.

Baer, Marc David. *The Dönme: Jewish Converts, Muslim Revolutionaries, and Secular Turks*. Stanford, CA: Stanford University Press, 2010.

Balling, J. Rafael. "Intimate Associations. Reading Community in Sasha Marianna Salzmann's *Außer sich* (2017) and Else Lasker-Schüler's *Der Malik* (1919)." *Feminist German Studies* 39, no. 1 (2023): 99–124.

Banki, Luisa. "Actuality and Historicity in Mirna Funk's *Winternähe*." In *German-Jewish Literature after 1990*, edited by Katja Garloff and Agnes Mueller, 169–86. Rochester, NY: Camden House, 2018.

Banki, Luisa, and Caspar Battegay. "Sieben Thesen zur deutschsprachigen jüdischen Gegenwartsliteratur." *Jalta. Positionen zur jüdischen Gegenwart* 1 (2019): 41–47.

Baranova, Olga. "Conceptualizations of The Holocaust in Soviet and Post-Soviet Ukraine and Belarus: Public Debates and Historiography." *East European Politics and Societies*, 34, no. 1 (2020): 241–60.

Baron, Ilan Zivi. *Obligation in Exile: The Jewish Diaspora, Israel and Critique*. New York: Oxford University Press, 2022.

Battegay, Casper. "German Psycho. The Language of Depression in Oliver Polak's *Der jüdische Patient*." In *German Jewish Literature after 1990*, edited by Katja Garloff and Agnes Mueller, 187–205. Rochester, NY: Camden House, 2018.

Bauer, Karin. "Erzählen im Augenblick höchster Gefahr: Zu Benjamins Begriff der Geschichte in Edgar Hilsenraths *Jossel Wassermanns Heimkehr*." *German Quarterly* 71, no. 4 (1998): 343–52.

Becker, Elisabeth. "A Revived Congregation's New Vision has Old Roots." *Tablet*, June 14, 2021. Online at https://www.tabletmag.com/sections/community/articles/revived-neue-synagogue-berlin. Last accessed July 25, 2024.

Becker, Franziska. *Angekommen in Deutschland: Einwanderungspolitik als biographische Erfahrung im Migrationsprozess russischer Juden*. Berlin: Dieter Reimer Verlag, 2001.

———. "Migration and Recognition: Russian Jews in Germany." *East European Jewish Affairs* 33, no. 2 (2003): 20–23.

Behler, Ernst. *Irony and The Discourse of Modernity*. Seattle: University of Washington Press, 1990.

Beiser, Frederick C. "Romantic Anti-semitism." In *Romanticism, Philosophy, and Literature*, edited by Michael N. Forster and Lina Steiner, 153–69. Cham: Palgrave Macmillan, 2020.

Belkin, Dmitrij. "Der Dialog muss weitergehen." *Jüdische Allgemeine*, November 8, 2020. Online at: https://www.juedische-allgemeine.de/polgitik/der-dialog-muss-weitergehen/. Last accessed July 25, 2024.

———. *Germanija: Wie ich in Deutschland jüdisch und erwachsen wurde*. Frankfurt: Campus Verlag, 2016.

———. "Jüdische Kontingentflüchtlinge und Russlanddeutsche." *Bundeszentrale für politische Bildung*, July 13, 2017. Online at: https://www.bpb.de/themen/migration-integration/kurzdossiers/252561/juedische-kontingentfluechtlinge-und-russlanddeutsche/. Last accessed July 25, 2024.

———. "Mögliche Heimat: Deutsches Judentum Zwei." In *Ausgerechnet Deutschland! Jüdisch-russische Einwanderung in die Bundesrepublik: Begleitpublikation zur Ausstellung im Jüdischen Museum Frankfurt*, edited by Dmitrij Belkin and Raphael Gross, 25–29. Berlin: Nicolai Verlag, 2010.

———. "Wir könnten Avantgarde sein: Die Zukunft des Patchwork-Judentums." In *Russisch-jüdische Gegenwart in Deutschland: Interdisziplinäre Perspektiven auf eine Diaspora im Wandel*, edited by Karen Körber, 153–61. Göttingen: V&R, 2015.

Ben-Rafael, Eliezer. "Germany's Russian-speaking Jews. Between Original, Present and Affective Homelands." In *Being Jewish in 21st-Century Germany*, edited by Haim Fireberg and Olaf Glöckner, 63–80. Berlin: de Gruyter, 2015.

———. "Russian Jews in Germany." In *Building a Diaspora: Russian Jews in Israel, Germany and the USA*, edited by Ben-Rafael et al., 93–108. Leiden: Brill, 2006.

———. "Russian-speaking Jews in Germany." In *The New Jewish Diaspora: Russian-speaking Jews in the United States, Israel, and Germany*, edited by Zvi Gitelman, 173–85. New Brunswick: Rutgers University Press, 2016.

Benz, Wolfgang. "The Legend of German-Jewish Symbiosis." *Leo Baeck Institute Year Book* 37, no. 1 (1992): 95–102.

Berghahn, Klaus L., and Jost Hermand, eds. *Goethe in German-Jewish Culture*. Rochester, NY: Camden House, 2001.

Bhabha, Homi K. "Unsatisfied: Notes on Vernacular Cosmopolitanism." In *Text and Nation: Cross-Disciplinary Essays on Cultural and National Identities*, edited by Laura Garcia-Morena and Peter C. Pfeiffer, 191–207. London: Camden House, 1996.

Bhabha, Homi K., and John L. Comaroff. "Speaking of Postcoloniality, in The Continuous Present: A Conversation between Homi Bhabha and John Comaroff." In *Relocating Postcolonialism*, edited by David Theo Goldberg and Ato Quayson, 15–46. Oxford: Basil Blackwell, 2002.

Biale, David. *Gershom Scholem: Master of The Kabbalah*. New Haven, CT: Yale University Press, 2018.

Biendarra, Anke S. "Cultural Dichotomies and Lived Transnationalism in Recent Russian-German Narratives (Gorelik, Bronsky, Grjasnowa)." In *Transnationalism in Contemporary German-Language Literature*, edited by Elisabeth Hermann, Carrie Smith-Prei, and Stuart Taberner, 209–27. Rochester, NY: Camden House 2015.

———. *Germans Going Global: Contemporary Literature and Cultural Globalization*. Berlin/New York: de Gruyter, 2012.

Biess, Frank. "Holocaust Memory and Postcolonialism: Transatlantic Perspectives on the Debate." *Central European History* 56, no. 2 (2023): 270–72.
Biller, Maxim. *Bernsteintage*. Cologne: Kiepenheuer & Witsch, 2004.
———. *Der gebrauchte Jude*. Frankfurt am Main: S. Fischer, 2011 [2009].
———. *Deutschbuch*. Munich: dtv, 2001.
———. "Deutscher wider Willen." In Biller, *Der perfekte Roman*, 115–34. Munich: dtv, 2003.
———. "Goodbye, Columbus: Randlage oder: Über die Voraussetzungen jüdischer Literatur." In *Deutschbuch*, 89–93. Munich: dtv, 2001. Originally published in *Frankfurter Rundschau*, March 2, 1995.
———. *Harlem Holocaust*. Cologne: Kiepenheuer & Witsch, 1998.
———. *Hundert Zeilen Hass*. Hamburg: Hoffmann und Campe, 2017.
———. *Land der Väter und Verräter*. Cologne: Kiepenheuer & Witsch, 1994.
———. *Liebe heute*. Cologne: Kiepenheuer & Witsch, 2007.
———. *Moralische Geschichte*. Cologne: Kiepenheuer & Witsch, 2005.
———. *Tempojahre*. Munich: dtv, 1991.
———. *Wenn ich einmal reich und tot bin*. Cologne: Kiepenheuer & Witsch, 1990.
———. "Wer nichts glaubt, schreibt." *Die Welt*, June 23, 2018. Online at: https://www.welt.de/kultur/literarischewelt/article178087386/Maxim-Biller-Wer-nichts-glaubt-schreibt.html. Last accessed July 25, 2024.
Birnbaum, David, and Martin S. Cohen, eds. *Tikkun Olam: Judaism, Humanism & Transcendence*. New York: New Paradigm Matrix Publishing, 2015.
Blalock, Hubert M. *Toward a Theory of Minority-Group Relations*. New York: Wiley, 1967.
Bock-Lindenbeck, Nicola. *Letzte Welten – Neue Mythen: Der Mythos in der deutschen Gegenwartsliteratur*. Cologne; Weimar; Vienna: Böhlau, 1999.
Bodemann, Y. Michal. "A Jewish Cultural Renascence in Germany?" In *Turning the Kaleidoscope: Perspectives on European Jewry*, edited by Sandra Lustig and Ian Leveson, 164–76. Oxford and New York: Berghahn Books, 2008.
———. "A Reemergence of Jewish Life?" In *Reemerging Jewish Culture in Germany: Life and Literature since 1989*, edited by Sander L. Gilman and Karen Remmler, 47–60. New York: New York University Press, 1994.
———. "Die Causa Max Czollek: Wer ist hier eigentlich Jude? Und wer nicht?" *Berliner Zeitung Online*, September 2, 2021. Online at: https://www.berliner-zeitung.de/wochenende/die-causa-max-czollek-wer-ist-hier-eigentlich-jude-und-wer-nicht-li.179949?pid=true. Last accessed July 25, 2024.
———. *Gedächtnistheater: Die jüdische Gemeinschaft und ihre deutsche Erfindung*. Hamburg, Rotbuch Verlag, 1996.
———. "Globale Diaspora? Europäisches Judentum? Die postmoderne Debatte gegen den Strich gebürstet." In *In den Wogen der Erinnerung:*

Jüdische Existenz in Deutschland, edited by Bodemann, 164–84. Munich: dtv, 2002.

———. *In den Wogen der Erinnerung: Jüdisches Leben in Deutschland*. Munich, dtv, 2002.

———. "Introduction." In *The New German Jewry and the European Context: The Return of the European Jewish Diaspora*, edited by Bodemann, 1–12. New York: Palgrave Macmillan, 2008.

———. "The State in the Construction of Ethnicity and Ideological Labor: The Case of German Jewry." *Critical Sociology* 17, no. 3 (1990): 35–46.

Bodemann, Y. Michal, and Gökce Yuedakel. "Learning Diaspora: German Turks and the Jewish Narrative." In *The New German Jewry and the European Context: The Return of the European Jewish Diaspora*, edited by Bodemann, 73–97. New York: Palgrave Macmillan, 2008.

Bodemann, Y. Michal, and Olena Bagno. "In the Ethnic Twilight: The Paths of Russian Jews in Germany." In *The New German Jewry and the European Context: The Return of the European Jewish Diaspora*, edited by Bodemann, 158–86. New York: Palgrave Macmillan, 2008.

Bower, Kathrin M. "Rafael Seligmann (1947–)." In *Holocaust Literature: An Encyclopedia of Writers and Their Work*, edited by S. Lillian Kremer, 1138–41. New York: Routledge, 2003.

Braese, Stephan. "Auf dem Rothschild-Boulevard: Olga Grjasnowas Roman *Der Russe ist einer, der Birken liebt* und die deutsch-jüdische Literatur." *Gegenwartsliteratur – Ein germanistisches Jahrbuch/A German Studies Yearbook* 13 (2014): 275–97.

———. "Writing against Reconciliation: Contemporary Jewish Writing in Germany." *Contemporary Jewish Writing in Europe*, edited by Vivian Liska and Thomas Nolden, 23–42. Bloomington: Indiana University Press, 2008.

Braidotti, Rosi, *Nomadic Subjects: Embodiment and Sexual Difference in Contemporary Feminist Theory*. New York: Columbia University Press, 2011.

Brenner, Michael. "A New German Jewry." In *A History of Jews in Germany since 1945*, edited by Michael Brenner, 417–31. Bloomington: Indiana University Press, 2018.

———. "East European and German Jews in Postwar Germany." In *Jews, Germans, Memory: Reconstructions of Jewish Life in Germany*, edited by Y. Michal Bodemann, 49–64. Ann Arbor: University of Michigan Press, 1996.

———. *In the Shadow of the Holocaust: The Changing Image of German Jewry after 1945*. Washington, DC: United States Holocaust Memorial Museum, 2010.

Brenner, Michael, and Norbert Frei. "German Jews or Jews in Germany?" In *A History of Jews in Germany since 1945*, edited by Michael Brenner, 202–27. Bloomington: Indiana University Press, 2018.

Breuer, Edward. "Rabbinic Law and Spirituality in Mendelssohn's 'Jerusalem.'" *Jewish Quarterly Review* 86, no. 3/4 (1996): 299–321.

Breuer, Mordechai. *Modernity within Tradition: The Social History of Orthodox Jewry in Imperial Germany.* New York: Columbia University Press, 1992.

Broder, Henryk. "Warum ich gehe." *Die Zeit*, February 27, 1981. Online at: https://www.zeit.de/1981/10/warum-ich-gehe. Last accessed July 25, 2024.

Brodkin Sacks, Karen. *How Jews Became White Folks and What That Says about Race in America.* New Brunswick, NJ: Rutgers University Press, 1998.

Brown, Madison. "Toward a Perspective for the Indian Element in Hermann Hesse's *Siddhartha*." *German Quarterly* 49, no. 2 (1976): 191–202.

Brudholm, Thomas. *Resentment's Virtue: Jean Amery and the Refusal to Forgive.* Philadelphia: Temple University Press, 2008.

Brumlik, Micha. *Judentum. Islam: Ein neues Dialogszenario.* Leipzig: Hentrich & Hentrich, 2022.

———. *Kritik des Zionismus.* Hamburg: Europäische Verlagsanstalt, 2007.

———. *Wann, wenn nicht jetzt? Versuch über die Gegenwart des Judentums.* Berlin: Neofelis Verlag, 2015.

———. *Zuhause, keine Heimat: Junge Juden und ihre Zukunft in Deutschland.* Gerlingen: Bleicher, 1998.

Buehler-Dietrich. Annette, "Relational Subjectivity: Sasha Marianna Salzmann's Novel *Außer Sich*." *Modern Languages Open* 1 (2020): 1–17. Online at: https://doi.org/10.3828/mlo.v0i0.287. Last Accessed December 1, 2024.

Caspari, Maya. "Subjunctive Remembering; Contingent Resistance: Katja Petrowkaja's *Vielleicht Esther*." In *Minority Discourses in Germany since 1990: Intersections, Interventions, Interpolations*, edited by Ela Gezen, Priscilla Layne, and Jonathan Skolnik, 196–227. Oxford and New York: Berghahn, 2022.

———. "'There Are No "Other" People': A Conversation with Katja Petrowskaja." *Los Angeles Review of Books*, March 7, 2018. Online at: https://lareviewofbooks.org/article/there-are-no-other-people-a-conversation-with-katja-petrowskaja/. Last accessed July 25, 2024.

Castronuova, Nadia. *Natalia Ginzburg: Jewishness as Moral Identity.* Leicester: Troubador, 2010.

Chase, Jefferson. "Part of the Story. The Significance of the Jews in Annette von Droste-Hülshoff." *Deutsche Vierteljahrsschrift für Literaturwissenschaft Und Geistesgeschichte* 71, no. 1 (1997): 127–46.

———. "Shoah Business: Maxim Biller and the Problem of Contemporary German-Jewish Literature." *German Quarterly* 74, no. 2 (2001): 111–31.

Chazan, Guy, Leila Abhoud, and Adrienne Klaser. "Israel-Hamas War unleashes Wave of Anti-semitism in Europe." *Financial Times*, October 15, 2023. Online at: https://www.ft.com/content/ed744535-d04f-4519-ac27-2be077cac912. Last accessed July 25, 2024.

Codrai, Bettina A. "Lost in Third Space? Narrating German-Jewish Identity in Maxim Biller's Autobiography *Der gebrauchte Jude* (2009)." *Jewish Culture and History* 14, no. 2/3 (2013): 126–39.

Cohen, Hadas, and Dani Kranz. "Israeli Jews in The New Berlin: From Shoah Memories to Middle Eastern Encounters." *Cultural Topographies of the New Berlin*, edited by Karin Bauer and Jennifer Ruth Hosek, 322–46. New York, Oxford: Berghahn Books, 2017.

Cohen, Richard I. "The 'Wandering Jew' from Medieval Legend to Modern Metaphor." In *The Art of Being Jewish in Modern Times*, edited by Barbara Kirshenblatt-Gimblett and Jonathan Karp, 147–75. Philadelphia: University of Pennsylvania Press, 2008.

Cohen, Yinon, and Irena Kogan. "Jewish Immigration from the Former Soviet Union to Germany and Israel in the 1990s." *Leo Baeck Year Book* 50 (2005): 249–65.

Cohen, Yinon, Yitchak Haberfeld, and Irena Kogan. "Who Went Where? Jewish Immigration from the Former Soviet Union to Israel, the USA and Germany, 1990–2000." *Israel Affairs* 17, no. 1 (2011): 7–20.

Cohen-Weisz, Susanne. *Jewish Life in Austria and Germany since 1945: Identity and Communal Reconstruction*. New York: Central European Press, 2016.

Corsten, Anna. "Jewish Left-Wing Intellectuals in Postwar Germany: The Case of Micha Brumlik and the Israeli Palestinian Conflict Between Antisemistism and Anti-Zionism." In *The European Left and the Jewish question, 1848–1992, between Zionism and Anti-semitism*, edited by Alessandra Tarquini, 262–82. Cham: Palgrave Macmillan, 2021.

Creuzberger, Stefan. "Freedom Fighter and Anti-Tsarist Rebel. Imam Shamil and Imperial Memory in Russia." In *Sites of Imperial Memory—Commemorating Colonial Rule in the Nineteenth and Twentieth Centuries*, edited by Dominik Geppert and Frank Lorenz Müller, 170–84. Manchester: Manchester University Press, 2015.

Cronin, Joseph. *Russian-speaking Jews in Germany's Jewish Communities, 1990–2005*. Basingstoke: Palgrave Macmillan, 2019.

———. "Wladimir Kaminer and Jewish Identity in 'Multikulti' Germany." *Skepsis* 9/10 (2018): 65–77.

Czollek, Max. *Desintegriert euch!* Munich: Carl Hanser Verlag, 2018.

———. "Tage der Jüdisch-Muslimischen Leitkultur." Online at: https://www.gorki.de/de/tdjml. Last accessed July 25, 2024.

Demetz, Peter. *After the Fires: Recent Writing in the Germanys, Austria and Switzerland*. New York: Harcourt Brace Jovanovich, 1986.

Desbois, Father Patrick. *The Holocaust by Bullets: A Priest's Journey to Uncover the Truth Behind the Murder of 1.5 Million Jews*. New York: Palgrave MacMillan, 2009.

Deutsch, Gotthard. "Hawkers and Peddlers." *Jewish Encyclopedia*. Online at: https://www.jewishencyclopedia.com/articles/7349-hawkers-and-pedlers. Last accessed July 25, 2024.

Deutscher, Isaac. "The Non-Jewish Jew." In Deutscher, *The Non-Jewish Jew and Other Essays*, 25–41. New York: Oxford University Press, 1968.

Dietz, Barbara. "German and Jewish Migration from the Former Soviet Union to Germany: Background, Trends and Implications." *Journal of Ethnic and Migration Studies* 26, no. 4 (2000): 635–52.

Diner, Dan. "Deutsch-jüdisch-russische Paradoxien oder Versuch eines Kommentars aus Sicht des Historikers." In *Ausgerechnet Deutschland! Jüdisch-russische Einwanderung in die Bundesrepublik: Begleitpublikation zur Ausstellung im Jüdischen Museum Frankfurt*, edited by Dmitrij Belkin and Raphael Gross, 18–20. Berlin: Nicolai Verlag, 2010.

———. "Negative Symbiose: Deutsche und Juden nach Auschwitz." *Babylon* 1 (1986): 9–20.

———. "Residues of Empire: The Paradigmatic Meaning of Jewish Trans-territorial Experience for an Integrated European History." In *The New German Jewry and the European Context: The Return of the European Jewish Diaspora*, edited by Y. Michal Bodemann, 33–49. New York: Palgrave Macmillan, 2008.

———. "Restitution and Memory: The Holocaust in European Political Cultures." *New German Critique*, 90 (2003): 36–44.

Dischereit, Esther. *Merryn*. Frankfurt am Main: Suhrkamp, 1992.

Dollinger, Rolland. "Anti-Semitism because of Auschwitz: An Introduction to the Works of Henryk M. Broder." In *Rebirth of a Culture: Jewish Writing and Identity in Austria and Germany*, edited by Hillary Herzog, Todd Herzog, and Benjamin Lapp, 67–82. New York: Berghahn, 2008.

Dweck, Yaacob. *Dissident Rabbi: The Life of Jacob Sasportas*. Princeton, NJ: Princeton University Press, 2019.

Edwards, David W. "Nicholas I and Jewish Education." *History of Education Quarterly* 22, no. 1 (1982): 45–53.

Efron, John M. *German Jewry and the Allure of the Sephardic*. Princeton, NJ: Princeton University Press, 2016.

Egger, Sabine. "The Poetics of Movement and Deterritorialisation in Katja Petrowskaja's *Vielleicht Esther* (2014)." *Modern Languages Open* 1 (2020): 1–18. Online at: https://doi.org/10.3828/mlo.v0i0.297. Last accessed July 25, 2024.

Endelman, Todd. "Assimiliation and Assimilationism." In Michelle B. Hart and Tony Michels, *The Cambridge History of Judaism*, 291–311. Cambridge: Cambridge University Press, 2017.

Eskin, Blake. *A Life in Pieces: The Making and Unmaking of Binjamin Wilkomirski*. New York and London: Norton, 2002.

Esformes, Maria. "The Sephardic Voice of Elias Canetti." *European Judaism: A Journal for The New Europe* 33, no. 1 (2000): 109–17.

Eulitz, Melanie. "Die jüdisch-liberale Bewegung in Deutschland nach 1990." In *Russisch-jüdische Gegenwart in Deutschland: Interdisziplinäre Perspektiven auf eine Diaspora im Wandel*, edited by Karen Körber, 37–59. Göttingen: V&R, 2015.

Eytan, Freddy. "The Complexity of the Relations between European Jewry and Israel." *Jewish Political Studies Review* 28, no. 3 (2017): 30–37.

Feiner, Shmuel. *The Jewish Enlightenment*. Philadelphia: University of Pennsylvania Press, 2004.

Ferziger, Adam S. "Feminism and Heresy: The Construction of a Jewish Metanarrative." *Journal of the American Academy of Religion* 77, no. 3 (2009): 494–546.

Fiero, Petra S. *Zwischen Enthüllen und Verstecken: eine Analyse von Barbara Honigmanns Prosawerk*. Tübingen: Niemeyer, 2008.

Finch, Helen. "Ressentiment beyond Nietzsche and Amery; H. G. Adler between Literary Ressentiment and Divine Grace." In *Re-thinking Ressentiment: On the Limits of Criticism and the Limits of its Critics*, edited by Jeanne Riou and Mary Gallagher, 71–86. Bielefeld: transcript, 2016.

Finkelstein, Miriam. "From German into Russian and Back. Russian-German Translingual Literature." In *Routledge Handbook of Translingual Literature*, edited by Steven Kellmann and Natasha Lvovich, 188–99. London: Routledge, 2021.

Fogel, Jeremy. *Jewish Universalisms: Mendelssohn, Cohen, and Humanity's Highest Good*. Hanover, NH, and London: Brandeis University Press, 2023.

Foroutan, Naika. *Die postmigrantische Gesellschaft: Ein Versprechen der pluralen Demokratie*. Bielefeld: transcript, 2019.

Freeborn, Richard. "The Nineteenth Century: The Age of Realism." In *The Cambridge History of Russian Literature*, edited by Charles Moser, 248–32. Cambridge: Cambridge University Press, 1992.

Funk, Mirna. "Am Ende eines langen Weges." *Zeit Magazin*, November 18, 2021: 58–61.

———. "Beänstigend." *Jüdische Allgemeine*, February 22, 2024. Online at: https://www.juedische-allgemeine.de/meinung/beaengstigende-empathielosigkeit/. Last accessed July 25, 2024.

———. "'Es gibt keine absolute Wahrheit.'" *Jüdische Allgemeine*, May 27, 2021: 3. Online at: https://www.juedische-allgemeine.de/kultur/es-gibt-keine absolute-wahrheit/. Last accessed September 30, 2024.

———. *Winternähe*. Frankfurt am Main: S. Fischer Verlag, 2015.

———. "'Wir brauchen Israel. Sonst sind wir alle tot.'" *Noz news*, November 7, 2023. Online at: https://www.noz.de/deutschland-welt/nahostkrieg/artikel/mirna-funk-die-hamas-verdient-geld-mit-jedem-kind-das-stirbt-45802288. Last accessed July 25, 2024.

Gammer, Moshe. *Muslim Resistance to the Tsar: Shamil and The Conquest of Chechnia and Daghestan*. London: Frank Cass & Co., 1994.

———. "Shamil in Soviet Historiography." *Middle Eastern Studies* 28, no. 4 (1992): 729–77.

Ganter, Ezster B., and Jay (Koby) Oppenheim. "Jewish Space Reloaded: An Introduction." *Anthropological Journal of European Cultures* 23, no. 2 (2014): 1–10.

Garloff, Katja. *Making German Jewish Literature Anew: Authorship, Memory, and Place*. Bloomington: Indiana University Press, 2022.

———. *Mixed Feelings: Tropes of Love in German Jewish Culture*. Ithaca, NY: Cornell University Press, 2016.

———. "The Power of Paratext: Jewish Authorship and Testimonial Authority in Benjamin Stein's *Die Leinwand*." In *Cross the Disciplinary Divide: Conjunctions in German and Holocaust Studies*, edited by Jennifer Kapczynski and Erin McGlothlin, 141–55. Rochester, NY: Camden House, 2016.

———. "What Is a German Jewish Author? Authorial Self-Fashioning in Maxim Biller, Esther Dischereit, and Barbara Honigmann." In *German Jewish Literature after 1990*, edited by Agnes Mueller and Katja Garloff, 19–37. Rochester, NY: Camden House, 2018.

Garloff, Katja, and Agnes Mueller. "Interview with Olga Grjasnowa." In *German Jewish Literature After 1990*, edited by Garloff and Mueller, 223–28. Rochester, NY: Camden House, 2018.

Gay, Peter. *Weimar Culture, the Outsider as Insider*. New York: Harper & Row, 1968.

Gelber, Mark H. "Thomas Mann and Anti-semitism." *Patterns of Prejudice* 17, no. 4 (1983): 31–40.

Gelbin, Cathy. "Nomadic Cosmopolitanism: Jewish Prototypes of Cosmopolitan in the Writings of Stefan Zweig, Joseph Roth and Lion Feuchtwanger, 1918–1933." *Jewish Culture and History* 16, no. 2 (2005): 157–77.

———. *The Golem Returns: From German Romantic Literature to Global Jewish Culture, 1808–2008*. Ann Arbor: University of Michigan Press, 2011.

———. "The Monster Returns: Golem Figures in The Writings of Benjamin Stein, Esther Dischereit and Doron Rabinovici." In *Rebirth of a Culture: Jewish Writing in Austria and Germany Today*, edited by Hilary Herzog, Todd Herzog, and Ben Lapp, 19–33. New York: Berghahn Books, 2008.

Gelbin, Cathy, and Sander Gilman. *Cosmopolitanism and The Jews*. Ann Arbor: University of Michigan Press, 2017.

Gelhard, Dorothee. *Mit dem Gesicht nach vorne gewandt: Erzählte Tradition in der deutsch-jüdischen Literatur*. Wiesbaden: Harrassowitz, 2008.

Georgiou, Myria, and Rafal Zaborowski. "Media Coverage of the 'Refugee Crisis': A Cross-European Perspective," Council of Europe, 2017. Online at: https://rm.coe.int/media-coverage-of-the-refugee-crisis-a-cross-european-perspective/16807338f7. Last accessed July 25, 2024.

Gilman, Sander. "Becoming a Jew by Becoming a German: The Newest Jewish Writing from the 'East.'" *Shofar* 25, no. 1 (2006): 16–32.

———. "Can the Experience of Diaspora Judaism Serve as a Model for Islam in Today's Multicultural Europe?" In *The New German Jewry and the European Context: The Return of the European Jewish Diaspora*, edited by Y. Michal Bodemann, 53–72. New York: Palgrave Macmillan, 2008.

———. "German Reunification and The Jews." *New German Critique* 52 (1991): 173–91.

———. "Introduction: Ethnicity-Ethnicities-Literature-Literatures." *PMLA* 113, no. 1 (1998): 19–27.

———. *Multiculturalism and The Jews*. New York: Routledge, 2006.
———. "The Case of Circumcision: Diaspora Judaism as a Model for Islam?" In *Anti-semitism and Islamophobia in Europe*, edited by James Renton and Ben Gidley, 143–64. London: Palgrave Macmillan, 2017.
———. "The Jewish Nose: Are Jews White? Or, the History of the Nose Job." In Gilman, *The Jew's Body*, 169–93. London: Routledge, 1991.
———. *The Jew's Body*. London: Routledge, 1991.
Gitelman, Zvi. "Homelands, Diasporas, and the Islands in Between." In *The New Jewish Diaspora: Russian-speaking Jews in the United States, Israel, and Germany*, edited by Zvi Gitelman. New Brunswick: Rutgers University Press, 2016.
Goethe, Johann Wolfgang. *Aus meinem Leben: Dichtung und Wahrheit*, vol. 1. Stuttgart: Reclam, 1991.
Goldish, Matt. "Sabbatai Zevi and the Sabbatean Movement." In *The Cambridge History of Judaism*, edited by Jonathan Karp and Adam Sutcliffe, 491–521. Cambridge: Cambridge University Press, 2017.
Gordis, Daniel. *We Stand Divided: The Rift Between American Jews and Israel*. New York: HarperCollins, 2019.
Gordon, Aleksandr V. "The Russian Enlightenment." *Russian Studies in History* 48, no. 3 (2009): 30–49.
Gorelik, Lena. "'Herr Grinblum, sie sind kein Jude!'" *Aufbau* 71, no. 1 (2005): 20–21.
———. "Jüdisch sein bedeutet nicht, Opfer zu sein." *Süddeutsche Zeitung*, January 27, 2014. Online at: https://www.sueddeutsche.de/politik/lena-gorelik-ueber-die-belagerung-von-leningrad-juedisch-sein-bedeutet-nicht-opfer-zu-sein-1.1872713. Last accessed July 25, 2024.
Goschler, Constantin, and Anthony Kauders. "1969–1989." In *A History of Jews in Germany Since 1945: Politics, Culture, and Society*, edited by Michael Brenner, 330–33. Bloomington: Indiana University Press, 2018.
———. "The Jews in German Society." In *A History of Jews in Germany since 1945*, edited by Michael Brenner, 325–76. Bloomington: Indiana University Press, 2018.
Göttsche, Florian, Jan Eberle, and Gunter Brückner. "Immigration into Germany from the Former Soviet Union." In *Migration from the Newly Independent States: Societies and Political Orders in Transition*, edited by Mikhail Denisenko, Salvatore Strozza, and Matthew Light, 243–75. Cham: Springer, 2020.
Gould, Rebecca. "Imam Shamil." In *Russia's People of Empire: Life Stories from Eurasia, 1500 to the Present*, edited by Steve Norris and Willard Sunderland, 117–28. Bloomington: Indiana University Press.
Green, Abigail. *Moses Montefiore: Jewish Liberator, Imperial Hero*. Cambridge, MA: Harvard University Press, 2010.
Grinberg, Marat. *The Soviet Jewish Bookshelf: Jewish Culture and Identity Between the Lines*. Waltham, MA: Brandeis University Press, 2022.
Grjasnowa, Olga. "Aus sicherer Entfernung." *Akzente: Zeitschrift für Literatur* 62, no. 2 (2015): 62–68.

———. *Der Russe ist einer, der Birken liebt*. Munich: Hanser, 2012.
———. *Der verlorene Sohn*. Berlin: Aufbau, 2020.
———. *Die juristische Unschärfe einer Ehe*. Munich: Carl Hanser Verlag, 2014.
———. *Die Macht der Mehrsprachigkeit*. Berlin: Duden, 2021.
———. *Gott ist nicht schüchtern*. Berlin: Aufbau Verlag, 2017.
———. "Privilegien." In *Eure Heimat ist unser Albtraum*, edited by Fatma Aydemir and Hengameh Yaghoobfirah. Berlin: Ullstein, 2019.
———. "Von Baku nach Berlin." *Die Presse*, February 13, 2021, I-II.
Gromova, Alina. "Eine heterogene Gruppe." In *Dossier—Judentum und Kultur*, in the *Zeitung des Deutschen Kulturrates*. Berlin: ConBrio Verlagsgesellschaft, 2016. Online at: https://www.kulturrat.de/wp-content/uploads/2016/10/Judentum_Kultur.pdf. Last accessed July 25, 2024.
———. *Generation "Koscher Light."* Bielefeld: transcript, 2013.
———. "Wir haben Juden erwartet und es kamen Russen. Umgang junger Juden mit Fremdbildern." In *Perspektiven jüdischer Bildung: Diskurse – Erkenntnisse – Positionen*, edited by Doron Kiesel, 20–33. Leipzig: Hentrich und Hentrich, 2017.
Guenther, Christina. "Exile and the Construction of Identity in Barbara Honigmann's Trilogy of Diaspora." *Comparative Literature Studies* 40, no. 2 (2003): 215–31.
———. "Julya Rabinowich's Transnational Poetics: Staging Border-Crossings in Theater and Fiction." *Women in German Yearbook* 33 (2017): 128–56.
———. "The Poetics of Ritual in Diaspora: Anna Mitgutsch's 'Familienfest' and Vladimir Vertlib's 'Letzter Wunsch.'" *Journal of Austrian Studies* 45, no. 1/2 (2012): 93–118.
Hamidouche, Martina. "The New Austrian Family Novel: Eva Menasse's *Vienna* (2005)." *Austrian Studies* 19 (2011): 187–99.
Harré, Rom, and Luk van Langenhove. "Varieties of Positioning," *Journal for the Theory of Social Behaviour* 21 (1991): 393–407.
Heine, Thomas. "*Der Schimmelreiter*: An Analysis of the Narrative Structure." *German Quarterly* 55, no. 4 (1982): 554–64.
Heiss, Lydia H. "Lena Gorelik's Autofictional Letter *Lieber Mischa*: A Guide to Being Jewish in Contemporary Germany." In *Contested Selves: Life Writing and German Culture*, edited by Katja Herges and Elisabeth Krimmer, 205–28. Rochester, NY: Camden House, 2021.
Helfer, Martha B. "The Male Muses of Romanticism: The Poetics of Gender in Novalis, E. T. A. Hoffmann, and Eichendorff." *German Quarterly* 78, no. 3 (2005): 299–319.
Hessing, Jacob. "Aufbrüche. Zur deutsch-jüdischen Literatur seit 1989." In *Handbuch der deutsch-jüdischen Literatur*, edited by Hans Otto Horch, 244–69. Berlin: de Gruyter, 2016.
Himmelfarb, Jan. *Sterndeutung*. Munich: C. H. Beck, 2015.
Hochman, Oshrat, and Sibylle Heilbrunn. "'I am not a German Jew. I am a Jew with a German passport': German-Jewish identification among

Jewish Germans and Jewish German Israelis." *Identities* 25, no. 1 (2018): 104–23.

Hödl, Klaus. *Entangled Entertainers: Jews and Popular Culture in Fin-de-Siècle Vienna*. Translated by Corey Twitchell. New York: Berghahn, 2019.

Hoffmann, Michael. "Translator's Preface." In Joseph Roth, *The Wandering Jews*. New York and London: W. W. Norton & Company, 2001.

Horowitz, David, ed. *Isaac Deutscher: The Man and His Work*. London: Macdonald, 1971.

Hughes, Aaron W. *Rethinking Jewish Philosophy: Beyond Particularism and Universalism*. Oxford: Oxford University Press, 2014.

Idel, Mosche. *Golem: Jewish Magical and Mystical Traditions on the Artificial Anthropoid*. Albany: State University of New York Press, 1990.

Igelhaut, Christina. "Young, Jewish and Queer." *Deutschland.de*, January 28, 2022. Online at: https://www.deutschland.de/en/topic/life/german-rabbi-helene-shani-braun-young-jewish-and-queer. Last accessed July 25, 2024.

Isterheld, Nora. *"In der Zugluft Europas" – Zur deutschsprachigen Literatur russischstämmiger AutorInnen*. Bamberg: University of Bamberg Press, 2017.

Jacobs, Susie. "Globalisation, Anti-globalisation and the Jewish 'Question.'" *European Review of History: Revue européenne d'histoire* 18, no. 1 (2011): 45–56.

Jeffreys, Tom. *The White Birch: A Russian Reflection*. London: Corsair, 2021.

Jeremiah, Emily. *Nomadic Ethics in Contemporary Women's Writing in German: Strange Subjects*. Rochester, NY: Camden House, 2012.

Jessen, Jens. "Die Kippa steht ihm schon mal gut." *Die Zeit*, December 8, 2016. Online at: https://www.zeit.de/2016/49/dmitrij-kapitelman-das-laecheln-meines-unsichtbaren-vaters. Last accessed July 25, 2024.

Jungmann, Alexander. *Jüdisches Leben in Berlin: Der aktuelle Wandel in einer metropolitanen Diasporagemeinschaft*. Bielefeld: transcript, 2007.

Kapitelman, Dmitrij. *Das Lächeln meines unsichtbaren Vaters*. Munich: dtv, 2018 [2016].

Kaplan, Aryeh. *Sefer Yetzirah: The Book of Creation in Theory and Practice*. San Francisco: Weiser Books, 1997.

Katlewski, Heinz-Peter. *Judentum im Aufbruch: Von der neuen Vielfalt jüdischen Lebens in Deutschland, Österreich und der Schweiz*. Berlin: Jüdische Verlagsanstalt, 2002.

Katsnelson, Anna. "Introduction to The New Wave of Russian Jewish American Culture," *East European Jewish Affairs* 46, no. 3 (2016): 241–44.

Katz, Elena M. *Neither With Them, Nor Without Them: The Russian Writer and The Jew in the Age of Realism*. Syracuse: Syracuse University Press, 2008.

Katz, Steven T. "Shoah." In *History of Jewish Philosophy*, edited by Daniel Frank and Oliver Leaman, 758–76. London: Routledge, 1997.

Kauders, Anthony. *Unmögliche Heimat: Eine deutsch-jüdische Geschichte der Bundesrepublik*. Munich: Deutsche Verlags-Anstalt, 2007.

Kaufmann, Kat. *Superposition*. Berlin: Ullstein, 2017 [2015].

Kermani, Navid. "Auschwitz morgen." *Frankfurter Allgemeine Zeitung*, July 7, 2017. Online at: https://www.faz.net/aktuell/feuilleton/debatten/auschwitz-morgen-navid-kermani-ueber-die-zukunft-der-erinnerung-15094667.html. Last accessed July 25, 2024.

Kessler, Judith. "Homo Sovieticus in Disneyland: The Jewish Communities in Germany Today." In *The New German Jewry and the European Context: The Return of the European Jewish Diaspora*, edited by Y. Michal Bodemann, 131–43. New York: Palgrave Macmillan, 2008.

Kilcher, Andreas B. "Diasporakonzepte." In *Handbuch der deutsch-jüdischen Literatur*, edited by Hans Otto Horch, 135–50. Berlin: de Gruyter, 2016.

———. "Exterritorialitäten. Zur kulturellen Selbstreflexion der aktuellen deutsch-jüdischen Literatur." In *Deutsch-jüdische Literatur der neunziger Jahre*, edited by Sander Gilman and Hartmut Steinecke, 131–46. Berlin: Erich Schmidt Verlag, 2002.

———. "Was ist 'deutsch-jüdische Literatur'? Eine historische Diskursanalyse," *Weimarer Beiträge* 45 (1999): 485–517.

Koehler, Daniel. "The Halle, Germany, Synagogue Attack and the Evolution of the Far-right Terror threat." *CTC Sentinel* 12, no. 11 (2019): 14–20. Online at: https://doi.org/10.17606/5z9d-w597. Last accessed July 25, 2024.

Kontje, Todd. *Thomas Mann's World: Empire, Race, and the Jewish Question*. Ann Arbor: University of Michigan Press, 2011.

Körber, Karen. "Conflicting Memories, Conflicting Identities. The Russian-Jewish Immigration and The Image of a New German Jewry." In *Migration, Memory and Diversity in Germany after 1945*, edited by Cornelia Wilhelm, 276–96. Oxford/New York: Berghahn, 2018.

———. "Puschkin oder Thora? Der Wandel der jüdischen Gemeinden in Deutschland." *Tel Aviver Jahrbuch für deutsche Geschichte* 37 (2009): 233–54.

———. "Widerstreitende Erinnerungen." In *Neues Judentum – altes Erinnern? Zeiträume des Gedenkens*, edited by Dmitrij Belkin, Lara Hensch, and Eva Lezzi, 79–94. Berlin: Hentrich & Hentrich Verlag, 2017.

———. "Zäsur, Wandel Oder Neubeginn? Russischsprachige Juden in Deutschland zwischen Recht, Repräsentation und Realität." In *Russisch-jüdische Gegenwart in Deutschland: Interdisziplinäre Perspektiven auf eine Diaspora im Wandel*, edited by Karen Körber, 13–36. Göttingen: V&R, 2015.

Körber, Karen, and Andreas Gotzmann, eds. *Lebenswirklichkeiten: Russischsprachige Juden in der deutschen Einwanderungsgesellschaft*. Göttingen: V&R, 2022.

Korey, William. "The Origins and Development of Soviet Anti-Semitism: An Analysis." *Slavic Review* 31 (1972): 111–35.

Kranz, Dani. "Das Körnchen Wahrheit im Mythos: Israelis in Deutschland – Diskurse, Empirie und Forschungsdesiderate." *Medaon* 14, no. 27 (2020): 1–15.

———. "Forget Israel—The Future Is in Berlin! Local Jews, Russian Immigrants, and Israeli Jews in Berlin and across Germany." *Shofar* 34, no. 4 (2016): 5–28.

———. "Where to Stay and Where to Go? Ideas of Home and Homelessness amongst Third-Generation Jews Who Grew Up in Germany." In *In The Shadows of Memory: The Holocaust and the Third Generation*, edited by Esther Jilovsky, Jordana Silverstein, and David Slucki, 179–208. London: Vallentine Mitchell, 2014.

Krasner, Jonanthan. "The Place of Tikkun Olam in American Jewish Life." *Jewish Political Studies Review* 25, no. 3/4 (2013): 59–98.

Krasuska, Karolina. *Soviet-born: The Afterlives of Migration in Jewish American Fiction*. New Brunswick, NJ: Rutgers University Press, 2024.

Krenz-Dewe, Linda. "Zum wechselseitigen Verhältnis von Identitätskonstruktion und (brüchiger) Überlieferung in Julya Rabinowichs *Spaltkopf*." *Yearbook for European Jewish Literature Studies* 5, no. 1 (2018): 67–85.

Laanes, Eneken, "Katja Petrowskaja's Translational Poetics of Memory." *New German Critique* 51, no. 2 (2024): 51–78.

Landry, Olivia. "Rethinking Migration: The Intervention of Theater." *German Quarterly* 90, no. 2 (2017): 222–24.

Langer, Armin. *Ein Jude in Neukölln: Mein Weg zum Miteinander der Religionen*. Berlin: Aufbau Verlag, 2016.

Layton, Susan. "Imagining a Chechen Military Aristocracy: The Story of The Georgian Princesses Held Hostage by Shamil." *Central Asian Survey* 23, no. 2 (2004): 183–203.

———. *Russian Literature and Empire: Conquest of The Caucasus from Pushkin to Tolstoy*. Cambridge: Cambridge University Press, 1994.

Lazier, Benjamin. *God Interrupted*. Princeton, NJ, and Oxford: Princeton University Press, 2008.

Lehmann, Jürgen. *Russische Literatur in Deutschland: Ihre Rezeption durch deutschsprachige Schriftsteller und Kritiker vom 18. Jahrhundert bis zur Gegenwart*. Stuttgart: Metzler-Verlag, 2015.

Lejeune, Philippe. "The Autobiographical Pact." In *On Autobiography*, edited by P. J. Eakin, 3–28. Minneapolis: University of Minneapolis Press, 1989.

Levesque, Paul. "The Double-Edged Sword: Anti-Semitism and Anti-Wagnerianism in Thomas Mann's 'Wälsungenblut.'" *German Studies Review* 20, no. 1 (1997): 9–21.

Levy, Daniel, and Natan Sznaider. *Human Rights and Memory*. Pittsburgh: Pennsylvania State University Press, 2010.

———. *The Holocaust and Memory in a Global Age*. Philadelphia, PA: Temple University Press, 2006.

Levy, Jack. *The Sephardim in the Holocaust: A Forgotten People*. Tuscaloosa: The University of Alabama Press, 2020.

Lorenz, Dagmar C. G., ed. *A Companion to the Works of Elias Canetti*. Rochester, NY: Camden House, 2004.

———. "Introduction." In *Rebirth of a Culture: Jewish Identity and Jewish Writing in Germany and Austria Today*, edited by Hillary Hope Herzog, Todd Herzog, and Benjamin Kapp, 1–17. New York: Berghahn Books, 2008.

Lowenstein, Steven M. "Jewish Intermarriage and Conversion in Germany and Austria." *Modern Judaism* 25, no. 1 (2005): 23–61.

Lubrich, Oliver. "Are Russian Jews Postcolonial? Wladimir Kaminer and Identity Politics." *East European Jewish Affairs* 33, no. 3 (203): 35–53.

Lundgren, Svante. *Particularism and Universalism in Modern Jewish Thought*. New York: State University of New York Press, 2001.

Lutjens Jr., Richard N. *Submerged on the Surface: The Not-So-Hidden Jews of Nazi Berlin, 1941–1945*. New York and Oxford: Berghahn, 2019.

Luz, Tilman. "Bei Lanz bringt Deborah Feldman alle gegen sich auf." *Die Welt*, July 5, 2024. Online at: https://www.welt.de/vermischtes/article252380544/Antisemitismus-Debatte-Deborah-Feldman-geraet-bei-Lanz-mit-Michael-Wolffsohn-aneinander.html. Last accessed July 25, 2024.

Maciejko, Pawel, ed. *Sabbatian Heresy: Writings on Mysticism, Messianism, and the Origins of Jewish Modernity*. Waltham, Mass.: Brandeis University Press, 2017.

Maechler, Stefan. *The Wilkomirski Affair: A Study in Biographical Truth*. New York: Schocken, 2001.

Mandel, Arthur. *The Militant Messiah: The Story of Jacob Frank and the Frankists*. Atlantic Highlands, NJ: Humanities Press, 1979.

Mangold, Iljoma. "Religion ist kein Wunschkonzert." *Die Zeit*, April 8, 2010. Online at: https://www.zeit.de/2010/15/Schriftsteller-Benjamin-Stein. Last accessed July 25, 2024.

Martynova, Olga. "Das Wort Jude im 21. Jahrhundert." *Jalta* 3 (2019): 76–82.

———. Interview with Jo Frank in the Literaturhaus, Berlin, on June 5, 2019. Online at: https://www.literaturhaus-berlin.de/programm/zwischen-unbehagen-und-aneignung. Last accessed July 25, 2024.

———. *Mörikes Schlüsselbein*. Graz: Droschl, 2013.

Mayr, Maria. "Europe's Invisible Ghettos: Transnationalism and Neoliberal Capitalism in Julya Rabinowich's *Die Erdfresserin*." In *Transnationalism in Contemporary German-Language Literature*, edited by Elisabeth Herrmann, Carrie Smith-Prei, and Stuart Taberner, 144–62. Rochester, NY: Camden House, 2015.

Mendelsohn, Ezra. *Painting a People: Maurycy Gottlieb and Jewish Art*. Hanover, New Hampshire: University Press of New England, 2002.

Mendes-Flohr, Paul. *Gershom Scholem: The Man and His Work*. Albany: State University of New York Press, 1994.

———. "The Emancipation of European Jewry. Why Was It Not Self-Evident?" *Studia Rosenthaliana* 30, no. 1 (1996): 7–20.

Mennel, Barbara. "Alina Bronsky, *Scherbenpark*: Global Ghetto Girl." In *Emerging German-Language Novelists of the Twenty-First Century*, edited by Lyn Marven and Stuart Taberner, 162–78. Rochester, NY: Camden House, 2011.

Metz, Erich. *Koscher Nostra: Jüdische Gangster in Amerika 1890–1980. Tod in Amerika*. Vienna: Jüdisches Museum der Stadt Wien, 2003.

Meyer, Michael A. *Response to Modernity: A History of the Reform Movement in Judaism*. New York: Oxford University Press, 1988.

Meyers, Jeffrey. *Thomas Mann's Artist-Heroes*. Evanston, IL: Northwestern University Press, 2014.

Michaelis-König, Andree. "Exterritoriale Visionen einer offenen Gesellschaft bei Olga Grjasnowa, Dmitrij Kapitelman und Sasha Marianna Salzmann: Generationelle Anknüpfungspunkte deutschsprachiger jüdischer Autor*innen der dritten Generation." *Yearbook for European Jewish Literature Studies* 10, no. 1 (2023): 71–88.

———. "Multilingualism and Jewishness in Katja Petrowskaja's *Vielleicht Esther*." In *German Jewish Literature after 1990*, edited by Katja Garloff and Agnes Mueller, 146–68. Rochester, NY: Camden House, 2018.

Michaels, Jennifer. "Confronting the Nazi Past." In *Beyond 1989: Re-reading German Literature since 1945*, edited by Keith Bullivant, 1–20. Providence, RI: Berghahn, 1997.

Michman, Dan. "Particularist and Universalist Interpretations of the Holocaust: A Complex Relationship." In *Beyond Ordinary Men: Christopher R. Browning and Holocaust Historiography*, edited by Thomas Pegelow-Kaplan and Jürgen Matthäus, 269–86. Paderborn: Ferdinand Schöning, 2019.

Millet, Kitty. "Our Sabbatian Future." In *Scholar and Kabbalist: The Life and Work of Gershom Scholem*, edited by Mirjam Zadoff and Noam Zadoff, 134–52. Leiden: Brill, 2018.

Mordell, Phineas. "The Origin of Letters and Numerals According to the Sefer Yesirah." *Jewish Quarterly Review* 2, no. 4 (1912): 557–83.

Morris, Leslie, and Karen Remmler. "Introduction." In *Contemporary Jewish Writing in Germany: An Anthology*, edited by Morris and Remmler, 18–20. Lincoln: University of Nebraska Press, 2002.

Moses, A. Dirk. *The Problems of Genocide – Permanent Security and The Language of Transgression*. Cambridge: Cambridge University Press, 2021.

Moses, Stéphane, and Ora Wiskind-Elper. "Gershom Scholem's Reading of Kafka: Literary Criticism and Kabbalah." *New German Critique* 77 (1999): 149–67.

Moyaert, Marianne. "Redemptive Suffering after the Shoah: Going back and forth between Jewish and Christian Traditions." In *Atonement and Comparative Theology: The Cross in Dialogue with Other Religions*, edited by Catherine Cornille, 189–213. New York: Fordham University Press, 2001.

Mueller, Agnes. "Israel as a Place of Trauma and Desire in Contemporary German Jewish Literature." In *Spiritual Homelands: The Cultural*

Experience of Exile, Place and Displacement among Jews and Others, edited by Asher D. Biemann, Richard I. Cohen, and Sarah E. Wobick-Segev, 233–52. Berlin, Boston: de Gruyter, 2020.

Murav, Harriet. *Music from a Speeding Train: Jewish Literature in Post-Revolution Russia*. Stanford, CA: Stanford University Press, 2011.

Myers, Jody. "Kabbalah in the Modern Era." In *The Cambridge History of Judaism*, edited by Mitchell Hart and Tony Michels, 988–1016. Cambridge: Cambridge University Press, 2017.

Nagy, Hajnalka. "Representations of the Other: An Intersectional Analysis of Julya Rabinowich's *Die Erdfresserin* (2012)." *Austrian Studies* 26 (2018): 187–201.

Neiman, Susan. *Learning from the Germans: Race and The Memory of Evil*. New York: Farrar, Straus and Giroux, 2019.

Nekula, Marek. *Franz Kafka and his Prague Contexts*. Prague: Karolinum, 2016.

Ngai, Sianne. *Ugly Feelings*. Cambridge, MA: Harvard University Press, 2005.

Niven, Bill. *Jüd Süß: Das lange Leben eines Propagandafilms*. Halle: Mitteldeutscher Verlag, 2022.

Nolden, Thomas. "Contemporary German Jewish Literature." *German Life and Letters* 47 (1994): 77–93.

———. *Junge jüdische Literatur*. Würzburg: Königshausen und Neumann, 1995.

Nöstlinger, Nette, "Germany records sharp rise in antisemitic incidents." *Politico*, June 25, 2024. Online at: https://www.politico.eu/article/sharp-rise-in-antisemitic-incidents-recorded-in-germany-october-7/. Last accessed July 25, 2024.

Nutt, Harry. "Der Identitätsschwindel des Fabian Wolff: Ein deutscher Fall." *Berliner Zeitung*, July 21, 2023. Online at: https://www.berliner-zeitung.de/open-mind/debatte-der-identitaetsschwindel-des-fabian-wolff-ein-deutscher-fall-li.371616. Last accessed July 25, 2024.

Ó Dochartaigh, Pól. *Germans and Jews since the Holocaust*. London: Palgrave Macmillan, 2016.

Oberwalleney, Barbara. *Heterogenes Schreiben: Positionen der deutschsprachigen jüdischen Literatur (1986–1998)*. Munich: Iudicium, 2001.

Oltermann, Philip. "Israeli Director receives Death Threats after Officials call Berlin Film Festival 'Antisemitic.'" *The Guardian*, February 27, 2024. Online at: https://www.theguardian.com/film/2024/feb/27/israeli-director-receives-death-threats-after-officials-call-berlinale-antisemitic. Last accessed July 25, 2024.

Ortner, Jessica. "The Reconfiguration of The European Archive in Contemporary German-Jewish Migrant-Literature: Katja Petrowskaja's novel *Vielleicht Esther*." *Nordisk Judaistik/Scandinavian Jewish Studies* 28, no. 1 (2017): 38–54.

———. *Transcultural Memory and European Identity in Contemporary German-Jewish Migrant Literature*. Rochester, NY: Camden House, 2022.

Osborne, Dora. "Encountering the Archive in Katja Petrowskaja's *Vielleicht Esther*." *Seminar: A Journal of Germanic Studies* 52, no. 3 (Sept. 2016): 255–72.
Ostow, Robin. "From Victims of Anti-semitism to Post-Modern Hybrids: Representations of (Post)Soviet Jews in Germany." *European Judaism: A Journal for the New Europe* 36, no. 2 (2003): 110–17.
———. "The post-Soviet Immigrants and the *Jüdische Allgemeine* in the New Millennium: Post-communism in Germany's Jewish Communities." *East European Jewish Affairs* 33, no. 2 (2003): 54–70.
Özyürek, Esra. *Subcontractors of Guilt: Holocaust Memory and Muslim Belonging in Postwar Germany*. Stanford, CA: Stanford University Press, 2023.
Pailer, Gaby. "Female Empowerment: Women's Crime Fiction in German." In *Contemporary German Crime Fiction: A Companion*, edited by Thomas Kniesche, 62–79. Berlin: de Gruyter, 2020.
Panagiotidis, Jannis. *Postsowjetische Migration in Deutschland: Eine Einführung*. Weinheim-Basel: Beltz-Juventa, 2020.
———. *The Unchosen Ones: Diaspora, Nation, and Migration in Israel and Germany*. Bloomington: Indiana University Press, 2019.
Paranyushkin, Dmitry. "Polysingularity of Itself." https://polysingularity.com/itself/. Last accessed July 25, 2024.
Patt, Avinoam. *Israel and the Holocaust*. London: Bloomsbury, 2024.
Peck, Jeffrey M. *Being Jewish in The New Germany*. New Brunswick and London: Rutgers University Press, 2016.
Petrowskaja, Katja. "'Die Stunde, zu spüren, was Frieden und Menschlichkeit bedeuten,' Katja Petrowskaja im Gespräch." *Politik und Kultur*, March 31, 2022. Online at: https://www.kulturrat.de/ukraine/aus-politik-kultur-ukraine/die-stunde-zu-spueren-was-frieden-und-menschlichkeit-bedeuten/. Last accessed July 25, 2024.
———. "Halten Sie Wort!" *Frankfurter Allgemeine Sonntagszeitung*, 15 (April 15, 2022): 33. Online at: https://www.faz.net/aktuell/feuilleton/hilfe-fuer-die-ukraine-petrowskajas-offener-brief-an-steinmeier-17960012.html. Last accessed July 25, 2024.
———. *Vielleicht Esther*. Berlin: suhrkamp taschenbuch, 2015 [2014].
———. "'Wie sonst möchten Sie Putin aufhalten?'" *Der Standard*, July 30, 2022. Online at: https://www.derstandard.de/story/2000137861146/katja-petrowskaja-wie-sonst-moechten-sie-putin-aufhalten. Last accessed July 25, 2024.
Pinkus, Benjamin. *The Jews of the Soviet Union: The History of a National Minority*. Cambridge: Cambridge University Press, 1988.
Pinto, Diana. "A New Jewish Identity for Post-1989 Europe." *JPR Policy Paper 1*. London: Institute for Jewish Policy Research, 1996. Online at: https://www.jpr.org.uk/reports/new-jewish-identity-post-1989-europe. Last accessed September 30, 2024.
———. "A New Role for Jews in Europe: Challenges and Responsibilities." *Turning the Kaleidoscope: Perspectives on European Jewry*, edited by

Sandra Lustig and Ian Leveson, 27–40. Oxford and New York: Berghahn Books, 2008.

———. "The New Jewish Europe: Challenges and Responsibilities." *European Judaism: A Journal for the New Europe* 31, no. 2 (1998): 3–15.

Platthaus, Andreas. "Brauchen Kritiker jetzt einen Ahnennachweis?" *Frankfurter Allgemeine Zeitung*, April 8, 2017. Online at: https://www.faz.net/aktuell/feuilleton/debatten/von-der-unfaehigkeit-des-maxim-biller-mit-kritik-umzugehen-14962443.html. Last accessed July 25, 2024.

Polak, Oliver. *Der jüdische Patient*. Cologne: Kiepenheuer & Witsch, 2014.

———. *Gegen Judenhass*. Berlin: Suhrkamp Verlag, 2018.

———. *Ich darf das—ich bin Jude*. Cologne: Kiepenheuer & Witsch, 2008.

Polonsky, Antony. "Nicholas I and the Jews of Russia, 1825–1855." In *The Jews in Poland and Russia: Volume I: 1350 to 1881*, edited by Polonsky, 355–91. Liverpool: Liverpool University Press, 2009.

Popescu, Diana I. "Performance, Memory and Identity: The Israeli Third Generation in Yael Ronen's *Third Generation* Play (2009)." In *In the Shadows of Memory: The Holocaust and the Third Generation*, edited by Esther Jilovsky, Jordana Silverstein, and David Slucki, 20–32. London & Portland, OR: Vallentine Mitchell, 2016.

Popkin, Richard H. "Jewish Messianism and Christian Millenarianism." In *Culture and Politics from Puritanism to the Enlightenment*, edited by Perez Zagorin, 67–90. Berkeley: University of California Press, 1980.

———. "Two Jewish Heresies: Spinozism and Sabbatianism." In *Histories of Heresy in Early Modern Europe*, edited by John Christian Laursen, 171–83. Palgrave Macmillan, New York, 2002.

Pörzgen, Yvonne. "Transgenerationale Traumatisierung durch Heim-Erfahrung in Olga Martynovas *Der Engelherd*, Lena Goreliks *Die Listensammlerin* und Mariam Petrosjans *Dom, v kotoro*." In *Trauma – Generationen – Erzählen: Transgenerationale Narrative in der Gegenwartsliteratur zum ost-, ostmittel- und südosteuropäischen Raum*, edited by Yvonne Drosihn, Ingeborg Jandl, and Eva Kowolli, 138–52. Berlin: Frank & Timme, 2020.

Preece, Julian. "Günter Grass, His Jews, and Their Critics: From Klüger and Gilman to Sebald and Prawer." In *Jews in German Literature since 1945: German-Jewish Literature?*, edited by Pól Ó Dochartaigh, 609–23. Amsterdam: Rodopi, 2000.

Presner, Todd Samuel. *Mobile Modernity: Germans, Jews, Trains*. New York: Columbia University Press, 2007.

Puar, Jasbir K. *Terrorist Assemblages: Homonationalism in Queer Times*. Durham, NC: Duke University Press, 2007.

Rapoport-Albert, Ada, ed. *Hasidism Reappraised*. Liverpool: Liverpool University Press, 1996.

Remennick, Larissa. "'Idealists Headed to Israel, Pragmatics Chose Europe': Identity Dilemmas and Social Incorporation among Former Soviet Jews who Migrated to Germany." *Immigrants & Minorities* 23, no. 1 (2005): 30–58.

———. "The New Russian-Jewish Diaspora in Israel and in The West: Between Integration and Transnationalism." In *Reconsidering Israel-diaspora Relations*, edited by Eliezer Ben-Rafael, Judit Bokser Liwerant, and Yosef Gorny, 267–90. Leiden: Brill, 2014.

———. "Transnational Community in The Making: Russian-Jewish immigrants of the 1990s in Israel." *Journal of Ethnic and Migration Studies* 28, no. 3 (2002): 515–30.

Remmler, Karen. "Encounters Across the Void." In *Unlikely History: The Changing German-Jewish Symbiosis*, edited by Leslie Morris and Jack Zipes, 3–29. New York: Palgrave, 2002.

———. "Maxim Biller. Das Schreiben als 'Counter-Memory.'" In *Shoah in der deutschsprachigen Literatur*, edited by Norbert O. Eke and Hartmut Steinecke, 311–20. Berlin: Erich Schmidt, 2006.

Rietveld-Van Wingerden, Marjoke, and Wim Westerman. "'Hear, Israel.' The Involvement of Jews in Education of The Deaf (1850–1880)." *Jewish History* 23, no. 1 (2009): 41–56.

Robbins, Bruce. *Perpetual War: Cosmopolitanism from the Viewpoint of Violence*. Durham, NC: Duke University Press, 2012.

Roberman, Sveta. "Haunting Images: Stereotypes of Jewishness among Russian Jewish Immigrants in Germany." *East European Jewish Affairs* 42, no. 2 (2012): 325–41.

———. "Impostors of Themselves: Performing Jewishness and Revitalizing Jewish Life among Russian-Jewish Immigrants in Contemporary Germany." *Social Identities: Journal for the Study of Race, Nation and Culture* 20, no. 2/3 (2014): 199–213.

———. "Performing Jewishness and Questioning The Civic Subject among Russian-Jewish Migrants in Germany." In *The New Jewish Diaspora: Russian-speaking Jews in The United States, Israel, and Germany*, edited by Zvi Gitelman, 186–95. New Brunswick: Rutgers University Press, 2016.

Robertson, Ritchie. *Kafka: Judaism, Politics, and Literature*. Oxford: Oxford University Press, 1985.

———. "The Problem of 'Jewish Self-Hatred' in Herzl, Kraus and Kafka." *Oxford German Studies* 16, no. 1 (1985): 81–102.

———. "Rafael Seligmann's *Rubinsteins Versteigerung*: The German-Jewish Family Novel before and after The Holocaust." *Germanic Review* 75, no. 3 (2000): 179–93.

———. *The "Jewish Question" in German Literature, 1749–1939: Emancipation and Its Discontents*. New York: Oxford University Press, 1999.

Roca Lizarazu, Maria. "Ec-static Existences: The Poetics and Politics of Non-Belonging in Sasha Marianna Salzmann's *Außer Sich* (2017)." *Modern Languages Open* 1 (2020): 1–19. Online at: https://modernlanguagesopen.org/articles/10.3828/mlo.v0i0.284. Last accessed July 25, 2024.

———. "'Integration Ist Definitiv Nicht Unser Anliegen, Eher Schon Desintegration.' Postmigrant Renegotiations of Identity and Belonging in Contemporary Germany." *Humanities* 9, no. 42 (2020). Online at: https://doi.org/10.3390/h9020042. Last accessed July 25, 2024.

———. "Moments of Possibility: Holocaust Postmemory, Subjunctivity and Futurity in Katja Petrowskaja's *Vielleicht Esther* (2014) and Robert Menasse's *Die Hauptstadt* (2017)." *Forum for Modern Language Studies* 56, no. 4 (2020): 406–26.
———. *Renegotiating Postmemory: The Holocaust in Contemporary German-Language Jewish Literature*. Rochester, NY: Camden House, 2020.
———. "The Family Tree, The Web, and The Palimpsest: Figures of Postmemory in Katja Petrowskaja's *Vielleicht Esther* (2014)." *Modern Language Review* 113, no. 1 (2018): 168–89.
Rohr, Susanne. "On Finding and Fabricating: Memory and Family History in Katja Petrowskaja's *Vielleicht Esther*." *German Life and Letters* 74, no. 4 (2021): 537–50.
Rosenthal, Gilbert S., and Walter Homolka. *Das Judentum hat viele Gesichter: Die religiösen Strömungen der Gegenwart*. Bergisch-Gladbach: Verlag Hentrich & Hentrich, 2006.
Rosenthal, Steven T. *Irreconcilable Differences: The Waning of the American Jewish Love Affair with Israel*. Hanover, NH: Brandeis University, 2003.
Rosman, Moshe. *Founder of Hasidism: A Quest for the Historical Ba'al Shem Tov*. Berkeley: University of California Press, 1996.
Roth, Joseph. "Jedermann ohne Pass." In *Werke*, vol. 3, 543–48. Cologne: Kiepenheuer & Witsch, 1991.
Roth, Sol. *The Jewish Idea of Ethics and Morality: A Covenantal Perspective*. New York: Yeshiva University Press, 2007.
Rothberg, Michael. "Lived Multidirectionality: 'Historikerstreit 2.0' and The Politics of Holocaust Memory." *Memory Studies* 15, no. 6 (2022): 1316–29.
———. *Multidirectional Memory: Remembering The Holocaust in the Age of Decolonization*. Stanford, CA: Stanford University Press, 2009.
Rothberg, Michael, and Yasemin Yıldız. "Memory Citizenship: Migrant Archives of Holocaust Remembrance in Contemporary Germany." *Parallax* 17, no. 4 (2011): 32–48.
Rubin-Dorsky, Jeffrey. "Philip Roth and American Jewish Identity: The Question of Authenticity." *American Literary History* 13, no. 1 (2001): 79–107.
Salloum, Raniah. "The Chocolate Pudding Exodus." *Spiegel International*, October 10, 2014. Online at: https://www.spiegel.de/international/world/olim-le-berlin-facebook-page-causes-an-uproar-in-israel-a-996503.html. Last accessed July 25, 2024.
Salzmann, Sasha Marianna. *Außer sich*. Berlin: Suhrkamp Verlag, 2017.
———. *Im Menschen muss alles herrlich sein*. Berlin: Suhrkamp Verlag, 2021.
———. "Unsichtbar." In *Eure Heimat Ist Unser Albtraum*, edited by Fatma Aydemir and Hengameh Yaghoobifarah, 13–26. Berlin: Ullstein, 2019.
Salzmann, Sasha Marianna, with Ofer Waldman. *Gleichzeit: Briefe zwischen Israel & Europa*. Frankfurt am Main: Suhrkamp Verlag, 2024.
Samuelson, Hava. "Kabbalah: A Medieval Tradition and its Contemporary Appeal." *History Compass* 6 (2008): 552–87.

Sandke, Randall. *Where the Dark and Light Folks Meet*. Lanham, MD: Scarecrow Press, 2010.
Schama, Simon. *Belonging: The Story of the Jews 1492–1900*. London: Random House, 2017.
Schmitz-Emans, Monika. "Der Roman und seine Konzeption in der deutschen Romantik." *Revue internationale de philosophie* 248, no. 2 (2009): 99–122.
Schoeps, Julius H. "Contemporary Philosophical and Ethical Fights over Jews, Judaism, and The State of Israel." In *Comprehending and Confronting Anti-semitism: A Multi-Faceted Approach*, edited by Lange, Kerstin Mayerhofer, Dina Porat, and Lawrence H. Schiffman, 235–46. Berlin: de Gruyter, 2020.
———. "How Anti-semitism, Obsessive Criticism of Israel, and Do-Gooders Complicate Jewish Life in Germany." In *Reconsidering Israel-diaspora Relations*, edited by Eliezer Ben-Rafael, Judit Bokser Liwerant, and Yosef Gorny, 296–308. Leiden: Brill, 2014.
———. "Russian-Speaking Jews and Germany's Local Jewry." In *Transnationalism: Diasporas and The Advent of a New (Dis)order*, edited by Eliezer Ben-Rafael and Yitzhak Sternberg, 295–302. Leiden: Brill, 2009.
———. "Saving the German-Jewish Legacy." In *Being Jewish in 21st-Century Germany*, edited by Haim Fireberg and Olaf Glöckner, 46–59. Berlin: de Gruyter, 2015.
Schoeps, Julius H., and Olaf Glöckner. "Fifteen Years of Russian-Jewish Immigration to Germany: Successes and Setbacks." In *The New German Jewry and the European Context: The Return of the European Jewish Diaspora*, edited by Y. Michal Bodemann, 144–57. New York: Palgrave Macmillan, 2008.
Schoeps, Julius H., Willi Jasper, and Bernhard Vogt, eds. *Ein neues Judentum in Deutschland? Fremd- und Eigenbilder der russisch-jüdischen Einwanderer*. Potsdam: Verlag für Berlin-Brandenburg, 1999.
———, eds. *Russische Juden in Deutschland: Integration und Selbstbehauptung in einem fremden Land*. Weinheim: Beltz Athenäum, 1996.
Scholem, Gershom. "Redemption Through Sin." In Scholem, *The Messianic Idea in Judaism and Other Essays on Jewish Spirituality*, 78–141. New York: Schocken, 1991 [1971].
———. *Sabbatai Sevi: The Mystical Messiah: 1626–1676*. London: Routledge, 1973.
Schrage, Eva-Maria. *Jüdische Religion in Deutschland—Säkularität, Traditionsbewahrung und Erneuerung*. Wiesbaden: Springer, 2019.
Schwartz, Yaakov. "Germany's 1st post-WWII Military Rabbi Aims to Open Door to More Jewish Recruits." *Times of Israel*, June 19, 2021. Online at: https://www.timesofisrael.com/germanys-1st-post-wwii-military-rabbi-aims-to-open-door-to-more-jewish-recruits/. Last accessed July 25, 2024.

Seligmann, Rafael. Interview with Steven Evans, "Anti-semitism still Haunts Germany." BBC, January 26, 2012. Online at: https://www.bbc.co.uk/news/world-europe-16708340. Last accessed July 25, 2024.

———. *Rubensteins Versteigerung.* Munich: dtv, 1991 [1989].

Shain, Yossi, and Barry Brisman. "Diaspora, Kinship, and Loyalty: The Renewal of Jewish National Security." *International Affairs* 78, no. 1 (2002): 69–95.

Sharifi, Azadeh, "Postmigrant Theatre and Its Impact on Contemporary German Theatre." In *The Palgrave Handbook of Theatre and Migration*, edited by Yama Meerzon and S. E. Wilmer, 79–90. Cham: Palgrave Macmillan, 2023.

Shatz, David, Chaim I. Waxman, Nathan J. Diament, and Robert S. Hirt, eds. *Tikkun Olam: Social Responsibility in Jewish Thought and Law.* New York: Rowmann and Littlefield, 1994.

Shavit, Yaacov. "Realism and Messianism in Zionism and the Yishuv." *Studies in Contemporary Jewry* 7 (1991): 100–27.

Sheaffer, Abby. "Olga Grjasnowa Discusses Her Stunning Debut Novel, *All Russians Love Birch Trees*, with Abby Sheaffer." *Chicago Now*, February 25, 2014. Online at: http://www.chicagonow.com/chicago-literati/2014/02/olga-grjasnowa-discusses-her-stunning-debut-novel-all-russians-love-birch-trees-with-abby-sheaffer. Last accessed July 25, 2024.

Sheffi, Na'ama. "Jews, Germans and the Representation of *Jud Süss* in Literature and Film." *Jewish Culture and History* 6, no. 2 (2003): 25–42.

Shneer, David. "The Third Way: German–Russian–European Jewish Identity in a Global Jewish World." *European Review of History: Revue européenne d'histoire* 18, no. 1 (2011): 111–21.

———. "Wie russischsprachige Immigranten, lesbische Geistliche und orthodoxe amerikanische Juden die Zukunft des deutschen und europäischen Judentums sehen." In *Ausgerechnet Deutschland! Jüdisch-russische Einwanderung in die Bundesrepublik: Begleitpublikation zur Ausstellung im Jüdischen Museum Frankfurt*, edited by Dmitrij Belkin and Raphael Gross, 102–5. Berlin: Nicolai Verlag, 2010.

Sinn, Andrea. "Returning to Stay? Jews in East and West Germany after The Holocaust." *Central European History* 53, no. 2 (2020): 393–413.

Skolnik, Jonathan. "'Jewish Writing' and The Place of Refugee: Olga Grjasnowa's *Gott ist nicht schüchtern.*" *Yearbook for European Jewish Literature Studies* 8 (2021): 148–57.

———. "Memory without Borders? Migrant Identity and The Legacy of The Holocaust in Olga Grjasnowa's *Der Russe ist einer, der Birken liebt.*" In *German Jewish Literature after 1990*, edited by Agnes Mueller and Katja Garloff, 123–45. Rochester, NY: Camden House, 2018.

Slodounik, Rebekah. "German, Jewish, and Female: Encounters with Anti-semitism in Mirna Funk's *Winternähe* (2015) and Deborah Feldman's *Überbitten* (2017)." *Feminist German Studies* 39, no. 1 (2023): 147–72.

Snyder, Timothy. *Bloodlands: Europe between Hitler and Stalin.* New York: Basic Books, 2010.

Sorkin, David. *Jewish Emancipation: A History Across Five Centuries.* Princeton, NJ: Princeton University Press, 2019.

Stanislawski, Michael. *Tsar Nicholas I and The Jews: The Transformation of Jewish Society in Russia, 1825–1855.* Philadelphia: Jewish Publication Society of America, 1983.

Stein, Benjamin. *Das Alphabet des Rabbi Löw.* Berlin: Verbrecher Verlag, 2014.

———. "Der Autor als Seelenstripper." June 3, 2008. Online at: https://turmsegler.net/20100603/der-autor-als-seelenstripper/. Last accessed July 25, 2024.

———. "Erstaunlicher Zufallsfund." June 23, 2008. Online at: https://turmsegler.net/20080623/erstaunlicher-zufallsfund. Last accessed July 25, 2024.

———. "Familiengeschichte." June 14, 2010. Online at: https://turmsegler.net/20100614/familiengeschichte/. Last accessed July 25, 2024.

Steinberg, Michael P., ed. *Walter Benjamin and The Demands of History.* Ithaca, NY: Cornell University Press, 1996.

Steinecke, Hartmut. "Deutsch-jüdische Literatur der 'Zweiten Generation' und die Wende: 'Geht jetzt wieder alles von vorne los'?" In *Mentalitätswandel in der deutschen Literatur zur Einheit (1990–2000),* edited by Volker Wehdeking, 189–200. Berlin: Erich Schmidt, 2000.

———. "'Deutsch-jüdische' Literatur heute. Die Generation nach der Shoah." In *Deutsch-jüdische Literatur der neunziger Jahre. Die Generation nach der Shoah,* edited by Sander L. Gilman and Hartmut Steinecke, 9–16. Berlin: Erich Schmidt, 2002.

———. "'Geht jetzt alles wieder von vorne los?' Deutsch-jüdische Literatur der 'zweiten Generation' und die Wende." In *Deutsch-jüdische Literatur der neunziger Jahre: Die Generation nach der Shoah,* edited by Sander L. Gilman and Hartmut Steinecke, 162–73. Berlin: Schmidt, 2002.

Steiner, Barbara. *Die Inszenierung des Jüdischen: Konversion von Deutschen zum Judentum nach 1945.* Göttingen: Wallstein Verlag, 2015.

Stephan, Felix. "Und manchmal bringen einen die Christen um." *Süddeutsche Zeitung,* August 23, 2019. Online at: https://www.sueddeutsche.de/kultur/dana-von-suffrin-otto-1.4573870. Last accessed July 25, 2024.

Stone, Alison. "Being, Knowledge, and Nature in Novalis." *Journal of the History of Philosophy* 46, no. 1 (2008): 141–63.

Stone, Brangwen. "Refugees Past and Present: Olga Grjasnowa's *Gott ist nicht schüchtern* and Sasha Marianna Salzmann's *Außer sich.*" *Colloquia Germanica* 51, no. 1 (2020): 57–74.

Strack, Christoph. "Muslims in Germany: Life post-Hamas-attack 'like after 9/11.'" *Deutsche Welle,* January 12, 2024. Online at: https://www.dw.com/en/muslims-in-germany-life-post-hamas-attack-like-after-9-11/a-67959092. Last accessed July 25, 2024.

Sutcliffe, Adam. *Judaism and Enlightenment*. Cambridge: Cambridge University Press, 2003.

———. "Judaism and the Politics of Enlightenment." *American Behavioral Scientist* 49, no. 5 (2006): 702–15.

———. "Quarreling over Spinoza: Moses Mendelssohn and The Fashioning of Jewish Philosophical Heroism." In *Renewing the Past, Reconfiguring Jewish Culture: From Al-Andalus to the Haskalah*, edited by Ross Brann and Adam Sutcliffe, 167–87. Philadelphia: University of Pennsylvania Press, 2004.

———. *What Are Jews For?: History, Peoplehood, and Purpose*. Princeton, NJ: Princeton University Press, 2020.

Sweeney, Marvin A. "Pardes Revisited Once Again: A Reassessment of The Rabbinic Legend Concerning the Four Who Entered Pardes." *Shofar* 22, no. 4 (2004): 43–56.

Sznaider, Natan. "Hannah Arendt's Jewish Cosmopolitanism: Between the Universal and the Particular." *European Journal of Social Theory* 10, no. 1 (2007): 112–22.

———. *Jewish Memory and The Cosmopolitan Order*. Cambridge: Polity Press, 2011.

———. "The Summer of Discontent: Achille Mbembe in Germany." *Journal of Genocide Research* 23, no. 3 (2021): 412–19.

Taberner, Stuart. "Germans, Jews, and Turks in Maxim Biller's Novel *Esra*." *German Quarterly* 79, no. 2 (2006): 234–48.

———. "Narrative and Empathy: The 2015 'Refugee Crisis' in Vladimir Vertlib's *Viktor hilft* and Olga Grjasnowa's *Gott ist nicht schüchtern*." *German Life and Letters* 74 (2021): 247–62.

———. "Redemption through Sin: Benjamin Stein's *Das Alphabet des Rabbi Löw* and the Heretical Dynamism of Contemporary German Jewish Literature and Identity." *Modern Language Review* 116 no. 3 (2021): 462–84.

———. "The Possibilities and Pitfalls of a Jewish Cosmopolitanism. Reading Natan Sznaider through Russian-Jewish Writer Olga Grjasnowa's German-language Novel *Der Russe ist einer, der Birken liebt* (All Russians Love Birch Trees)." *European Review of History: Revue européenne d'histoire* 23 (2016): 912–30.

———. "Towards a 'Pragmatic Cosmopolitanism': Rethinking Solidarity with Refugees in Olga Grjasnowa's *Gott ist nicht schüchtern* (2017)." *Modern Language Review* 114, no. 4 (2019): 819–40.

———. *Transnationalism and German-language Literature in the Twenty-first Century*. London: Palgrave MacMillan, 2017.

———. "Worldliness, Jewish Purpose, and the Non-Jewish Jewish Narrator in Olga Grjasnowa's *Der verlorene Sohn* (2020)." *Seminar* 58, no. 4 (2022): 424–45.

Tormos, Fernando. "Intersectional Solidarity." *Politics, Groups, and Identities* 5, no. 4 (2017): 707–20.

Traverso, Enzo. *The Jews and Germany: From the Judeo-German Symbiosis to the Memory of Auschwitz*. Lincoln: University of Nebraska Press, 1995.
Tress, Madeleine. "Foreigners or Jews? The Soviet Jewish refugee populations in Germany and the United States." *East European Jewish Affairs* 27, no. 2 (1997): 21–38.
———. "Germany's new 'Jewish question' or German-Jewry's 'Russian question'?" *New Political Science* 12, no. 1/2 (1993): 75–86.
———. "Jewish Immigrants from the Former Soviet Union in Germany: History, Politics and Social Integration." *East European Jewish Affairs* 33, no. 2 (2003): 7–19.
———. "Soviet Jews in the Federal Republic of Germany: The Rebuilding of a Community." *The Jewish Journal of Sociology* 37, no. 1 (1995): 39–54.
Trzebiner, Channah. *Die Enkelin, oder wie ich zu Pessach die vier Fragen nicht wusste*. Frankfurt am Main: Weissbuch GmbH, 2013.
Vertlib, Vladimir. "Nichtvorbildliche Lieblingsautoren." In *Helden wie ihr: junge Schriftsteller über ihre literarischen Vorbilder*, edited by Jürgen Jakob Becker and Ulrich Janetzki, 198–204. Berlin: Quadriga, 2000.
———. *Viktor hilft*. Vienna: Deuticke, 2018.
Vital, David. *A People Apart: The Jews in Europe, 1789–1939*. Oxford: Oxford University Press, 1998.
Voigtländer, Nico, and Hans-Joachim Voth. "Married to Intolerance: Attitudes toward Intermarriage in Germany, 1900–2006." *American Economic Review* 103, no. 3 (2013): 79–85.
Vowinckel, Dana. "In my Jewish Bag." In *L'Chaim: Schreib zum jüdischen Leben in Deutschland!* Online at: https://www.kulturrat.de/wp-content/uploads/2022/10/Begleitheft_Schreibwettbewerb_LChaim.pdf. Last accessed July 25, 2024.
Wanner, Adrian. "Journeys of Identity: From Soviet Jew to German Writer." In *Migration and Mobility in the Modern Age: Refugees, Travelers, and Traffickers in Europe and Eurasia*, edited by Anika Walke, Jan Musekamp, and Nicole Svobodny, 301–20. Bloomington: Indiana University Press, 2017.
———. *Out of Russia: Fictions of a New Translingual Diaspora*. Evanston, Illinois: Northwestern University Press, 2011.
Waxman, Dov. *Trouble in The Tribe: The American Jewish Conflict over Israel*. Princeton, NJ: Princeton University Press; 2016.
Weinberg, Robert. "The Politics of Remembering: The Treatment of The Holocaust in The Soviet Union." In *Lessons and Legacies VII: The Holocaust in International Perspective*, edited by Dagmar Herzog, 314–32. Evanston, Ill.: Northwestern University Press, 2006.
Weiss, Yfaat, and Lena Gorelik. "The Russian-Jewish Immigration." In *A History of Jews in Germany since 1945*, edited by Michael Brenner, 393–411. Bloomington: Indiana University Press, 2018.
Weiss-Sussex, Godela. "'Dass die tauben Geschichten aufflattern': Narrative, Translingual Creativity and Belonging in Katja Petrowskaja's *Vielleicht*

Esther." *Modern Languages Open* 1 (2020): 1–18. Online at: http://doi.org/10.3828/mlo.v0i0.281. Last accessed July 25, 2024.

Willeke, Stefan. "Der Unzumutbare." *Zeit-Magazin*, February 17, 2017. Online at: https://www.zeit.de/zeit-magazin/2017/10/maxim-biller-biografie-kritik-schriftsteller-literarisches-quartett. Last accessed July 25, 2024.

Wilke, Peter. "Bavaria Premier Keeps Deputy Aiwanger in Office Despite Nazi Scandal." *Politico.eu*, September 3, 2023. Online at: https://www.politico.eu/article/hubert-aiwanger-nazi-antisemitic-scandal-markus-soder-bavaria/. Last accessed July 25, 2024.

Wilson, Dan, *Goethe und die Juden: Faszination und Feindschaft*. Munich: C. H. Beck Verlag, 2024.

Wistrich, Robert S. "Zionism and Its Jewish 'Assimilationist' Critics (1897–1948)." *Jewish Social Studies* 4, no. 2 (1998): 59–111.

Wolfe, Alan. *At Home in Exile: Why Diaspora Is Good for the Jews*. Boston: Beacon Press, 2014.

Wolffsohn, Michael. "Jews in Divided Germany (1945–1990) and Beyond." In *Being Jewish in 21st-Century Germany*, edited by Haim Fireberg and Olaf Glöckner, 13–30. Berlin: de Gruyter, 2015.

Wolfson, Eliot. "Structure, Innovation, and Diremptive Temporality: The Use of Models to Study Continuity and Discontinuity in Kabbalistic Tradition." *Journal for The Study of Religions and Ideologies* 6, no. 18 (2007): 143–67.

World Jewish Congress. "Germany." In *Resolutions Adopted by The Second Plenary Assembly of the World Jewish Congress, Montreux, Switzerland, 27 June–6 July 1948*. London, 1948.

Yıldız, Erol, and Marc Hill, eds. *Nach der Migration: Postmigrantische Perspektiven jenseits der Parallelgesellschaft*. Bielefeld: transcript, 2015.

———, eds. *Postmigrantische Visionen: Erfahrungen – Ideen – Reflexionen*. Bielefeld: transcript, 2018.

Zipes, Jack. "The Contemporary German Fascination for Things Jewish: Toward a Jewish Minority Culture." In *Reemerging Jewish Culture in Germany: Life and Literature since 1989*, edited by Sander Gilman and Karen Remmler, 15–46. New York and London: New York University Press, 1994.

Index

Abraham, Yuval, 180
Adelson, Leslie, 169
Adler, H. G., 40
Aggadah, 65, 69
Aiwanger, Hubert, 13
Al Qaeda, 175
Albé, Francesco, 6, 138, 140
Alderman, Naomi, 121
Altaras, Adriana: allusion to the Mitscherlichs, 44; arrival in Germany, 36; early life, 36, 42–44; marriage, 39; reaction to October 7, 177, 180; reference to Biller, 40; transgression theme, 39, 42
Altaras, Adriana works by: *Doitscha: Eine jüdische Mutter packt aus*, 36; *Jud Sauer*, 36; *Die jüdische Souffleuse*, 37; *Das Meer und ich waren im besten Alter*, 36–37; *titos brille*, 36–46; *Trauer to go*, 36, 44
Améry, Jean, 40, 71, 91
Antmann, Debora, 11
Arendt, Hannah, 178
Auschwitz. *See* Funk, Himmelfarb, Petrowskaja, Trzebiner
Ausländer, Rose, 51

Babi Yar. *See* Petrowskaja
Bagno, Olena, 17
Bakunin, Mikhail, 150, 154
Balla, Mordechai, 9
Ballhaus Naunynstraße theater, 168
Balling, J. Rafael, 6, 138, 140
Banki, Luisa and Battegay, Caspar, 119
Barsilay, Rabbi Levy, 20
Becker, Franziska, 19
Becker, Jurek, 70
Beckermann, Ruth, 2
Behrens, Katja, 2

Belkin, Dimitrij, 11, 55–56, 59, 82, 118
Benjamin, Walter, 93, 96
Ben-Rafael, Eliezer, 16, 18, 21, 52
Bergen-Belsen. *See* Trzebiner
Bhabha, Homi, 2, 170–71
Biendarra, Anke, 47, 141
Biller, Maxim, 2, 3, 4, 5, 15, 34, 35, 124; arrival in Germany, 47; criticism of Czollek, 22, 171; as "provocateur by profession," 33, 165; relationship with Germany, 40
Biller, Maxim works by: *100 Zeilen Hass*, 3; *Biografie*, 33, 35; *Esra*, 169; *Der gebrauchte Jude*, 33, 40, 128; *Harlem Holocaust*, 3; *Sechs Koffer*, 35, 47; *Sieben Versuche zu lieben*, 47; *Die Tochter*, 33
Bobrowski, Johannes, 70
Bodemann, Y Michal, 9, 10, 17, 20, 31, 78, 118
Braese, Stephan, 2, 28
Braidotti, Rosi, 6–7
Braun, Helene Shani, 12
Brecht, Berthold, 163, 173
Broder, Henryk, 15, 34, 40
Bronsky, Alina, 48; allusions to Dostoyevsky, 49
Bronsky, Alina works by: *Baba Dunjas letzte Liebe*, 48; *Die schärfsten Gerichte der tatarischen Küche*, 47–48; *Scherbenpark*, 47; *Der Zopf meiner Großmutter*, 50
Brumlik, Micha, 14, 24, 121
Bühler-Dietrich, Annette, 6, 138, 140
Butler, Judith, 172

Canetti, Elias, 43, 46
Castronuova, Nadia, 158

Celan, Paul, 51
Central Council of Jews in Germany, 11, 21, 40
Central Jewish Council of Germany. *See* Central Council of Jews in Germany
Chabad-Lubavitch, 9
Chechyna, 148, 149
Chernomyrdin, Viktor Stepanovich, 149
Cohen, Hadas, 10
Cold War, end of, 6, 7, 38, 118, 159
Communist show trials, 39
conservative Judaism, 8, 12, 161
cosmopolitan memory, 6, 81, 112, 113
COVID-19, 12
Cronin, Joseph, 20, 49
Czollek, Max, 11, 22, 140, 146, 171; collaborations with Salzmann "Desintegrationskongress" and "Radikale Jüdische Kulturtage," 171; comparison to Benjamin Wilkomirski, 22; Integrationstheater, 31; Jewish background, 22, 171

Danylko, Andriy Mykhailovych / Serduchka, Verka, 135, 136
Deutscher, Isaac, 29, 117, 148, 157
Diner, Dan, 17, 118
Dischereit, Esther, 2, 4, 34, 167
Dischereit, Esther, works by: *Blumen für Otello*, 79; *Joëmis Tisch: Eine jüdische Geschichte*, 3; *Merryn*, 3, 9
Döblin, Alfred, 79
Droste-Hülshoff, Annette von, 59

Egger, Sabine, 110
emancipation of the Jews, 109, 149, 151, 155
Enlightenment, 24, 71, 109, 151, 152, 154, 155. *See also* Jewish Enlightenment
established community, 9, 12, 16–18, 20–21, 35, 39, 45, 47, 55, 61, 76–77, 81, 165
Eulitz, Melanie, 8

exogamy, or marrying out, 22, 42
expulsion of Jews from Spain in 1492, 42

Feldman, Deborah, 10, 127–28, 176
Feuchtwanger, Lion, 79, 163
Finkelstein, Miriam, 49
Fleischmann, Lea, 2–4
Fleischmann, Lea, works by: *Dies ist nicht mein Land:Eine Jüdin verlässt die Bundesrepublik*, 4; *Meine Sprache wohnt woanders: Gedanken zu Deutschland und Israel* (with Chaim Noll) 4
Foroutan, Naika , 30, 160, 161, 168
Frenk, Marina, 51
Freud, Sigmund, 157
Friedmann, Alexandra, 51
Fukelman, Larisa, 20
Funk, Mirna, 23, 29, 90, 93, 159, 161, 170; reaction to October 7, 176–77, 180; references to Auschwitz, 91; references to Biller, 90
Funk, Mirna, *Winternähe*, 27–28, 63, 77, 81–82, 89–99, 116, 120, 129, 136, 162, 164–66, 170, 176

Gammer, Moshe, 148
Gaponenko, Marjana, 49
Gardi, Tomer, 10
Garloff, Katja , 4, 5, 6, 173
Gaza, Israel's invasion of. *See* October 7, 2023
Gelbin, Cathy, 66, 71–72, 79
Gelhard, Dorothee, 66–67
gender identity, transgender identity, 12, 120, 129–30, 134–35, 143, 162
German perpetrators and Jewish victims, 28–29
German Romanticism, 56, 73, 149
Gilman, Sander, 32, 48, 70, 118, 135
Ginzburg, Natalia, 158
Glöckner, Olaf, 18
Gogol, Nikolai, 151, 157
Gorelik, Lena, 5, 6; allusions to Dostoyevsky, 49; arrival in

Germany, 19; tour of Germany with Emcke and Zaree 2023, 20; with Yftat Weiss, 16, 22
Gorelik, Lena, works by: *Herr Grinblum, Sie sind kein Jude!*, 22; *Lieber Mischa . . . Du bist ein Jude*, 50; *Hochzeit in Jerusalem*, 50; *Die Listensammlerin*, 48; *Meine weißen Nächte*, 47, 49, 50; *Verliebt in Sankt Petersburg: Meine russische Reise*, 48; *Wer wir sind*, 48
Goschler, Constantin and Kauders, Anthony, 32
Gottlieb, Maurycy, 172
Gould, Rebecca, 148
Grjasnowa, Olga, 6, 81, 100, 159, 161, 163; comparison to Werfel, 163; reference to Isaac Deutscher, 157; reference to Kafka, 163–64; reference to Loewe, 155–6; references to Montefiore, 152–56; references to Russian literature, 148–49; references to Syria civil war, 148, 157, 172–73
Grjasnowa, Olga, works by: *Aus sicherer Entfernung*, 173; *Gott ist nicht schüchtern*, 79, 80, 148, 163; *Die juristische Unschärfe einer Ehe*, 148, 164, 171; *Die Macht der Mehrsprachigkeit*, 173; *Privilegien*, 174, *Der Russe ist einer, der Birken liebt*, 23, 80, 148; *Der verlorene Sohn*, 29, 80, 89, 117, 120, 128, 146–58, 159, 162, 164, 174
Gromova, Alina, 78, 82
Grushko, Alexandra, 16

halachic tradition, 12, 22–23, 54, 63, 64, 68, 74, 76, 81, 147, 166
Harré, Rom and Langenhove, Luk van, 35
Haskalah. *See* Jewish Enlightenment
Heine, Heinrich, 157, 163
Hesse, Hermann, 59, 72
Hessing, Jakob, 14
Hilsenrath, Edgar, 71
Himmelfarb, Jan, 62, 159, 161, 163, 165, 170, 178; arrival in Germany, 5,6; references to Auschwitz, 54, 60; references to Goethe, 57, 59, 163; references to Grass, 57, 59, 60, 163; references to Kafka, 59, 163–64; references to Treblinka, 54–55, 60; references to Rwanda genocide, 60–61, 77, 170; transgression theme, 76–77
Himmelfarb, Jan, *Sterndeutung*, 27, 36, 46–62, 67, 76, 77, 82, 89, 120, 129, 162, 164–65, 169
historians' controversy (Historikerstreit) 15
Holocaust by bullets, mass shootings, 19, 53, 55, 76, 104, 109–10
Holocaust trauma, 44, 81, 96, 97, 99, 120–21, 123–24, 127, 129, 165
Honigmann, Barbara, 2, 3, 4, 5, 34
Horch, Hans Otto, 14

Isterheld, Nora, 48, 50

Jacobi, Friedrich Heinrich, 71
Jewish Enlightenment (Haskalah), 25, 66, 71, 75, 101, 108, 109, 116, 149
Jewish particularism and universalism, 7, 21, 24, 27, 77, 80, 89, 99, 103, 109, 116–17, 120, 147, 151, 166
Jewish purpose, 25, 117, 119, 148, 152, 156, 167
Jewish quota refugees, 7 8, 15–16, 47, 161
Jewish sensibility, 29, 52, 61, 78, 93, 104, 147
Jewish victimhood, 3, 124, 166
Jews as chosen people, 79, 119
Jews in public discourse, 22, 32, 78, 161, 176
jüdische Kontingentflüchtlinge. *See* Jewish quota refugees
Jurjew, Oleg, 49, 51

Kabbalah, 27, 64–65, 68–70, 116, 166
Kaminer, Wladimir, 48, 49, 50, 84; arrival in Germany, 48; references to Gogol, 49

Kaminer, Wladimir, works by: *Es gab keinen Sex im Sozialismus*, 48; *Goodbye, Moskau: Betrachtungen über Russland*, 48; *Mein deutsches Dschungelbuch*, 48; *Onkel Wanja kommt: Eine Reise durch die Nacht*, 48; *Russendisko*, 48
Kapitelman, Dimitrij, 5, 6, 23, 51, 163, 170; allusions to Kafka, 163
Kapitelman, Dimitrij, works by: *Eine Formalie in Kiew*, 23, 51; *Das Lächeln meines unsichtbaren Vaters*, 23, 163, 170
Kauders, Anthony. *See* Goschler, Constantin
Kaufmann, Kat, 159, 161, 169, 170, 178
Kaufmann, Kat, *Superposition*, 82–89
Kermani, Navid, 79
Kessler, Judith, 18, 22
Kietz, Barbara, 18
Kilcher, Andreas, 3, 79–80, 116, 163
Körber, Karen, 12, 15, 19
Kranz, Dani, 4, 10, 18

Laanes, Eneken, 103
Langenhove, Luk van. *See Harré*
Langer, Armin, 11
Langhoff, Shermin, 168
Lazier, Benjamin, 75
Lejeune, Philippe, 39
Levy, Daniel and Sznaider, Natan, 6, 81, 112
LGBTQ culture, 10, 12, 127, 134–5, 145, 146, 161–62, 166, 172
liberal/Reform Judaism, 1, 8, 22, 45–6, 63, 76, 98, 125–26
Limmud Deutschland, 12
Lubrich, Oliver, 17, 118
Lux, Lana, 79, 167
Luxemburg, Rosa, 157

Mandelstam, Osip, 51
Mangold, Iljoma, 63
Martynova, Olga, 49–51, 167; arrival in Germany, 49
Martynova, Olga, works by: *Das Wort Jude*, 51; *Der Engelherd*, 51; *Mörikes Schlüsselbein*, 49, 79; *Sogar Papageien überleben uns*, 49, 50, 58
Marx, Karl, 157
Maxim Gorki Theater, 146, 168
Mbembe, Achille, 13
Menasse, Eva, 23
Menasse, Robert, 2, 3, 15
Mendelssohn, Moses, 109
Michaelis-König, Andree, 100, 163
Muchina, Lena, 19
Mueller, Agnes, 173
multidirectional memory, 6, 13, 81, 110. *See also* Rothberg
Murav, Harriet, 18–19

Nachmann, Werner, 40
Nama and Herero, extermination of, 13
Neiman, Susan, 9
Netanyahu, Benjamin, 177
Nolden, Thomas, 2
non-Jewish Jew. See also Deutscher

October 7, 2023, Hamas attack, 13, 14, 25, 30, 117, 146, 158, 160–61, 175–76, 179–80; Gaza, Israel's invasion following October 7 , 2023, 14, 23–25, 30, 160, 175–76, 178
Ohel Hachidusch, 8
Orthodox Judaism, 1, 4, 8, 12, 22, 25–28, 32, 40–41, 45, 62–65, 67, 70, 73–74, 75–76, 81, 85, 98, 112, 120–23, 125, 127–29, 157, 159, 161
Ortner, Jessica, 52, 111, 115
Ostow, Robin, 17
Ottoman Empire, 42, 74–75
Özdamar, Sevgi, 79

patchwork Judaism, 56, 119
Pears Jewish Campus Berlin, 9
Petrowskaja, Katja, 4–6, 147, 159, 161, 163, 165, 170, 176, 178; arrival in Germany, 5, 100; references to Auschwitz, 114; references to Babi Yar, 56, 102, 105, 109–15; references to

Russian literature, 100; references to Treblinka, 106; subjunctive remembering / subjunctive approach, 101–2, 109
Petrowskaja, Katja, *Vielleicht Esther*, 28, 56, 77, 99–117
Pinkus, Benjamin, 16
Pinto, Diana, 118
Pitt, Brad, 126–27
Poland, partition of, 151
pop aesthetic, 29, 35, 82–83, 99, 162
postmigrant society, 15, 30, 160, 161–81
postmigrant theater, 168
Presner, Todd, 74
Puar, Jasbir K, 172

queer culture. *See* LGBTQ culture
queering Jewish identity, 35, 138
queering history, 130–32, 136, 139–40
queering narratives, 128, 130, 132, 136, 140

Rabinovici, Doron, 2, 4, 6, 15, 34; arrival in Austria, 5
Rabinovici, Doron, works by: *Andernorts*, 21; *Suche nach M: Roman*, 3
Rabinowich, Julya, 5, 6, 167; arrival in Austria, 47
Rabinowich, Julya, works by: *Erdfresserin*, 78; *Spaltkopf*, 47
Reform Judaism, 8, 12, 24, 26, 41, 46, 62, 63, 75, 81, 93, 161
Remarque, Erich Maria, 163, 173
Remennick, Larissa, 18
Remmler, Karen, 32
repairing the world (tikkun olam), 7, 25, 66, 74, 81, 116–17, 147, 158
reunification of Germany. *See* unification
Rietveld-Van Wingerden, Marjoke, and Westerman, Wim, 108
Roberman, Sveta, 17
Roca Lizarazu, Maria, 6, 110, 138, 140
Ronen, Yael, 10, 11

Rohr, Susanne, 110
Rosenthal, Steven, 23
Roth, Joseph, 50, 58, 59, 79
Roth, Philip, 33
Rothberg, Michael, 81
Russian Empire, 148, 151–52, 174
Russian German Jewish identity, 20, 35, 52, 62
Russian Jewish identity, 47, 50, 178
Russian literature, Russian literary tradition, 26, 49, 100, 148–49, 162
Russlanddeutsche - ethnic Germans, 16

Salzmann, Sasha Marianna, 6, 29, 81, 89, 100, 117, 146, 159, 161, 163, 170, 172, 176, 180; allusions to Kafka, 51, 163–64; collaboration with Waldman, Ofer, *Gleichzeit*, 177–79; gender identity theme, 129–30, 135, 143; references to Russian literature, 133; references to Syria civil war, 142
Salzmann, Sasha Marianna, works by: *Außer sich*, 29, 89, 117, 120, 128–46, 159, 162, 164, 166, 171, 178–79; *Im Menschen muss alles herrlich sein*, 51
Sand, George, 154
Schindel, Robert , 2, 15, 34
Schoeps, Julius, 10, 18, 118
Scholem, Gershom, 75
Seghers, Anna, 70, 163, 173
self-effacement, 29, 148, 175
self-positioning, 27, 35, 36, 52, 61, 76, 77, 81, 117, 120, 147, 158–60, 164, 166–68, 176–77, 179
Seligmann, Rafael, 2, 15, 34, 40, 124
Seligmann, Rafael, works by: *Lauf, Ludwig, lauf! Eine Jugend zwischen Synagoge und Fußball*, 40; *Hannah und Ludwig—Heimatlos in Tel Aviv*, 34; *Der Milchmann*, 34; *Rubinsteins Versteigerung*, 8
Sephardic Jews, 4, 26, 40, 42–46, 76
September 11, 2001 (9/11), 175
Shapira, Shahak, 10

Shneer, David, 12, 118
Six-Day War 1967, 157
Skolnik, Jonathan, 163
Slodounik, Rebekah, 91
Spiegelman, Art, 95
Spinoza, Baruch/ Benedictus de, 157
Stallinger, Julia, 11
Stein, Benjamin, 4, 28, 159, 161, 163; allusions to Kafka, 72, 163–64; allusions to Mann, 72; transgression theme, 67, 71, 74–75
Stein, Benjamin, works by: *Das Alphabet des Rabbi Löw, Das Alphabet des Juda Liva*, 27, 36, 62–75; *Die Leinwand*, 63
Steinecke, Hartmut, 14
Steinke, Ronen, 11
Stephan Balliet, Halle synagogue shooting, 13
Sutcliffe, Adam, 25, 80, 119, 148, 151, 167
Syria, civil war. *See* Grjasnowa, Salzmann
Sznaider, Natan. *See* Levy

tikkun olam. *See* repairing the world
transgender identity. *See* gender identity
transgression, 27, 29, 34–5, 77, 119, 157. *See also* Altaras, Himmelfarb, Stein, Trzebiner
Treblinka. *See* Himmelfarb, Petrowskaja
Trotsky, Leon, 157
Trzebiner, Channah, 28, 29, 46, 100, 117, 120, 161; references to Auschwitz, 121, 127; references to Bergen-Belsen, 121, 123, 127; transgression theme, 123
Trzebiner, Channah, *Die Enkelin, oder Wie ich zu Pessach die vier Fragen nicht wusste*, 120–28, 136, 159, 162, 165–66

Tsar Nicholas I, 149, 151, 154–55
Tsarist Russia. *See* Russian Empire
Turgenev, 151, 153, 157
twentieth century modernism, 82, 163

Ukraine, invasion by Russia, 146, 147, 176
unification of Germany, 9, 14, 15, 31, 46

Vertlib, Vladimir, 5, 6, 167; arrival in Austria, 47
Vertlib, Vladimir, works by: *Letzter Wunsch*, 32; *Victor hilft*, 46, 79
Vowinckel, Dana, 32

Waldheim scandal, 15,
Wanner, Adrian, 48,
Weiss-Sussex, Godela, 110
Weiss, Yfat. *See* Gorelik
Westerman, Wim. *See* Rietveld-Van Wingerden
Wilkomirski, Benjamin, 22
Wolfe, Alan, 24
Wolfenstein, Alfred, 163
Wolff, Fabian, 22
Wolffsohn, Michael, 78, 177
Wolfson, Elliot, 69
World Jewish Congress, 9

Yevtushenko, Yevgeny, 115
Yildiz, Erol, 15, 30, 159, 161, 168. *See also* postmigrant society
Young Jewish Literature, 2, 5, 28
Yuedakel, Gökce, 118

Zevi, Sabbatai, 65, 67, 74–5, 165, 169
Zipes, Jack, 31
Zuckmayer, Carl, 79
Zweig, Stefan, 79

www.ingramcontent.com/pod-product-compliance
Lightning Source LLC
Chambersburg PA
CBHW070803230426
43665CB00017B/2469